EXPERIENCE
OF THE
INNER WORLDS

A COURSE IN CHRISTIAN QABALISTIC MAGIC

GARETH KNIGHT

SKYLIGHT PRESS

© Gareth Knight 1975, 2010

This edition published in Great Britain in 2010 by Skylight Press,
210 Brooklyn Road, Cheltenham, Glos GL51 8EA

First published in Great Britain by Helios Book Service, 1975.

Designed and typeset by Rebsie Fairholm
Printed and bound in Great Britain by Lightning Source, Milton Keynes

www.skylightpress.co.uk

ISBN 978-1-908011-03-9

CONTENTS

AUTHOR'S PREFACE

My aim in this book has been to provide a system of occult teaching and practice that is founded on a framework of Christian tradition and belief. I realise that there may be many who would consider occultism and Christianity to be incompatible, and there are others who might wonder why I should bother.

However, until the late nineteenth century Western magic and occultism was firmly based on Christian tradition, from the Florentine magicians of the Renaissance to the Rosicrucian Brotherhood, Robert Fludd and Eliphas Levi. Before that, the Hermetic literature, allied to the theology of pseudo-Dionysius, was an amalgam of the divine revelation of Christianity and the highest spiritual insights of the pagan Mystery tradition. The great mystical vision of Dante; the contributory streams of other 'peoples of the Book' (the Old Testament) whether Jewish Qabalism, or the Alchemical, Courtly Love and Holy Grail traditions from Islamic sources; all combine in a rich tapestry that forms the occult and mystical heritage of the West.

That the science and art of magic should have become divorced from orthodox science and orthodox religion is, in my view, regrettable. Magic is deprived of some rational discipline and guidance, science loses its soul, and religion much of its vitality.

It is my hope that this book will enable a body of students to recover the threads of a vital tradition that is an indispensable part of our spiritual and cultural birthright. To use the book to greatest advantage, the serious student should read it through at leisure or fairly quickly, then proceed to do the exercises about one chapter per month—preferably night and morning—and using extracts from the chapter as readings. It is important that the order of studying the exercises and chapters is preserved.

I wish to record my thanks to the Reverend Tony Duncan for his helpful midwifery during the long gestation of the manuscript, and for his ready permission for it to be built around the exercises first formulated in his essay on mysticism entitled *The Lord of the Dance,* and from whose *The Sword in the Sun* the extracts at the head of the exercise sections are drawn, and also the 'angelic' scripts. Also to the band of volunteers who originally validated the exercises and worked through the manuscript with me, particularly Michael and Brenda Bartholomew, Leanne Lee Miller and Calla Haack.

Finally, my thanks to my family, Roma, Richard and Rebecca, who have, in their understanding and forbearance, helped immeasurably in

the preparation of this book. May it be a help to others in the degree that they have been a help and inspiration to me.
Amor vincit omnia.

ADDENDUM TO NEW EDITION

Since first publication, this book has gone through two editions: one in Britain and one in America, and the hopes expressed above for its future have been to a large extent attained, insofar that in the subsequent thirty-five years it has served to train personal students of mine in the Gareth Knight Group who have since gone on to write books or to run groups of their own on both sides of the Atlantic. Of particular mention should be Wendy Berg and Mike Harris in Britain and Coleston Brown and Jim McBride in the United States.

For this edition I have taken the opportunity to make a few corrections of fact and to tidy up some infelicitous expressions, otherwise all is as it was in the beginning. It may now be revealed that 'Douglas Warren' is in fact the late Anthony Duncan, and *The Sword in the Sun* did achieve publication, along with a number of other works of his, by Sun Chalice Books between 1999 and 2002.

I count Anthony Duncan as one of the most formative influences upon my interior life and thought and this book arose out of ten years' hard slog between us when he, as a psychically gifted curate in the Church of England seeking some rationale for some of his inner experiences, met up with an initiate out of Dion Fortune's Society of the Inner Light, currently engaged with the magical dynamics being formulated by the redoubtable old occultist W.G. Gray, and looking for the right relationship of Western occultism with Western religious experience.

How far we got things right is not for us to say. But coming back to the text after all these years I find it packing quite a punch at several levels, to the point that all later books I have written should be regarded as largely supplementary to its main theme.
Kyrie Eleison. Christe Eleison. Kyrie Eleison.

'Well, now that we have seen each other,' said the Unicorn, 'if you'll believe in me, I'll believe in you. Is that a bargain?'
'Yes, if you like,' said Alice.

Lewis Carroll
Through the Looking Glass

CHAPTER I

The Sphere of Light

Occultism is a branch of science. Just as physical science is a study of physical forces and forms, so occult science is a study of occult forces and forms — that is, those hidden forces and forms that are not immediately apparent to physical perception. (Occult comes from the Latin *occultus*, meaning 'hidden'). The fact that many people do not recognise the existence of occult forms and forces is beside the point; this does not mean they do not exist. The findings of occult science are simply not so readily demonstrable as those of physical science. One difficulty, for instance, is that physical instruments do not directly register occult forces.

But because occult science does not have easily demonstrable physical results, it has, at any rate since the eighteenth century, been rejected from orthodox academic study. This has resulted in its becoming a rag-bag of all rejected matters — both scientific and religious — and it has been regarded as the happy hunting ground of the quack, the charlatan, the inadequate, the deranged, the credulous and the perverse.

However, much of this academic dead letter will not lie down! It has a certain vitality that keeps it alive despite its lack of official patronage. This suggests that beneath all the rejected and distorted ideas there are some very lively truths that, by their very truth, remain alive in spite of their abuse and neglect.

Unfortunately, when things are thrown higgledy-piggledy together like this, they can in their growth become almost inextricably tangled. Thus one has, from time to time, strange popular growths springing up, given rude vitality by the truths within them, but doomed to a rapid growth, deterioration and death by the many errors within that growth.

Thus one has the history of heresies throughout the ages — whether the heresies be scientific or religious. It is our purpose to select from these manifestations what exactly are the fundamental truths that cause their perpetual recurrence.

In order to do this we must define our terms. We must first decide upon the difference between the religious and the scientific in what we have to deal with. Another way of putting this in the context of occult science is to define the difference between the *mystical* and the *magical*. For mystical is practical *religious* experience of an inner nature, and magical is practical *scientific* experience of an inner nature. And what we are here concerned about fundamentally is *experience of an inner nature,* of whatever kind, though it is vitally important to define the various kinds.

Briefly, the religious, or the *mystical,* is the approach of the soul to God, and the experience thereof. The scientific, or the *magical,* is the approach of the soul to the Inner Creation. We must get this distinction clear. If we do not we will be in danger of setting up archetypes or intelligent agencies of the occult worlds as gods; or of coming to them without proper orientation or authority. And in occult science, for the most part, it is not possible to attain to a proper understanding of the forms and forces with which it deals without a true belief and faith in God. While a student of the subject denies the existence of God, either categorically or provisionally, its higher reaches are not for him. And this awareness of the reality of God must be of a personal nature.

Here we must announce our parting of the ways from that form of occult study that is very prevalent in our times — that of the arm-chair cosmologist. This carries with it an outmoded idea of God, that was somewhat fashionable in the nineteenth century, as a remote kind of 'life force' or 'evolutionary urge'. Stemming largely from Hindu speculation via an influx of such teaching to the West in the late nineteenth century, it contents itself with speculating upon conditions of life and existence in other worlds, solar systems and galaxies, in previous, present or future times. It is a kind of intellectual exercise which has a certain fascination by its very complexity, and is invested with certain glamorous pretensions, such as being of extreme antiquity, and handed down by generations of secret adepts —thus feeding curiosity with a subtle form of pride.

The only practical good that may come from such activities is that the material, by its vast imaginative extent, may train the mind — even if it does not inform it. It has a mental callisthenic use of developing a faculty of intuition as long as the information is not taken too seriously. Regrettably, it is usually regarded as more sacrosanct than Holy Writ and thought to be the preserve of the 'highly evolved'; though the ability to read such lengthy tomes is more a sign of an uncritical mind and mis-spent leisure than of 'high evolution' or supernormal powers.

It is a phase that many occult enquirers go through — and is harmless as long as it is *gone through.* What is a little sad is to see the amount of time the average 'seeker' spends in going through one system after another. It may make business more lucrative than it otherwise might be for the occult bookseller, but is also a sad reflection upon the quality of the wares being purveyed. They excite curiosity, and promise truth to those who seek, but seldom give long satisfaction. This is because they are not practical. If they were to descend to the practical their lack of reality would soon be revealed.

There are, of course, aspects of occult study which are intensely practical and that do not partake of the mystical element which is an important feature of higher occult work. These are the areas of rejected, semi-physical sciences that may have been rejected for good reasons or for bad. The kind of subject areas we mean are, for instance, astrology, hypnotism, dowsing, auric diagnosis, acupuncture and so on.

Each has its own history of coming in or out of scientific fashion. Hypnosis, for instance, has virtually come back into medical respectability after a very chequered career during which it has featured as music hall entertainment and been the subject of romantic novels, and has gone through a variety of names from 'animal magnetism' to 'induced auto-suggestion'.

The investigation of the human aura was undertaken by Dr W. J. Kilner, a physician at St Thomas's Hospital, London, who wrote *The Human Atmosphere* as an aid to medical diagnosis. It became by-passed by progress however, in that superior and easier methods of medical diagnosis made it unnecessary. It has relapsed into the province of the occult — where it is pursued in a desultory fashion, rather in a spirit of unscientific credulity than as disciplined investigation. Though, who knows, it might well be accepted back into the orthodox scientific canon at some future time and would then cease to be 'occult'.

There are grounds for taking astrology, the influence of the stars on human affairs and personality, seriously. Though as prediction it is highly unreliable, and as character description is of a vagueness that makes it impractical for commercial use, so it is outside the scientific canon. But those who have investigated it have generally been impressed by the occasional staggering lucky shot of prediction, or by the general validity of character description. It is as true to say there are zodiacal characteristics (according to time of birth) as to say there are national character traits but the information cannot be put to concrete use nor proven in laboratory conditions.

Dowsing is a shadowy science that is hardly recognised by the scientific community because it is not readily explained by currently acceptable theories. But there is strong evidence that it does work, otherwise commercial companies would hardly be prepared to pay high fees to those who are able reliably to trace water or minerals by such methods. Science particularly tries to dig its head in the sand when dowsers get results by swinging pendulums over maps. It just does not accord with modern (allegedly 'scientific') prejudice.

In the examples we have cited, the sciences are those that are on a borderline between the physical and the non-physical. Because of their non-physical affiliations they tend to be unpredictable and dependent upon subjective considerations which physical science finds difficult to accept.

We see physical science's difficulty in relation to those areas of knowledge that are on the borderline of the material and the non-material. Here areas become occult or non-occult according to how physical they are. But there are areas that are wholly non-physical and can be investigated only by subjective means.

Of these, an example is magic. And we need to realise that magic is a science. It is akin to the science of psychology (itself not an 'exact' science, because it does not deal with inanimate matter) but it is something more than psychology.

We may realise the scientific nature of magic in referring to the aims of a typical Renaissance magician such as Johannes Trithemius, Abbot of Sponheim, whose aims included using a telepathic network for transmitting messages at a distance, and for being aware of occurrences in other parts of the world. In this, his aims — if not his results—were but foreshadowings of the electric telegraph, the telephone, radio and television. As it happened, such aims were the better to be achieved by physical science than occult science —though for all we know he may have achieved his aims by occult means and been unable or unwilling to prove it!

In these times occult and physical science were closely intertwined, astronomers were astrologers as well, chemists were alchemists. Dr John Dee, who investigated the occult communication with spirits through a psychic and a crystal ball, was also a mathematician of considerable importance and a devout Christian to boot.

The great leap which humanity took at the Renaissance in its grasp of the scientific method was intimately connected with occult as well as physical science. The ancient classical world had made no major scientific or technological strides, not because they were stupid or less 'evolved' than us, but because their preoccupation was with rational and philosophical speculation, rather than base mechanical investigation. The Middle Ages, when they emerged from barbarism, held theology and religious contemplation to be the peak of man's activity and any wish to manipulate or question God's creation, the work of the devil.

When the spirit of the Renaissance upset this psychological orientation, men such as Ficino, Pica della Mirandola and Cornelius Agrippa turned to the 'impious' manipulation of matter on their own account. The church tended to look upon all with great distrust, whether they were occult scientists like Bruno or Campanella, or physical scientists like Galileo or Copernicus. Many of course, such as Kepler, Cardano, Paracelsus and Newton, were both.

We find ourselves today, however, in a position where physical science, having outstripped occult science in terms of physical results, is now regarded as the *only* science, and occult science is part of a rag-bag of misunderstood rejected things partly confused with heretical and deviant religion.

With man finding that in spite of his mastery of physical science, major and frightening problems still exist, it may be that the time has come for the reappraisal of what occult science has to offer. But we must first disentangle it from much pseudo-science and much pseudo-religion.

This is not an easy task, for a proper appreciation of the validity of occult science lies in a restoration of a broken relationship with reality that was caused when physical investigation became an end in itself.

The investigation of the inner worlds is a discipline that involves the whole of an individual's being and demands a synthesising rather than an analytic approach. The whole can hardly be perceived through the eye-piece of a microscope, and even a telescope is but a microscope of the skies.

The approach that is required is rather that of the alchemists of old, by no means all of whom were the superstitious dullards that our modern arrogance and prejudice tends to make of them. Their attitude is well summed up in the chemist E. J. Holmyard's *Alchemy:*

> The unity of the world and all things in it was an unshakable belief; there was thus nothing illogical in the combination of mystical theology with practical chemistry, however incongruous it may seem to us today.

One may see a little further into this 'incongruity' by reference to the psychologist C. G. Jung's *Psychology and Alchemy,* where he says:
'… just because of this intermingling of the physical and the psychic, it always remains an obscure point whether the ultimate transformations in the alchemical process are to be sought more in the material or more in the spiritual realm. Actually, however, the question is wrongly put; there was no "either-or" for that age, but there did exist an intermediate realm between mind and matter, i.e. a psychic realm of subtle bodies whose characteristic it is to manifest themselves in a mental as well as a material form. This is the only view that makes sense of alchemical ways of thought, which must otherwise appear nonsensical. Obviously, the existence of this intermediate realm comes to a sudden stop the moment we try to investigate matter in and for itself, apart from all projection:

and it remains non-existent so long as we believe we know anything conclusive about matter or the psyche. But the moment when physics touches on the "untrodden, untreadable regions" and when psychology has at the same time to admit that there are other forms of psychic life besides the acquisitions of personal consciousness — in other words, when psychology too touches on an impenetrable darkness — then the intermediate realm of subtle bodies comes to life again, and the physical and psychic are once more blended in an indissoluble unity. We have come very near to this turning point today.'

And he goes on to say that 'the earlier talk of the "aberration" of alchemy sounds rather old-fashioned today, when the psychological aspects of it have faced science with new tasks. There are very modern problems in alchemy, though they lie outside the province of chemistry.'

The same may be said of occult science generally, which in its various specialities and degrees is much akin to alchemy. A change in direction of approach associated with the scientific method put these matters out of fashion by causing them to appear 'nonsensical'. And now the scientific method has gone as far as it is possible for it to go in certain directions, and we find it no longer so nonsensical and unfashionable to approach such things in a former light.

The pendulum has swung back again — or at any rate is about to start its swing.

In speaking of 'the unity of the world and all things in it', we must, however, avoid the error of oriental monism which denies the dual existence of Creator and created. According to this view the universe and all the inner worlds therein have been self-created, or at best emanated from a central source. This means that God is *in* everything, in the holiest of holies and in the dust on the sandals of the worshipper at the temple gate. As a child of an acquaintance put it with devastating childlike logic, 'When I stamp on the ground am I stamping on God?' To this the monist would rush to reply 'Yes', but the theist would say 'No'. The monist would go on to say that as God is also in the child's foot, sock and shoe, God was stamping on God. The theist would go on to say that although God is not *in* everything he is omniscient as far as the creation is concerned and is therefore aware of the child stamping and in empathy with both the child and the ground.

All this is not academic, theological or philosophical hair splitting, for the consequences of believing one thing or the other are profound. If we are going to build a philosophical or theological edifice we need to be very certain of the rock upon which it is founded.

To believe that all things unfurl of their own accord from nothing is to assume that man is capable of expanding his consciousness until he becomes eventually as God, comprehending all — and that animals expand their consciousness to become humans, plants likewise to become animals, even minerals to become plants. This is a theory that is, in fact, held by many students of the occult, based on the monist philosophical assumptions of the East. It has its superficial attraction as a logical sounding kind of arrangement. It takes in the ideas of human progress and general life evolution that were newly formulated and current in the nineteenth century, and it is hardly surprising that these ideas in occult form were first promulgated in the West in the late nineteenth century by the efforts of the newly formed Theosophical Society. What Madame Blavatsky, its founder, did really was to take nineteenth-century materialist evolutionary theory as formulated by Darwin and stand it on its head as a spiritual evolutionary theory, in much the same way that Marx had inverted the spiritual dialectic of Hegel to form the dialectical materialism of Marxism. Both Marxism and Theosophy have a great spurious appeal as seeming to answer many questions by this agile topsy-turveydom. Unfortunately both are wrong — though this does not alter the fact that Marxism as a political philosophy came to dominate a third of the world and Theosophical monism dominates much of modern occult thought.

It is not our task to try to judge why certain particular nineteenth-century philosophical ideas should retain such a hold into modern times, though in the case of oriental monism and occultism its influence spread because a whole generation of occult students sat at the feet of Madame Blavatsky and imbibed her principles even if they later rejected some of the superstructure of her philosophy. They later taught others and so the basic assumptions spread — with various modifications to and arguments about the superstructure, but with the entire theological foundations taken for granted and accepted unchallenged.

The whole Western occult tradition, which had followed an underground course for centuries, burst out into the open, only to be thoroughly mixed, swamped and diluted with Eastern ideas deriving from Hinduism and Buddhism. The true occult heritage of the West stems, however, along with the religion of the West, from Christian and Judaic tradition — or rather from *revealed* as opposed to *natural* religion.

If one examines the points in Western history where the occult tradition rose to the surface — in fourth-century Gnosticism, twelfth-century Holy Grail tradition, seventeenth-century Rosicrucianism, medieval alchemy — one finds a Christian orientation, or failing that, a Jewish or Islamic, all three of which stem from the *revealed* religion of the Old Testament.

It is important therefore that we draw a distinction between revealed and natural religion. In short, *natural* religion is man's approach to God, whilst *revealed* religion is God's approach to man.

Natural religion takes many forms but the ground base is the same, and the psychic structure and needs and desires of man being generally similar throughout the world, so do natural religions have a generally similar aspect beneath the local variations. It stems from the desire of man to have some explanation for the forces in the world about him that he does not understand, and following from this, some way of dealing with them.

In its primitive form it is called 'animism' — the idea that all external objects have souls — that there are spirits in trees, or in stones, or in features of the landscape. This naturally extends to a formulation of gods of the wind, the rain, the sun, the sea, the rivers, the forests, the crops, the hunted beasts, the fire and so on. One sees something of the same psychological process happening when people with small knowledge of the workings of the motor car, possessed of an old jalopy of uncertain reliability, fondly invest it with a name to be cajoled or petted by — 'Old Bess will see us through! Come on, old girl!' as the springs sag and the gaskets blow. How much more imperative was the need for primitive man to get onto some kind of familiar terms with the precious seeds which, when planted, might or might not come up again and with uncertain yield — or with the terrors of the dark forest about his hill encampment — or the efficacy of his club or sling shot or spear or arrowhead in making the kill and saving him from starvation.

We must qualify these remarks by hastening to add that we do not suggest that primitive man was deluded. He was naturally and intuitively groping towards a truth. To the occult investigator there *are* such spirits of natural things. As we have already quoted from Jung ... *'there are other forms of psychic life besides the acquisitions of personal consciousness ...'*

The point we wish to make is that it is very important that we get right our own relationship to these 'other forms of psychic life'. Primitive man's natural, and understandable, reaction was first to supplicate, then to worship them. We cannot put ourselves entirely into primitive man's mind and say exactly how, or even if, he was aware of subject/object relationships, and Owen Barfield's *Saving the Appearances* puts some fascinating ideas on this question. But certainly when civilisation progresses and concepts became more defined and conceptualised we do find the god forms springing up — in the human image —and being worshipped by man. What we need to establish is, if they are his own creations, why should he be worshipping them?

In the religious myths of the various ancient civilisations we find gods being worshipped which are, or to all intents and purposes appear to be, projections of aspects of the personality of man; and which also, from being gods of local topology or flora and fauna, have developed into a more philosophical role as gods of earth, sky or sea. There are Sky Fathers, Earth Mothers, Virgins of Wisdom, Moon Goddesses, Hermaphroditic Gods of Communication, Trade and Knowledge, Goddesses of Sexual Desire, Gods of War and Saviour Gods.

There is a similarity between the various types of god that can be made readily apparent when such a yardstick of relationships as the Qabalistic Tree of Life is used when, in spite of the apparent teeming diversity of the pagan god pantheons, common relationships and functions appear. This similarity is because the projections of various peoples of the earth are basically similar because of their common human psycho-biological heritage.

The family relationships and adventures of various gods in various pantheons is, in most cases, the result of tribal or national movements, migrations or conflicts, where one people's gods had to be integrated with those of a conquering people. Sometimes the gods or goddesses became identified with and 'took over' other gods of a similar nature. The goddess Isis, for instance, swallowed up numerous other local goddesses. But where assimilation is impossible then family relationships are formed — brothers, sisters, husbands, wives, mothers, fathers, daughters, sons, to say nothing of lovers, homosexual, heterosexual and/or incestuous. Something of the kind of thing that went on can be read in considerable detail in Robert Graves' *The Greek Myths*.

A major and simple philosophical relationship that occurs over and again is that of Father, Mother, Son, Adversary. The Father Sky-God mates with the Mother Earth-goddess and a Son-hero is born. The Adversary kills the Sky-god, who is mourned by the Earth-goddess, but avenged by the Son-hero. This is the basic quaternity relationship that can be seen, for example, in the Egyptian Osiris, Isis. Horus and Set. Here we have attempts to form a religious philosophy or cosmology.

It is the same mechanism that we found in primitive man trying to account for and to control the forces of the elements and nature, and for similar reasons many of the pagan mystery religions were concerned with sexuality and with death. These are the two great gateways to and from this earthly life and so the natural ways to come to an understanding and possible control of that which lies beyond is by trying to penetrate either the gates of conception or the gates of death.

A stage in the religious development of man comes when the old gods begin to be questioned. This happened in Ancient Greece with the teaching of Plato and Socrates, and in India and China with Gautama the Buddha and Confucius and Lao Tse. The Greek drama that has come down to us shows the steady erosion of faith in the old gods from the majestic belief in them of Aeschylus, through the beginnings of doubt in Sophocles, to the open questioning of Euripides and burlesquing of them in Aristophanes.

In the main areas of advanced civilisation this awakening happened in approximately 500 B.C. and it is relatively soon after this that the Pagan Mysteries were instituted, which made of the old popular religions a personal system of secret initiation for spiritual rebirth. In these, the candidate, blindfolded and bound, underwent various tests of faith and fortitude and a symbolic death and subsequent regeneration. Their vestiges remain in certain types of Masonic ritual to this day, and in such occult initiation systems as that of the Hermetic Order of the Golden Dawn and its derivatives.

In the West the national systems of old gods were not able to survive the social results of the conquests of Alexander the Great. These, as Professor Angus in *The Mystery Religions and Christianity* points out, 'form a turning-point in the history of the race with which may not be compared even the rise of the Roman empire, the coronation of Charles the Great at Rome in 800, or in the Renaissance, or the Reformation. Alexander made all things new; the results of his work have affected all the religious history of the Mediterranean world and the civilisations descended therefrom.'

The reasons for Alexander's importance are several. His conquests, which spanned most of the then known world, had as a larger aim the 'marriage of East and West'. He was also probably the first ancient conqueror to concede any rights to the conquered and he used a cosmopolitan army with which to unite the world. He eventually allowed himself to be declared a god, and this, though seemingly an uncharacteristic act of oriental despotism, had a profound effect upon the progress of religious thought. Some of these effects were unfortunate, such as the later deification of Roman Emperors and the doctrine of Divine Right of Kings by which an English king lost his head two thousand years later.

By his conquests he imposed a conception of unity upon the human race that could be physically seen, and thus led to the establishment of a common language of international communication — the *koine* — or common Greek, which was a fusion of the various dialects of the different Greek city states. The intellectual and religious intercommunication which this allowed developed a trend of syncretism on a large scale, where various local gods were compared one with another and found to be similar.

There had already been some amalgamation of similar gods as a result of migration and conquest but the breaking down of national barriers in the empire of Alexander, and the availability of a common language, increased this trend a hundredfold, without the need for conquest or migration. It was a time of considerable and remarkable religious tolerance, with Eastern and Western gods and their priests and temples existing side by side.

In the face of this evidence of a multiplicity of gods there naturally grew up a philosophical desire to rationalise them in some way, and the more thoughtful began to regard them all as various aspects of the One God. The idea of the One God took on popular support as a by-product of Alexander's apotheosis — for as he was plainly the one great ruler of the known world then there before the eyes of the pagan world was a physical demonstration of what might well be theological reality.

In this relatively happy period of religious amalgamation and tolerance one race stood out starkly and painfully — that of the Jews. We shall examine their strange behaviour and the reasons for it in our next chapter — for they were the custodians of what they considered to be Revealed Religion — as opposed to the Natural Religion that was followed by the whole world around them.

We must also take a brief look at the East in our survey, for the Eastern religions become important for us in relation to their later and comparatively recent influence on Western occult thought.

In ancient India, just as in the West, or indeed any part of the world, mankind produced a teeming profusion of gods, and these comprise the many pantheons of Hinduism, if indeed Hinduism can be described as an 'ism', for it contains so much, so diverse, within it. Like the pagan Western religions after the time of Alexander it tends towards a system of great mutual religious tolerance. This, to our particular present times, when in Europe we have emerged from some centuries of religious intolerance, appears to be very modern and enlightened. It is in reality, however, very ancient, and not necessarily particularly enlightened. There is a narrow but important distinction between enlightened tolerance and easy-going disinterest or apathy, or, what is perhaps worse, a combination of sloppy thought and sentimentality that is unable to perceive and evaluate differences and boundaries.

The Western pagan religions in their multiplicity developed eventually into formal observances with moral decadence on the part of the priesthood. This resulted in the rise of Greek moral philosophers such as Plutarch, Dion, Epictetus and Marcus Aurelius. So, in the East did one have a similar reaction to Vedic and Brahman priestcraft in the rise of the teachings of Siddartha Gautama. There were, in fact, many *buddhas* or holy men in those times — as in most times — but the greatness of Siddartha Gautama caused him to appropriate the title Buddha almost entirely to himself.

His teaching was a spiritual and humane one. Shocked and repelled by the pain and corruption of the world, he taught that detachment would release one from 'the wheel of birth and death'. By rising above desire, no longer would one be a part of the world conceived by Hindu speculation — an endless round of lives in which one reincarnated time and again, reaping the sins or good deeds of one life in the pains or pleasures of the next, on an eye for an eye, a tooth for a tooth basis, a crude formulation but one which at least in some kind of logical fashion explained the existence of pain and injustice in the world. Eventually, the Buddha taught, one might rise so far above it, beyond desire, as to be absorbed into a kind of blissful Cosmic Nothingness — a state of Nirvana.

It was an amalgam of these concepts that was taught by Madame Blavatsky in her newly formed Theosophical Society in the 1870s. Slightly spiritualised, and with the worst of the crudities removed, it appealed to many who were repelled by the naïve and sentimental transcendentalist phase that the Victorian Protestant Churches were going through. As we have said, it still remains the ground base of assumed axioms in much modern occult belief and speculation.

Buddhism itself gradually became priest-ridden and showed a tendency to align itself with the original indigenous religions of India prior to the Vedic, the daimon worshipping Turanian sects. From these we have the various forms of Tantric Yoga and developments far from the original lofty conceptions of Gautama.

Yoga itself is a Hindu phenomenon and not so much a religion as a form of occult science in which the aim is discovery of the inner worlds, and mastery of the self. The various forms of it emphasise the levels at which mastery is attained, whether via the mind, the emotions, the subtle and physical bodies (for instance *raja yoga, bakhti yoga, karma yoga).* Other forms (like *laya yoga* or *mantra yoga*) are based on particular techniques.

Yoga means 'union' and its disciplines may be valuable, as indeed any system of callisthenics of mind or body may be valuable, but it is not necessarily a means of union with God. The union it prescribes is more a union or integration of various parts of the soul or psyche, and self-conquest is its general aim. The danger is that systems of callisthenics may be elevated into religious philosophies and they are not necessarily well fitted for the task.

One great attraction of Hindu religious philosophy to a particular type of Western mind is its great speculative daring and seeming all-inclusiveness. It is in fact all-inclusive to the point of self-contradiction. This is all very well as long as it is recognised for what it is — human speculation. But it is often given a charismatic patina by being regarded as a complex of great secret truths that have been handed down for millennia in secret archives under the custodianship of infallible brotherhoods of high adepts. Attractively romantic as this may sound (though it is equally off-putting to others), even if the monkish civilisations of the Himalayas or the Andes should have records of ancient teaching, it is no less fallible for being ancient, or secret, or for being transmitted by psychic or clairvoyant means. The teachings, on analysis, are but the typical speculations of Natural Religion.

The speculations of Natural Religion, fascinating and even educative as they may be, should be realised for what they are — intrinsically the product of the human mind and imaginative faculty — but not necessarily any nearer the truth for that. It is true that the freely ranging imagination may indeed have a worth, and access to a reality, that is little suspected, but that is another matter that we, in this book, shall investigate. But it is important that we do not overlay a real and profound occult tradition, based on Revealed Religion, that is our heritage in the West, with a man-made system of conjecture, however 'spiritual' in tone or intuitively perceptive in some respects, this conjecture might be.

The tenets of occult philosophy that are taught in many of the schools are similar in appeal to early speculative science — the Newtonian atomic theory for instance. Newton's atomic theory seems wholly reasonable, and appeals to common sense in regarding atoms as small particles of matter of different kinds. However, a more technically advanced science, able to investigate matter at closer quarters, found itself not with a commonsense kind of theory but with a complex field of energies, again at first sight apparently simple in its terms of electrons and neutrons and positrons but in fact exceedingly complex in its mechanisms, of random instantaneous orbital changes and so on.

The first broad human guesses are generally capable of being approximately right. The atomic theory had been proposed by Democritus in ancient Greece. But although such intuitions look more or less in the right direction, reality itself turns out to be considerably more intractable, complex and unexpected than the speculations of man's commonsense mind would ever have first suspected. The mind, used to dealing with sense perceptions of the outside world, tends to build up ideas by use of pictures. But actual truth is rarely, if ever, comprehended in this fashion. In fact an advanced knowledge of pure mathematics is now required to approach a valid explanation of the physics of matter. It has developed totally beyond any simple diagrammatic representation. For instance, the popular *idea* of how the atom is structured (Figure 1), which most people think still holds true, is based on an idea put forward by Bohr in 1913. Yet this was superseded in 1927 as a result of Schrödinger's work, when it was discovered that electrons have properties of particles *and* waves, and so the wave-mechanical model had to be introduced which can not be so conveniently represented on paper — the electron no longer being a particle in orbit but a 'probability distribution' of energy.

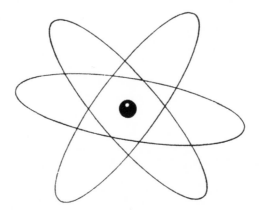

Figure 1

The 'truths' that are frequently the basis of modern occult speculation are akin to these early picture speculations of physical science. But again and again on closer investigation one finds that these 'truths' are sweeping and formless generalities, that only achieve some kind of universalism because they blur distinctions and follow uncritically a wide gamut of pictorial analogies.

It is a regrettable, and indeed ironic, fact that because most of these ideas, in the West at any rate, are met in adult life, and compared to an idea of Christian belief that was received, usually quite distortedly, in childhood, they appear to be profundities when opposed to the 'childish' pictorial ideas of the Western Christian heritage. C.S. Lewis has put it well in *Miracles*, a book of particular interest to the occult student, particularly in Chapter 11, wherein this argument is expanded:

> The true state of the question is often misunderstood because people compare an adult knowledge of Pantheism with a knowledge of Christianity which they acquired in their childhood. They thus get the impression that Christianity gives the 'obvious' account of God, the one that is too easy to be true, while pantheism offers something sublime and mysterious. In reality it is the other way round. The apparent profundity of pantheism thinly veils a mass of spontaneous picture-thinking and owes its plausibility to that fact.

The term *pantheism* covers most, if not all, forms of current occult speculation even though many occult teachers would deny the term, saying that they do not worship Nature, which is what the term directly implies. However, if the monist belief is held to, that God is in nature, and the natural world is a part of, or manifestation of, God himself (instead of a creation separate from the Creator), then this is, *ipso facto,* a worship of Nature, under somewhat thin disguise.

We shall investigate the claims of Revealed Religion and an 'adult' appreciation of Christian ideas in our next chapter. For the moment we simply wish to establish the idea of God as Creator, and man, and the world he lives in, inner and outer, as the Creation.

EXERCISE FOR CHAPTER I

Secure within a sphere of Light, O Man!
Abide in peace and knowledge of my love.

The exercise that we take as the summation of this chapter, which is really a clearing of the ground for laying true foundations, is the building of a Sphere of Light.

On the work upon which we are about to embark it is not enough to involve simply the conscious mind. The whole of our being must become involved. Like the alchemy of old it is a total commitment to the Work, not a rational 'investigation' of it, that is alone able to bring it to a successful conclusion.

Identification with a basic symbol is a first step in this process and the most appropriate one is a Sphere of Light. This is a symbol of the whole of creation, it speaks to the soul as being the basic shape upon which worlds are formed, from their smallest part to their largest, from the energy sphere of the atom to the bowl or hemisphere of the night sky.

It is a personal symbol too of recollection and withdrawal, of concentration about a centre. It is, if one likes, a three-dimensional magic circle or *mandala* — in which the soul can safely rest and no harm can approach from the outside. In another sense it is a hygienic clearing of a sterilised place for work, as in a surgery or laboratory.

However, we have emphasised that the simple rational approach is not enough, and that love is also required — for this is a religious as well as a scientific quest. We should feel the reality of the symbol with our heart as well as picturing it in our imagination and speculating about it mentally.

Rest assured that subjective though this may seem, the Sphere of Light has an objective reality on the inner side of Creation.

Within this sphere it will be possible to penetrate all time and space, and the inner planes of Creation, as well as to approach the Creator. In one sense it is akin to a crystal ball, in another sense to a spaceship or magic carpet. Its efficacy will depend upon the faith, hope and love of the one who builds it.

Right religious orientation is essential otherwise a whole and most important dimension is lost. There are worldly wise men who would regard this activity as delusory fantasy. There are others, a little more sagacious, who would regard it as applied psychology. There are yet others who, with more perception, would see it as an approach to inner realities. But the wisest will realise it as an orientation and approach of the personal will to the Will of God.

By giving the exercise a contemplative as well as a meditative aspect there are two most important results that accrue. The regular performance of such an activity conforms the personal Will in freedom to the Will of God, which corrects and sanctifies the present moment. And the sustained regular practice of it helps the personal Will to attain a habit of free conformity to the Will of God as a general way of life. The benefits of this have to be experienced to be believed — but they cannot be proved to the unbeliever. As we said before — and will no doubt say again — faith, hope and love are the essential means of progress in this work. The objectivity of the scientific method is a barrier to any progress — for though apposite to examining the inanimate creation, it is dehumanising and the human personality is the flower of creation. It is our aim not that we should *control* or even *understand* life — but that we should *have* life more abundantly.

So for the first practical application of this Course, set aside a time and place, free from interruption, where you may, sitting, kneeling or standing, as you will, formulate a Sphere of Light about you in the imagination. Then relax your tensions, physical and mental, in the midst of it, breathing regularly and deeply. Put the mind and body at rest in an attitude of faith, hope and love of the Creator — who created you.

Do this preferably night and morning for about ten minutes each time. With practice you may find a longer or a shorter period more suitable. Everyone is different, with different needs and requirements. You will also probably find it useful, once practice is attained, to build the Sphere at any time of day in times of stress. In this way, if the full contemplative aspect has been pursued, God will be with you, with all the attendant spiritual comfort and strength, through any difficulties of life. This is not a pious hope but a proven experience.

Ideas or pictures may come into mind while you are thus 'waiting on God'. They should not be deliberately encouraged or sought for, nor, on the other hand, suppressed or discouraged. If the orientation of the soul in faith, hope and love is correct, anything that comes into mind in this way, however seemingly inappropriate, has a bearing on the life of the soul and its approach to God.

The Password and first injunction of the ancient Mysteries was *Know Thyself.* Without this the higher reaches of our Work are impossible. The regular formulation of the Sphere of Light in the way we have described is a means towards this knowledge.

CHAPTER II

The Fiery Spear

We have already said that we must — in any but the most material forms of occult science — have a religious foundation for it, and that this foundation should be Revealed Religion rather than Natural Religion.

Revealed Religion is the revelation of God about himself to man; Natural Religion is man's speculation about God.

Revealed Religion stems from the historical experience of a certain small part of humanity — the Jews — the 'chosen' race — and the Revelation of God as shown in their history, which is contained in the books which we know as the Old Testament.

To many attracted to occult studies Natural Religion tends to have a great appeal. This is partly because it is based on the structure of the human psyche, projected outwards, and this reveals an underlying universality which appeals to the modern temperament. Also many such students have had an unfortunate experience of Revealed Religion, or what passes for it, in childhood. But we have stressed that it is important not to compare childish ideas received in childhood about Revealed Religion with mature ideas received in maturity about Natural Religion.

Let us then examine the Old Testament to see how useful a book it may be to guide us on our way, and if the ideas coming from it really are so unique in the field of man's religions.

It is, of course, not just a book but a whole library of books. It ranges from history to tribal laws, from moralistic novels to erotic and devotional poetry, from philosophical speculation to collections of proverbs and wise saws. In the modern state of Israel children can be taught almost every subject from this one collection of books. It is the history of the Jews, their geography, grammar and religion.

Some of the books that once comprised it have been lost altogether. Others have been crudely amalgamated so that events are sometimes described twice or three times. In reading it a cover to cover approach is hardly to be recommended. A good unbiased explanatory guide is advisable — such as Professor Bernhard Anderson's *The Living World of the Old Testament*. And an opportunity to read it in contemporary modern language is offered in the *New English Bible*, which is the version we have used in quotations here, although other more colloquial versions, such as the *Good News Bible* also exist.

The material of the Bible was written down and formulated at a fairly late date. It contains material that is comparatively recent and material that is very archaic and common to other ethnic groups within the area of its origin. Thus the Flood is known in the legends of Sumaria and Babylon. In other parts ancient historical events can be discerned. The Egyptian Pharaoh who made the Hebrews slave at making bricks without straw was probably the pyramid builder Rameses II.

Miracles abound, though some may be adduced to natural causes. The Red Sea, for instance, is in reality a reed sea — a shallow, swampy area where high wind and tide could have the effect of preparing the way for the fleeing tribes, with a change of conditions cutting off the Egyptian pursuit. The miraculous part, if such there be, would have been in the timing rather than the mode of execution. Similarly, manna from heaven is a not uncommon event in the Middle East. It is an edible honey-like dewy product of certain insects. Common too is the migration of quails. And the Israelites were in the wilderness for forty years.

M. J. Field, an ethno-psychiatrist with experience of primitive tribes in Africa, has pointed out in *Angels and Ministers of Grace* the readiness of primitive man (and the civilised for that matter) to prefer a supernatural explanation to a natural one. Thus when Mr Field appeared unexpectedly at a certain native village by walking along the sea-shore instead of arriving by motorised transport in accustomed European fashion, the natives insisted on believing him to be a supernatural visitor who had come up from the sea.

There is much to suggest that many of the angels that appear in the Old Testament were similarly quite solid men — agents of landlords, or itinerant holy men — and Field gives interesting evidence for this, if in the end he does appear to drive his theory to the staggers.

The mythologising element in human popular memory is common to all nations. It may be the divinisation of early men of genius, such as Imhotep, architect of the pyramids and inventor of the pillar, who later became identified with the Greek god Asclepios. Or in the romantic glow of the tales of King Arthur and his Knights that collected round the resistance to Saxon invasion of post-Roman Britain. Even Saints Paul and Barnabus were hailed, to their faces, by the citizens of Lystra as the gods Mercury and Zeus, on account of some charismatic healing that they did. The Holy Ghost did the work but the pagan gods got the credit.

Alongside the Biblical historical material that is miraculously embroidered there are also traces of myth, though most of the mythology has been edited out, and many pious Jews and Christians tend to be sensitive about it. Robert Graves and Raphael Patai in *Hebrew Myths: The Book of Genesis* point out some. The story of Ham, for instance, seeing his father's nakedness, has much in common with the castration of Cronos by Zeus.

> Zeus, the youngest, alone dared castrate him, and as a result became King of Heaven. But Ham's (or Canaan's) castration of Noah has been excised from Genesis just before the line: "Noah awoke from his wine, and knew what his little son had done to him." The revised version, a moral lesson in filial respect, sentences Ham to perpetual servitude under his elder brothers for no worse a crime than accidentally seeing his father's nakedness.

The story, as revised, helps also to justify the Hebrews' enslavement of Canaanites.

But of course much can be interpolated into scriptural writings by the attitude of mind of the interpreter. Freemasonry draws much strange allegoric teaching from the Temple of Solomon and the help Solomon obtained from Hiram. Much mystical Christian exegesis has been drawn from the love songs of the Canticles. And it is even possible to make a good case for evidence of visits by beings from other planets in space craft in, say, the first chapter of Ezekiel: 'I saw a storm wind coming from the north, a vast cloud with flashes of fire and brilliant light about it: and within was a radiance like brass, glowing in the heart of the flames … etc.' Though one could equally adduce other visions to the use of hallucinogenic drugs.

But amid all this welter is running a single thread. The Jews' belief that their God was the God of Gods — the Creator of the Worlds — and that he had chosen them as a vehicle for a particular transcendent mission to the rest of mankind.

They later doctored their history and their legends to conform to this belief. They fell away from the ideal often, but beneath it all runs this golden thread of a particular revelatory purpose. If a kind of cosmic message was being given, let us try to decipher what it was.

In the Old Testament we have a history of how the community of Hebrew tribes kept faith with the Covenant with God that they reckoned had been made initially by Abraham, and later ratified by Moses when they received the main body of the Law after they had escaped from bondage in Egypt.

Once they had got into the Promised Land of Canaan, the constant temptation was to abandon the Covenant Law and the worship of IHVH, the One God, for the custom and law of the indigenous population. This was the more attractive in that whereas before they had been wandering herdsmen, they were now settled agriculturalists and thus under some incentive to worship and mollify a vegetation divinity.

Those who did follow this line, the ten tribes that formed the Northern Kingdom, were subsequently absorbed by the surrounding nations and lost to history. The remaining two tribes, those under the kingdom of David and Solomon, in spite of much falling back into the ways of the Canaanites about them, remained faithful to the Covenant and are the ancestors of the Jews we know today. (Though it would be more accurate to say that *some* of them remained faithful; that is, those who were taken in exile to Babylon and those of their descendents who elected to return to rebuild the temple at Jerusalem some seventy years later. These, in fact, were only a 'remnant' of the whole original twelve tribes of the Hebrews. The others were also, in time, absorbed. Some became the despised Samaritans.

The local nature and vegetation gods, against the worship of whom the prophets of the Old Testament inveigh at tedious length (though with some great invective, oratory and poetry), were principally two in number — Baal and Ishtar. These were in fact two quite ordinary nature gods no better or worse than the many other nature gods met with throughout the history of man in any part of the world. It is true that human sacrifice and ritual prostitution were not unknown in connection with these cults, at any rate in their decadent aspects, but read in the context of the times they were not unduly barbarous. Some of the early Jewish practices were just as bad, from collecting foreskins as battle trophies to merciless genocide and butchery in the name of God.

Baal was the male vegetation god, who died and was reborn every year; Ishtar was his female consort. Their worship varied along with the state of the civilisation of the time, but during the period we are considering they were mostly worshipped in hill-top shrines and sacred groves. Some of their liturgy was of great aesthetic beauty. The Song of Solomon which became incorporated in Hebrew canon and is used by later commentators to signify the mutual love of God and his faithful is obviously taken from Baal and Ishtar worship.

> Hark! My beloved! Here he comes,
> bounding over the mountains, leaping over the hills.
> My beloved is like a gazelle
> or a young wild goat:
> there he stands outside our wall,
> peeping in at the windows, glancing through the lattice.
> My beloved answered, he said to me:
> Rise up, my darling; my fairest, come away.

For now the winter is past,
the rains are over and gone;
the flowers appear in the countryside;
the time is coming when the birds will sing.
and the turtle-dove's cooing will he heard in our land;
when the green figs will ripen on the fig-trees
and the vines give forth their fragrance.
Rise up, my darling; my fairest, come away.

Here the mysterious Bridegroom is seen behind the symbolism to be a god of vegetation and Spring. And in the following, the Bride, like the Egyptian goddess Isis, or the Greek Demeter, the mother of Persephone, wanders in search of him.

Night after night on my bed
I have sought my true love;
I have sought him but not found him.
I have called him but he has not answered.
I said, 'I will rise and go the rounds of the city,
through the streets and the squares,
seeking my true love.'
I sought him but I did not find him,
I called him but he did not answer.
The watchmen, going the rounds of the city, met me,
and I asked, 'Have you seen my true love?'

This overtly erotic poetry is, of course, capable of a spiritual interpretation, whether Jewish, Christian, or pagan.

At times the tendency was to combine the Hebrew worship of the One God with the better parts of the local pagan cults. This might well be looked upon as an enlightened ecumenical policy nowadays; however, by the prophets of God it was roundly condemned. Israel — a title for the worshipping community — was likened to a young virgin, betrothed to the One God, who was unfaithful and playing the harlot with strange gods. It is no doubt the importance of this imagery — first formulated by the prophet Hosea —that allowed, through a certain irony, the hymn of Baal and Ishtar to be incorporated into the Hebrew canon.

Did God really have such an uncompromising, even jealous, attitude anyway? Were the prophets his real spokesmen? Let us look a little closer at their credentials.

In Old Testament times official bands of prophets were employed to interpret the word of God to the reigning monarch. This was much in the pagan tradition of having 'wise men' at court or even oracular facilities such as the Delphic Oracle where professional priestesses, psychedelically drugged by vapours, gave forth ecstatic utterances which were interpreted by resident priests. The prophets who appear in the Old Testament are not such as these however. They were indeed frequently in conflict with them. A prophet is not incidentally, one who foretells the future, as the word has come to be used in modern times. It derives from the Greek words *pro* and *phetes*, meaning to speak on behalf of a god.

The mark of an Old Testament prophet was almost invariably that he was an amateur — not one of the court employed professionals who tended only to reflect what they thought that the king wanted to hear. Also, he tended to receive his 'call' to go and prophesy reluctantly. This was partly on account of a becoming and impressive — and indeed essential — modesty at being apparently a special one, chosen by God: 'Why should it be me?' And also partly because the message was, in most cases, likely to bring little but tribulation to its bearer.

The usual message was that Israel was breaking the Covenant — a message that bad conscience on the part of the nation would tend to find irritating at best. The popular or official feeling against what was felt to be the interfering and inflated conscience of an apparently self-appointed 'do-gooder' was as strong then as it has ever been. In some cases it could appear downright treason — as when Jeremiah preached the fall of the beleaguered Jerusalem with the enemy at the gates. Not-withstanding the fact that he may have been a direct representative of God, political and military expediency were reckoned — as always — more important than the hifaluting ideas of the God of the Universe, and Jeremiah was duly flung into a noisesome dungeon and barely escaped with his life. According to a late tradition, he was eventually stoned to death.

Christians might well see in this that prophets were, in the pattern of their vocation, forerunners of Jesus. According to the followers of Islam, Jesus himself was no more than a prophet, who came after the last Old Testament prophet but before Mahomet. Jews would tend not to give credence either Jesus or Mahomet as being in the prophetic line. Christians themselves would, of course, see Jesus as considerably more than a prophet, as an incarnation in some unique way of God himself.

If this is so, how does the line of Old Testament Law and the Prophets bear out with it? The Law was laid down originally in the time of Moses, written down and codified during the reign of David (about 1000 B.C.). What was the point of having this particular Law and custom? And why was it so important that a line of prophets should have sprung up over a thousand years to try and present it? Again, why is this idea of God different from the ideas of the Canaanites and indeed of most of the rest of mankind?

The only reasonable answer to this is that in this particular instance God was being revealed — or was revealing himself — through the conscience of a nation. A chosen nation.

And to find out how and why this might be so, we need to make ourselves familiar with what was familiar to the Jews of those times — particularly the pattern of worship through sacrifice that was adopted by them, and what it meant.

Hebrew worship, from the beginning, as with all the surrounding tribes, was based on the concept of sacrifice. It was felt that the blood was the vehicle of life, in so far that when blood is spilt, life is extinguished, and thus blood belongs to God.

From this developed the slaughter of meat animals in a way that drained the blood from the carcase. It was, and is, taboo for the Jews to consume blood in any form, hence the continued need for the *kosher* butcher.

The wealth of wandering tribes is measured by the herds they keep. A sacrifice —as opposed to agricultural communities who offer the grain and the grape, or bread and wine — is thus in the form of an animal taken from the herd.

Amongst the Jews there were two main types of sacrifice — the *Peace Offering* and the *Sin Offering*.

The *Peace Offering* was a communal feast, meant to cement the existing good relationship between men and God. The meat of the killed beast was roasted and everyone had a share, including God, whose portion was burned upon the altar.

The *Sin Offering* was made when man had, for one reason or another, offended in some way against God. On these occasions the sinner, in an effort to make amends, laid his hands on the sacrificial beast, thus ritually placing the burden of sin upon it instead of upon himself and his family. The whole carcase was then burnt (hence this was also sometimes called a Burnt Offering), or offered to God, and there was no feast. From these two basic forms of sacrifice developed two others of historical significance to the Jews. These were the *Covenant Offering* and the *Passover Offering*.

The *Covenant Offering* commemorated what the Jews regarded as the especial and unique relationship with God — promised to Abraham and ratified under Moses. Many, no doubt, thought, and possibly still do, that this meant an eventual theocratic Jewish world empire under the military, political and spiritual leadership of a Messiah. Such a concept ironically would seem to have something of the fascist about it. Christians would consider that the Messiah has come in the person of Jesus, but was unrecognised by his own people, and that the new Israel is not a nation but the body of the faithful believers, and the Second Coming, whenever that is, will see the final glory of God and the Heavenly Jerusalem coming down to Earth.

Be this as it may, whatever the Jewish speculations about it at the time, the Covenant Offering affirmed their acceptance of the bargain they had struck with God. In form it was a combination of Sin Offering and Peace Offering.

The *Passover Offering* commemorated their deliverance from bondage in Egypt. A lamb was sacrificed, a cross of its blood put upon the doorposts, and the roasted lamb eaten whole, in order to sustain them on the first part of their journey through the Wilderness, where they were to receive the Covenant Law on Sinai and eventually proceed to the Promised Land. This was a re-enactment of the traditional prelude to their escape from Egypt when the Angel of the Lord was said to have gone through Egypt slaying the firstborn.

In all of these Offerings, the blood of the victim was set apart as being sacred to God. It would have been the height of blasphemy for anyone but a priest to touch it, and it was usually sprinkled about the altar, or, in the Covenant Sacrifice, on the Book of the Law and the worshippers, as emblematic of the Spirit and God-given life. All of these four forms of Offering were known to the Jews of New Testament times, to Jesus of Nazareth and to his Apostles, and to the early Christian church — which in its early days was in practical terms a Jewish sect.

We have lost sight of their significance in our own times, but they throw a unique light upon just what Jesus meant when he did the rather out-of-the-way things mentioned in the Gospel accounts of the Last Supper. If the Christian contention is right, that God did have a special relationship with the Jews, and that this came to fruition, or at any rate to a crisis point, with the life of Jesus (as incarnation of God himself), then whatever meaning it may have will have been brought to a focus by the events of the Passion of Jesus Christ. His own reading of the situation was exemplified, in action as well as words, on the eve of his execution.

In Christian eyes, what Jesus said and did at the time, the occasion of the Last Supper, is so significant that it has been commemorated ever since in the celebration of the Mass or Holy Communion.

> Who in the same night that he was betrayed, took Bread, and when he had given thanks, he brake it, and gave it to his disciples, saying, "Take, eat. This is my Body which is given for you. Do this in remembrance of me."

In this Jesus was identifying the bread with himself and himself with the sacrificial lamb. This is confirmed and further expanded in his next action and statement.

Likewise after supper he took the Cup; and, when he had given thanks, he gave it to them, saying, "Drink ye all of this: for this is my Blood of the New Testament, which is shed for you and for many for the remission of sins. Do this, as oft as ye shall drink it, in remembrance of me."

There is a blasphemous enormity about this statement which is not apparent today. The enormity is that the blood is, and always had been, *God's* portion of the sacrifice. What are the implications of all this?

What we have are the principle types of Jewish sacrificial worship being amalgamated into one. It is a Peace Offering — for all are partaking of a feast together. It is a Sin Offering — or a sacrificial substitution is being made for the remission of sin. It is a Covenant Offering — in that here we have the institution of a new Covenant.

It must be a *new* Covenant because man is being taken on to a level with God — by sharing the wine (or blood). Those who accept the New Covenant exchange the loyalty of the creature to its Creator, for identity or at-one-ment with the Creator. The incarnation of God in the life of Jesus effected a unifying relationship between Creator and created, as the Athanasian Creed subsequently put it, 'not by conversion of Godhead into flesh, but by taking manhood into God'.

There is also the element of the Passover Feast — and these events took place at the actual time of the Passover celebrations — in that under the terms of the New Covenant man is delivered from bondage. Not from the bondage of the Egyptians but from the bondage of time and death.

The message of the Messiah plainly is, that they who believe in the word of the Lord, who by faith and repentance place their sins on the sacrificial victim, and then eat it as a peace offering, will be delivered from the bondage of their own sin and from the existential boundaries of the human condition. At the same time, this Covenant, whereby man is taken onto a new level (into God), is sealed by man's taking God's portion of the sacrifice —the part which signifies eternal life.

Small wonder that the word *gospel* derives from the old words meaning 'good news'. However, there are corollaries to this, the implications of which took some time to be realised and which are possibly not realised in their entirety yet. For by being taken up into Godhead man takes on some of the responsibilities of Godhead. By becoming united with God he becomes united with the sacrificed and the bearer of the sin. In all it is a kind of cosmic coming of age.

When he came to the territory of Caesarea Philippi, Jesus asked his disciples. "Who do men say that I, the Son of Man, am?" They answered, "Some say John the Baptist, others Elijah, others Jeremiah, or one of the prophets."

"And you," he asked. "Who do you say I am?"

Simon Peter answered: "You are the Messiah, the Son of the living God."

Then Jesus said: "Simon son of Jonah, you are favoured indeed! You did not learn that from mortal man; it was revealed to you by my heavenly Father. And I say this to you: You are Peter, the Rock; and on this rock I will build my church, and the powers of death shall never conquer it. I will give you the keys of the kingdom of heaven; what you forbid on earth shall be forbidden in heaven, and what you allow on earth shall be allowed in heaven."

Upon this dictum from the Gospel of St. Matthew many ecclesiastical institutionalists may well have felt the sweet pang of organisational self-righteousness rise within them. But of course an organism of likeminded believers is not necessarily the same thing as a sacerdotal organisation. What is being said here, and in the context of a joke (Peter = *petros* = rock) — and the pun still holds in the original Aramaic, is simply that Peter is the first of many to realise the implications of the Incarnation. The keys of the kingdom are given to whoever recognises and believes in the Messiah. The process is virtually automatic, because it results in an alteration of emphasis of the will. That which was twisted and misdirected is brought into right orientation.

The roots of this are to be found in the very earliest assumptions of the Hebrew canon, in Genesis, where Adam and Eve lose their place in paradise because of their disobedience to their Creator — a disobedience that has characterised the sons and daughters of Adam and Eve ever since. This is a concept succinctly — though at present unfashionably — known as Original Sin. The result is the Fall into bondage of time, disease and death — the 'wages of sin'.

Basically it is a matter of a false direction of the will, to its own ends and purposes rather than to those of the Father. The cure, as presented by Jesus, is a turning of the will back to its true direction. Hence all that man is called upon to do, in order to unwarp his will and regain the paradisal state, is to admit his error and believe in God and the God-Man who has saved him. This belief brings right orientation of will, and opens the soul to the action of God the Holy Spirit; and acts and powers and good works flow from it.

Good works on their own are not really the same thing. Man cannot raise himself to heaven by tugging his own boot-straps. The whole thing is anyway rather more complex than just improving peoples' general behaviour. We are concerned with some other types of relationship — with the state of eternity, and with God, together with a kind of cosmic civil war in the whole of creation.

We had better begin with first things. Assuming that the worlds did not just grow from a series of blind coincidences, without purpose or intention, there has to be some Prime Author of it all — in short, God.

We have tried to trace this revelation of himself as generally accepted by a large proportion of the human race, and from a consideration of the claims of Jesus of Nazareth we need to describe the One God in three forms — as Divine Father, Son (or God-Man), and Holy Spirit.

There are many difficulties in all this. It tramples pretty hard on a variety of different prejudices. What is good sense to the goose is a stumbling block to the gander, and vice versa. It took the Church centuries of debate to sort out some kind of rational and understandable answer.

The Trinity is nonetheless the One. But with the fragmented understanding that we possess we cannot approach any rational appreciation of the One unless we try to split it. So let us deal in turn with Father, Son and Holy Spirit, but trying to remember that what we say of one we are saying of the others, although they are neither identical nor yet separate. Words and ideas tend to fall apart as one tries to define that which is beyond them.

God the Father is common to almost all religions. He is the Creator and Sustainer of the whole Universe. The All-seeing Eye that, if it blinked, would cause the worlds momentarily to vanish. The natural speculation of early man, after civilisation and religious ideas had developed away from primitive hunting and animistic fetishes or ancestor worship, was to see God the Creator and Sustainer as a great emperor or magnate — with innumerable minions running to obey his slightest whim. Though there may well be some truth in this image, it is far from being the whole story, certainly as presented by Jesus, who was insistent upon the real presence of a loving Father as concerned for each one of his creatures as for the Creation as a whole.

> 'Are not sparrows two a penny? Yet without your Father's leave not one of them can fall to the ground. As for you, even the hairs of your head have all been counted. So have no fear; you are worth more than any number of sparrows.'

This differs markedly from the concept of a remote transcendent being light-years and light-years away — a God that was formulated by some of the early Gnostic heretics and which has some kind of dim credence today in that it seems to some people to be somehow more 'scientific'. Buddhism also tends towards this conception — God as a kind of attenuated impersonal interstellar gas. In place of the words of the old hymn 'Eternal Father strong to save', it tends to substitute 'Oh rootless ground of everything / To which we tentatively sing'.

To Jesus, God the Father is no abstract principle (at least he *might* be that, but he is a great deal more besides). He interferes in what we would consider quite an arbitrary way in history, selects an obscure group of nomadic tribes to be a Chosen People (*'How odd of God, to choose The Jews'*, as some rhyming wit has put it), tests their faith and takes them through terrible tribulations when they fall away from the Covenant (being the Chosen of God is no soft option), and has generally far more to do with concrete problems of morals and manners, law and liturgy, people and politics, than seems altogether proper for the Creator of a Cosmos.

One is tempted to feel that if he is really a person of such particularity he ought to be off some several zillion light years away, maybe in a different space-time continuum, organising some other benighted universes. Perhaps he is. We should not limit the powers of the Creator to what seem to us the limits of the Creation. God may well be able to be as aware of the Brownian movements of atoms in a minute particle of substance (and even before Brown discovered them) as he is of Middle Eastern politics, the morals of the West End stage, or the state of evolution of prehistoric monsters on fifteen million planets.

We are faced with a vast range of consciousness in our own small world. For instance, what does a dog realise of the contents of his master's bookshelf or the output of his television? But it is there staring him in the face. Again, what kind of contemporary prehistoric life is going on in the insect world of our own house and garden? We do well to beware of setting hypothetic limits on celestial beings, based upon the scale of our own consciousness.

But what happens when this terrifyingly complex, vast, multi-faceted, omniscient, omnipotent and omnipresent being decides to come upon the earth — to take on the life of one of his created beings on one of his created planets? And also on a redeeming mission to save that species from itself?

The mind begins to boggle. Would any of us, say a cat-lover, take on the body and consciousness of a cat, knowing that apart from the appalling constriction of power and consciousness we would end up being booted to death in a back alley by hooligans? One is faced with a magnitude of love that transcends the magnitude of power and reduces it to voluntary impotence. This is rather different from the 'gentle Jesus meek and mild' so sentimentally portrayed by Victorian hymn-writers.

The sayings of Jesus about himself in the New Testament are either the self-revelations of the Messiah or the ramblings of a megalomaniac. For instance:

Whoever then will acknowledge me before men, I will acknowledge him before my Father in heaven; and whoever disowns me before men, I will disown him before my Father in Heaven.

You must not think that I have come to bring peace to the earth. I have not come to bring peace, but a sword. I have come to set a man against his father, a daughter against her mother, a son's wife against her mother-in-law: and a man will find his enemies under his own roof!

No man is worthy of me who cares more for father and mother than for me; no man is worthy of me who cares more for son or daughter; no man is worthy of me who does not take up his cross and walk in my footsteps. By gaining his life a man will lose it: by losing his life for my sake, he will gain it.

To receive you is to receive me, and to receive me is to receive the One who sent me. Whoever receives a prophet as a prophet will be given a prophet's reward, and whoever receives a good man because he is a good man will be given a good man's reward. And if anyone gives so much as a cup of cold water to one of these little ones, because he is a disciple of mine, I tell you this: that man will assuredly not go unrewarded.

According to this hardly meek and mild passage one can take one's choice over calling him divine or demented, or opting for various other interpretations — such as good man or prophet. And much would appear to hang on the choice.

It is a matter of spiritual affection and relationship. To accept the Messiah as simply a good man is a sign of some health in the soul. To accept him as a prophet of God is a sign of a greater contact with reality. But it is receiving him in the heart, as the Son of God, that is for the soul a cure and achievement of eternal life. Eternal life, we should add, is not simply life that goes on forever and ever for a very long time; it is a particular quality of life that is outside our conception of time and space.

As an aid to belief — and possibly for other reasons we are in no place to fathom — Jesus performed some supra-human actions. There was the Transfiguration soon after Peter had recognised him to be the Messiah.

Jesus took Peter, James, and John the brother of James, and led them up a high mountain where they were alone; and in their presence he was transfigured; his face shone like the sun and his clothes became white as the light. And they saw Moses and Elijah appear, conversing with him ... a bright cloud suddenly overshadowed them, and a voice called from the cloud: "This is my Son, my Beloved, on whom my favour rests; listen to him." At the sound of the voice the disciples fell on their faces in terror. Jesus then came up to them, touched them, and said, "Stand up; do not be afraid." And when they raised their eyes they saw no one, but only Jesus.

Then there are the events of the Passion, having their own particular enacted meaning, and finally the Resurrection and subsequently the Ascension.

Some modern theologians feel the necessity to try to explain away these later events in whole or in part so as not to offend modern scientific sensibilities. The sensibilities are not entirely modern — the philosophically minded Greeks of the time also found them a stumbling block. Whether we decide to like it, lump it, or try to ignore it, the record is that after his death Jesus appeared and disappeared at will before his followers, sometimes to one or two, sometimes in private to the assembled apostles, at other times to five hundred people at a time. He was solid enough to share a meal with them (and whoever heard of a gastronomic ghost?) and for doubting Thomas to physically examine the wounds of his execution. Finally, after promising that the Holy Spirit, the Comforter, would come, he disappeared in a cloud. And there are many mystics throughout the ages who can testify that disappearance does not necessarily mean an absence. By the help of this book, or by any other way, we hope that others will be able to testify too.

We will postpone a consideration of the Holy Spirit until our next chapter, when we shall need to deal with 'the powers of the Spirit' and other supernormal phenomena. For the moment, we may rest and decide just what the implications are for us in re-orientating the will by belief in the incarnation of God.

The concept has been described by St. Paul in two great images — the Body of Christ, and the Bride of Christ. These are concepts which have wide and deep ramifications and to which we shall need to return as we progress in our work.

St. Paul's primary idea is that the Church (that is, all true believers — we do well to leave religious organisations and denominations out of the matter for the time being), is the mystical Bride of Christ, and as a consequence of this, groom and bride becoming one 'flesh', the body of believers is the Mystical Body of Christ.

In his first letter to the Corinthians he says. 'Now you are Christ's body and each of you a limb or organ of it.' And this is no mere allegory. His ideas are closely akin to the philosophy of Plato where in *The Republic* a similar idea is expressed in regard to the perfect State — 'when any individual citizen experiences good or evil, such a State will assuredly maintain that she herself is the sufferer, or will rejoice or grieve as a whole'. And it is because of this Platonic cast of mind, wherein Christ and the Church are the realities, and the affairs of men and women but shadows of them, that Paul seems to have made such rulings on the relations between the sexes that tend to offend modern liberal thought.

It was not that he was a 'typical oriental' or one who looked down upon women, but that he regarded women as emblematic of the fallen human race and men as emblematic of the Christ. And thus he bid wives be subject to their husbands and respect them and bid husbands love their wives. It is, in its proper understanding, a ritual act or attitude, rather than anti-feminism. And to Paul and his contemporaries the Second Coming and end of the world was expected imminently, which put a rather different complexion on things than our longer term viewpoint two thousand years later.

Paul's ideas parallel somewhat the symbolism of the Old Testament prophets but there are some radical differences. The prophets spoke of the Virgin Israel (beginning with Hosea) as a fallen wife 'whoring after strange gods', whereas Paul sees the Church as a new bride, party to a New Covenant, not falling away from an Old Covenant. The prophets called Israel the mother of her children whereas Paul speaks as all Christians *being* a part or members of the Bride. And the prophets talk in terms of allegory, whereas for Paul it is actual reality.

We have spoken of the Christ being a Bridegroom of the Church — that is, to Christians collectively — but it also has a personal significance, particularly in the light of Jesus' remark that husband and wife become 'one flesh' — despite the other remark about there being no giving in marriage in heaven. Similarly one's own body (including the soul that indwells it) becomes a vehicle for Christ as its head, directing it.

When God the Son ascended to God the Father in Heaven, *'to prepare a place for his followers'*, he left his followers acting in his place, guided by God the Holy Spirit. The human being under the New Covenant is therefore offered a high calling to be the representative of God in the world. Though, as we have said, it is something more than being a representative, it is a mystical union, which can be best described in terms of great intimacy — as a marriage or physical union. It will call therefore for commitment on all levels of being, a redirection of the will or purpose in life, in the mind or mentality, in the feelings, and in the physical life in the world.

There is a similarity here with some of the ideas of the pagan mysteries — an identification of the world with God. But here again there are certain seemingly slight but radically important differences.

The pagan mysteries tended to regard the world as created by a demiurge — a kind of intermediary god who had created things wrongly.

Thus it was up to man to rise above the evils of the world by identifying with a mystical saviour hero and thus to be 'reborn' into higher worlds.

There is a great similarity here with the ideas of St. Paul. So much so that he has been accused of importing ancient Pagan Mystery ideas into Christianity. He may have been so influenced and, if so, this makes him rather less the Pharisaic bigot that he is sometimes made out to be. But what is more important is that the similarities show a coming together of Revealed and Natural Religion in a way that had never been before and never has been since. It was as if, when the Creator and Lord of All came nearer and nearer to that crisis point in time where he actually appeared physically in the world (an actor within his own play) there was a growing ability of the pagan world at large to pick up his coming in their speculations.

The Pagan Mysteries commenced about three hundred years before Christ and ceased about three hundred years after. We have already stated how the general tenor of affairs in the world (a worldwide empire, a *lingua franca* etc.) had made the conditions for the advent of a universal religion favourable. This general effect is also to be seen in the religious psychology of the pagan world.

The old pagan religions had become sterile and institutionalised into bureaucratic priestcrafts and the growth of the Mysteries was at the same time a reaction from this, an attempt to inject some mystical reality into formal observances and a foreshadowing of the coming of a real Saviour. Not a mythical being but an actual flesh and blood appearance of God within the world.

It took some time of course for the early Church to work things out. To begin with, it was expected that the end of the world was imminent, and there was also considerable disagreement as to whether the coming of the Messiah was an event only of significance to the Jews, or of importance to the Gentiles also. And if so, whether this meant enforcing the Old Covenant Law upon Gentile converts —with circumcision, *kosher* meat, and all the other observances detailed in the Levitical code.

Then there was the question of the pagan religions. The prevailing state cults were spiritually dead letter, although formal subscription to their beliefs was expected as a proof of loyalty to the state. Many early Christians were martyred for refusing to make this formal token observance to the deified Roman emperors. Of more importance were the Mystery Religions, and in particular the one that sprang into pre-eminence and travelled wherever the Roman army went, the cult of Mithra This was so close to Christian observance that it was often confused with Christianity.

Mithraism came close to becoming the religion of the Roman Empire instead of Christianity. In one sense it could be regarded as the last brilliant flicker of a dying paganism in a near-Christian compromise. And there are two points of view. It can be seen as a commendable height of paganism (man's approach to God) just short of Christianity (God's approach to man), or on the other hand as a diabolical subtlety of the devil to divert converts from the true religion by imitation of its surface features.

The god Mithra is of considerable antiquity and like all pagan god forms, underwent considerable modification during his evolution. By the beginning of the Christian era he had absorbed a number of similar rival gods and come to be regarded as god of light. He was represented most frequently as a young man in a cap in the act of slaying a divine bull, from whose wounded side was coming, not blood, but wheat and fruits of the earth. The cult had its primitive side. It was a type of Mystery religion for men (an attitude somewhat more anti-feminist than Paul's Christianity is sometimes made out to be), with various grades of initiation — Soldier, Raven, Persian, Lion, Hidden One, Sun, Father. A particularly gory aspect was the initiatory bath in the blood of a slaughtered bull. The candidate stood in a pit under a grating while the bull was slaughtered immediately above him. This aspect of the worship probably goes back to the ancient Minoan civilisation of Crete, and survives to this day in the bull-fighting of the Spanish peninsula.

Its remarkable similarity to Christianity lay in its other sacraments — of bread and wine. Also, both Christianity and Mithraism tended to use the Sun as a symbol of their Lord.

The similarity of the two religions was often remarked upon by contemporaries, though the similarity was more superficial than may have appeared to uncommitted onlookers. Even a distinguished commentator has gone astray in saying that Christianity and Mithraism had differing mythologies but the same theology. The converse is in fact more accurate — they had differing theologies but similar mythologies.

According to both, a 'divine man' acted as Saviour of the righteous, and this could be represented by similar liturgies and symbols. For instance, both chose December 25th (immediately after the Winter Solstice when the days begin to get longer) as the day to celebrate the Saviour's birth.

But there were other, more fundamental, differences. Mithra was a mythical being; Jesus was an historical figure. Mithra brought god-head down to man; Jesus brought manhood up to god. Mithra was a protagonist in a perpetual battle between equal principles of good and evil; Jesus once and for all conquered the evil that had been perpetrated by some of the created. The Mithra elect were saved by their own efforts — salvation was earned; the Christian was saved by grace, following upon belief, and although virtue and merit were important to strive for, the Christian did not consider it possible for man to attain to heaven by his own efforts.

There is, of course much high teaching in the Mithraic system and it enfolded within itself most of the better teachings of paganism. It embraced the original blood mystique of the primitive hunter and the vegetation rites of the primitive agriculturalist. It included the more philosophical stellar worship of the Babylonians, a complex inner cosmology based upon the symbolism derived from groupings of the stars. All this had been grafted on to a Persian Zoroastrian basis of dual, basically equal, forces of Good and Evil fighting for power over creation. Earthly life tended to be equated with evil (it *was* frequently unpleasant!) and heavenly other-worldliness with good. To this had been added the more sophisticated philosophical speculations of the Greeks, embodied for instance in the Stoic's view of man as a noble creature making his own balanced life and values in the face of a warring universe — which has a parallel in modern existentialism.

Thus as well as being a rival to young Christianity from without, it also became, by its superficial similarity, an heretical rival within. Mithraism as such was eradicated at the end of the fourth century through the influence of the Christian Church which had just come into political power. But beliefs as deep rooted and of such antiquity are not so easily dismissed from human consciousness.

There were those within the Christian Church, and by no means an eccentric minority, who strove to combine the best of the old religion with the new. Unfortunately it did not quite succeed. It was a time of considerable intellectual challenge to the Church, trying to sort out the implications of the Incarnation without having the situation made even more complex by pre-Christian speculation.

One difficulty was that pre-Christian speculation of various types tended to be taken as self-evidently true, into which Christian history should be made to fit. Thus implicit pagan belief in the utter duality of spirit and matter would be unable to accept the possibility of God becoming man. It would insist that Jesus was some kind of cosmic phantom or divine 'projection'. Alternatively. it might refuse to see Jesus as anything more than an inspired man — the best of the prophets or *gurus.*

Those pagans who espoused a complex doctrine of inner worlds to be circumnavigated after death by the judicious use of secret words of power conferred at initiation ceremonies would also insist on trying to formulate an inner tradition of esoteric Christianity for the elect.

There is, of course, just sufficient truth in these positions to make them the more dangerous in perverting the real truth. The early Fathers finally hammered out the facts of the Incarnation to mean that God had walked the earth as man; he had once and for all conquered evil; and all who believed in him would, by the simple remedial act of will, conquer death; that as God of all, his message was for *all* men, and there were no first class and second class citizens in the Kingdom of Heaven.

The Incarnation *could* be foreshadowed by recourse not only to prophecy in the Old Testament but also to parallels in the pagan myths. Being dreams of an unfulfilled reality, the sacrificed god of the primitive hunters and the resurrected god of the primitive agriculturalists, no less than the cosmic mediator of more sophisticated pagan belief, were fulfilled historically in the coming of the Christ. This led to a danger of putting the cart before the horse and trying to force the Christian story into conformity with prior belief, rather than modify the early speculative beliefs according to the corrective Incarnate fact.

All of these half truths were capable of giving birth to a heresy and most of them did. Arianism, Nestorianism, Pelagianism, Paulicianism — some with very considerable followings, and even persisting to this day — to say nothing of various revivals through the ages under different names and guises. However tedious the apparently over-subtle bickerings of the early Church may appear to us, they were vitally important in getting the basic truths of Christian belief hammered out. This occurred in the first four Ecumenical Conferences from Nicea to Chalcedon and resulted in the Nicene and Athanasian Creeds. For Christianity to hope to survive as an entity it was essential to get things right from the start, otherwise errors would grow by geometric progression and eventually burst the Church apart. Human nature is not perfect and therefore neither was perfection in this attained. A single word, *filioque,* caused the great separation between the Catholic and Orthodox churches, centuries later.

Also the early Fathers in their rigorous search for the essential basic truth tended to throw out the baby with the bathwater in a number of instances. The rejection of some truths could be dangerous. It is possible that those heresies that have come back to haunt the Church again and again through the ages, should not be regarded as persistent weeds to be stamped out rigorously every time they re-appear, but rather the embodiment of vital truths that the Church needs to assimilate in order to fulfil its mission. The old law, whether pagan or Old Testament Hebrew, remains true where it does not conflict with the teaching and life of Jesus, who said of it himself: I am come not to destroy but to fulfil—though also, Behold, I make all things new.

An occult study of Christianity is much concerned with examining rejected heresies to identify the truths that give them their vitality but which could not be accepted, for one reason or another, by the official ecclesiastical authorities of the time.

EXERCISE FOR CHAPTER II

The spear which pierced my side shall run you through
And make of you a reed through which my Grace shall flow.

Our next exercise in building a magical armamentarium is the visualising of a fiery spear. This must be realised as embodying the love of God for all his creation, channelled through man. By its means man is a priest to all the lower orders of life that come within his jurisdiction, including the consciousness in the very atoms that comprise his own body and the animal and vegetable aspects that go to make up his own physical means of manifestation.

There is a deep and important teaching here concerning the Planetary Being, which is the aggregate of all these consciousnesses, a kind or great 'Generating Elemental', something akin to the 'biosphere' formulated by Teilhard de Chardin, and without which a higher consciousness would have no ground for terrestrial existence. Its archetypal prototype is held within human consciousness as the Garden of Eden, or the former mythical Golden Age of innocence. Its archetypal destiny, as formulated in human consciousness, should be the New Jerusalem (as personally prefigured in the Transfiguration), coming down from Heaven to Earth, adorned like a Bride for her Bridegroom.

A proper realisation of its necessity and beneficence might have avoided many weird Christian and pagan ultra-ascetic and flagellant sects of the past.

The construction of the Fiery Spear in the imagination, and the consciousness of its coming from the All Highest and penetrating every level of being, passing symbolically through the top of the head above, transfixing the spine and going deep into the heart of the Earth, is an act of will in accordance with the Will of God, and an invocation of the Reality that the symbol represents — the Love and Grace of God to all Creation through Man. It has to be Man in Christ however. The Manhood taken up into Godhead by the passion of Jesus.

The archetype of the Spear that we visualise is the one that is prominent also in the Holy Grail legends — the spear that was suspended over the Holy Grail dripping with three drops of blood. It is also the Spear which dealt the Dolorous Stroke when it was misused and thus caused the whole Land of Logres to fall under a dreadful curse and enchantment. The Land of Logres is our physical planet — the effects of its continuing curse and enchantment are all about us — plain to all who can read newspaper headlines. In other words, we have in the Grail Legends a presentation, in alternative symbolic form, of the Fall of Man through misuse of the God-given free will.

We will examine the meaning of the Grail Legends in more depth later. For the meantime we may be content to concentrate on the original spear (traditionally that of the centurion Longinus — he who said: 'Truly this man was a son of God') that was stabbed into the side of the dead Jesus to ensure his death and from which came a flow of blood and water emblematic of the water of baptism and the redeeming sacrifice.

As Emma Jung and Marie Louise von Franz take pains to emphasise in their book *The Grail Legend*, 'When, in most of the versions, the bleeding lance appears as appertaining to the Grail, this is because *it is the instrument by which the redeeming blood was brought forth into manifestation.*'

This will give food for thought on the deep implications of this symbol of the Fiery Spear, some of which we shall examine later, and others which will become apparent to whoever undertakes the exercises of the Sphere of Light and the Fiery Spear in faith. They are, like all the exercises in this book, to be used in conjunction one with another — and in the order given.

The first two exercises of the Sphere and the Spear are of particularly basic importance, as regular performance of them will prove by personal experience.

CHAPTER III

The Serpent Flame

Having dedicated ourselves to be a channel for the works of God, it follows that we should develop our powers to be as effective an instrument as our natural gifts allow. Some powers may be bestowed by grace, others acquired by slow learning. Some confusion also exists as to which are valid and which are not. To those who are called to be doctors, the exercise of their medical skill is a channel for their own will guided by the Holy Spirit. The same might be said of any human science. But what happens in the case of those whose calling is not to physical but to occult science?

The confusion that exists in this area is caused principally because of a failure to distinguish between the *mystical* and the *magical* — between that which is of God and that which is of the inner side of creation.

To begin with, this confusion arises because various kinds of unusual phenomena may attend the presence and workings of the Holy Spirit. This has led to a tendency to identify such phenomena with the working of God. But speaking more strictly, these phenomena may really be but side-effects on the inner creation of the direct activity of God.

As an illustrative metaphor, the action of the Holy Spirit has been likened to a great wind (no doubt deriving from *pneuma* — spirit or wind in Greek; *ruach* — spirit or breath in Hebrew) but the Holy Spirit works upon the minds and hearts of men, and the attendant phenomena are as the dust raised by that wind. Whirling dust may show the presence of a whirlwind, but is not an active part of it. Conversely, anyone who by any means is able to raise a figurative storm of dust, is not necessarily invoking or associated with the Holy Spirit.

The types of phenomena that may attend the active manifestation of the Holy Spirit have been described in the New Testament. The Acts of the Apostles account of its first coming to the Christian church is that:

> ... suddenly there came from the sky a noise like that of a strong driving wind, which filled the whole house where they were sitting. And there appeared to them tongues like flames of Fire, dispersed among them and resting on each one. And they were filled with the Holy Spirit and began to talk in other tongues, as the Spirit gave them power of utterance ... at this sound the crowd gathered, all bewildered because each one heard his own

language spoken. They were amazed … others said contemptuously, "They have been drinking!"

St. Paul refers to the various manifestations of the Holy Spirit in a letter to the early Church in Corinth:

There are varieties of gifts, but the same Spirit … In each of us the Spirit is manifested in one particular way, for some useful purpose. One man, through the Spirit, has the gift of wise speech, while another, by the power of the same Spirit, can put the deepest knowledge into words. Another, by the same Spirit, is granted faith; another, by the one Spirit, gifts of healing, and another miraculous powers; another has the gift of prophecy, and another ability to distinguish true spirits from false; yet another has the gift of ecstatic utterance of different kinds, and another the ability to interpret it. But all these gifts are the work of one and the same Spirit, distributing them separately to each individual at will.

And it was because the 'gifts' or 'activities' of the Spirit were put into higher regard by the members of the congregation at Corinth that Paul was led to make that famous injunction:

I may speak with the tongues of men or of angels, but if I am without love, I am a sounding gong or a clanging cymbal. I may have the gift of prophecy and know every hidden truth; I may have faith strong enough to move mountains; but if I have no love, I am nothing … Are there prophets? Their work will be over. Are there tongues of ecstasy? They will cease. Is there knowledge? It will vanish away … Now we see only puzzling reflections in a mirror, but then we shall see face to face. My knowledge now is partial: then it will be whole, like God's knowledge of me. In a word, there are three things that last for ever; faith, hope, and love; but the greatest of these is love.

Something of the confusion into which the Corinthians were falling can be read between the lines in his development of this theme where he distinguishes between 'ecstatic utterance' which was often meaningless to others, and 'prophecy' which was the interpretation of the word of God, as we have already seen in the previous chapter. As he goes on to say:

Even with inanimate things that produce sounds — a flute, say, or a lyre — unless their notes mark definite intervals, how can you tell what tune is being played? … In the same way if your ecstatic utterance yields no precise meaning, how can anyone tell what you are saying? You will be talking into the air … if I do not know the meaning of the sound the speaker makes, his words will be gibberish to me, and mine to him. You are, I know, eager for gifts of the Spirit; then aspire above all to excel in those which built up the church … Thank God, I am more gifted in ecstatic utterance than any of you, but in the congregation I would rather speak fine intelligible words, for the benefit of others as well as myself, than thousands of words in the language of ecstasy … if the whole congregation is assembled and all are using the "strange tongues" of ecstasy, and some instructed persons or unbelievers should enter, will they not think you are mad? … If it is a matter of ecstatic utterance, only two should speak, or at most three, one at a time, and someone must interpret. If there is no interpreter, the speaker had better not address the meeting at all, but speak to himself and to God.

The trouble with the Corinthians would seem to be that they fell victims of having a greater regard for the gifts than for the giver. And they mistook the purpose of those gifts for a sign of personal prestige at worst, and in a spirit of uncritical 'enthusiasm' at best.

That the gifts of the Holy Spirit were a very real thing and not to be trifled with is indicated elsewhere in the New Testament. Jesus refers to it himself on sending his disciples off on their various missions, instructing them: 'when you are arrested, do not worry about what you are to say; when the time comes, the words will be given you; for it is not you who will be speaking; it will be the Spirit of your Father speaking in you.'

And it is of the Holy Spirit that Jesus made that dark saying: 'Anyone who speaks a word against the Son of Man will receive forgiveness; but for him who slanders the Holy Spirit there will be no forgiveness.'

The Holy Spirit was essentially that part of God that came upon man as part of his 'spiritual rebirth' when the will turned back to the ways of God the Father by the acceptance of God the Son. According to the New Testament this is a birth to wisdom, faith, righteousness, joy and peace, and a deliverance from sin, death and the Law. By deliverance from the Law one means an abandonment of an 'I — it' attitude to God and the creation, for an 'I — thou' relationship. The mechanistic, inhuman object becomes the organic personal love.

The 'converted' or 'reborn' man or woman ceases to be cut off in a delusory world of intellect and superstition but becomes aware of the true state of the universe—as a good earth, the creation of an ever loving Father for his children, that has been made into a place of dark shadows, pain and sorrows only by their turning away from him. St. John identifies Spirit with Truth, and also says:

Though God has never been seen by any man, God himself dwells in us if we love one another, his love is brought to perfection within us. There is the proof that we dwell in him and he dwells in us; he has imparted his Spirit to us.

The Holy Spirit is thus the proof as well as the means of 'conversion' or 'rebirth' — which is perhaps why the Corinthian Christians set such great store on showing this proof. But, as Paul went to great pains to point out, as well as bringing powers it should also show itself as love — of God and man and fellow creatures.

The disciples at Pentecost talked with many tongues, the Christian martyrs went singing to their deaths, the apostles worked miracles of healing, Philip was even teleported. At the same time the powers of the Holy Spirit could be destructive, as Ananias and Sapphira found. The early Christians held property in common. Ananias and Sapphira secretly withheld a portion of theirs. In the act of proclaiming their deceit they were struck dead. Not unnaturally 'a great awe fell upon the whole church, and upon all who heard of these events'.

The powers of the Holy Spirit also had a hand in Church government. The successor to fill the apostleship abandoned by Judas was chosen in this manner:

> Two names were put forward; Joseph, who was known as Barabbas, and bore the added name of Justus; and Matthias. Then they prayed and said, "Thou, Lord, who knowest the hearts of all men, declare which of these two thou hast chosen to receive this office of ministry and apostleship which Judas abandoned to go where he belonged." They drew lots and the lot fell on Matthias, who was then assigned a place among the twelve apostles.

One can hardly imagine the government of Church affairs being conducted in such a manner nowadays. There are even denominations of the Church who would condemn the process as gambling if not sorcery. Whether the institutional churches today lack this kind of implicit faith, or all signs of the early manifestations of the Holy Spirit, is a matter for their own conscience.

Sufficient has been said to indicate that we are dealing with an important matter that can be looked at in a number of different lights. Basically it is — if the Holy Spirit has brought supernormal powers in the past:

a) does the lack of those powers mean that there is no contact with the Holy Spirit?

b) does the presence of those powers mean that they come from the Holy Spirit?

c) does the cultivation of those powers for their own sake constitute a sin or blasphemy against the Holy Spirit?

To all of these we can give a single answer — No.

Confusion and error has existed only because men have confused the presence of the Holy Spirit with the ancillary powers or perception that such a presence might (but on the other hand might not) bring. It is, as we said, a confusing of the wind with the dust that is raised by it; of the cause with the effects. And the same effects could result from different causes. They could result from the presence and activity of a spirit that is other than the Holy Spirit; a visitation from other dimensions of existence, good, evil, indifferent, or wholly 'other' than life as we physically know it. Alternatively man himself might, by his own efforts, bring about such powers and perceptions — which might be a difficult procedure, perhaps even a dangerous procedure, but not necessarily having anything to do with the Holy Spirit or, for that matter, any other spirit but his own.

The Holy Spirit may very well work without the side effects of supernormal powers, and frequently does, through the hearts of men. It has led and inspired men to lives of great dedication and courage in pursuit of a Christian calling. This less immediately spectacular working of the Holy Spirit has been misunderstood in two ways.

In one way it has been 'ordinarified' into a kind of stamp of historical infallibility upon whatever denomination of the Church the commentator happens to approve.

On the other hand, the lack of the enthusiastic spectacular has led to the formation of some Christian sects who deliberately set out to show signs of the Spirit. These are the Pentecostal churches, which appeal to congregations of a particularly emotional fervour. They range in their 'evidence' from a fairly normal 'speaking with tongues' to more circus-like performances such as the handling of deadly snakes.

This, however, is not necessarily the work of the Holy Spirit, for as much might be witnessed in primitive religious festivities. Although again, of course, it *could* be the work of the Holy Spirit — and each case needs to be judged on its merits — assuming that we are in a position to pass a judgement. It is at root a confusion of an effect with a particular cause — and not necessarily the right cause. As we have said, just as a lack of unusual powers does not necessarily mean there is a lack of the presence of the Holy Spirit, so the presence of unusual powers does not necessarily mean the presence of the Holy Spirit.

As to the deliberate cultivation of such powers, much will depend upon motive; but it is of course needful also to get the technicalities right.

Another cause of confusion has been the periodical upsurge of 'Holy Spirit' movements. They are in fact always with us but come to the fore more at some times than at others. In the history of the Christian West they come forward as a claimed re-stimulation of the working of the Holy Spirit, and embrace a more mystical approach to religious observance than the more orthodox pattern of institutional church worship usually appears to encourage.

They have, at their height, in for instance the early Franciscan Order, achieved a real re-stimulation of the conscience of the Church. But they have also at other times degenerated into weird and unhealthy eccentric forms such as the Flagellants. They are not without considerable significance in social history, for they formed in medieval times perhaps the first mass movement towards popular social democratic forms of government, in however crude a way.

They are also linked with eschatological hopes — the coming of the end of the world with the final overthrow of evil by the reappearance of the Messiah and his saints.

This again is a religious tradition that goes back far into Jewish history, and stems from the conception of the Jews being a chosen race. Although this was conceived by the prophets as a divinely appointed destiny in which the Jews would enlighten the whole world, the various misfortunes that their nation went through caused there to be compensatory dreams of a future when the Lord would come and reconstitute a new Eden upon Earth and exalt them in the face of their enemies. At first this was conceived in the narrow national limits of a new Eden in the land of Palestine. Later this was extended to a worldwide vision in, for instance, the Book of Daniel, written about 150 B.C. in response to a crisis when the Syrian Greek monarchy, to which the Jews were then subject, forbade all Jewish religious observances and so sparked off the Maccabean revolt.

The general pattern or archetype of this belief has been admirably summed up in Professor Norman Cohn's analysis of the social history of such movements, *The Pursuit of the Millennium*:

'The world is dominated by an evil, tyrannous power of boundless destructiveness — a power moreover which is imagined not as simply human but as demonic. The tyranny of that power will become more and more intolerable — until suddenly the hour will strike when the Saints of God are able to rise up and overthrow it. Then the Saints themselves, the chosen, holy people who hitherto have groaned under the oppressor's heel, shall in their turn inherit dominion over the whole earth. This will be the culmination of history; the Kingdom of the Saints will not only surpass in glory all previous kingdoms, it will have no successors.'

This vision passed, in time, from the Jewish race to the Christian Gentile world, bridged by the increasing Jewish emphasis on the coming Messiah who would lead the righteous on the Last Day and save his people. This idea had come particularly to the fore in the immediately pre-Christian era of the Roman annexation of Palestine by Pompey in 63 B.C. It also resulted in the disastrous revolt against the Roman power in A.D. 66-72 when the Temple at Jerusalem was physically destroyed. The last Jewish hero in the struggle for national independence on whom such Messianic hopes lay was Simon bar Kokhba in A.D. 131, after which time the Christians took over increasingly the Jewish apocalyptic beliefs, in the doctrine of the Second Coming.

The early Christians firmly believed in this cosmic event in their own lifetimes, and unless it is a later interpolation, according to the Gospels so did Jesus:

> For whoever is ashamed of me and my words, the Son of Man will be ashamed of him, when he comes in his glory of the Father and the holy angels. And I tell you this: there are some of those standing here who will not taste death before they have seen the kingdom of God.

However, this could equally refer to the Transfiguration, which immediately follows this passage, or the Resurrection, or the coming of the Holy Spirit at Pentecost. Be this as it may, the early Christians expected an imminent end of the world, and this was foretold in a number of apocalyptic documents of which the Book of Revelations is the only one to survive in the Christian canon — because it was attributed (erroneously) to the apostle John. In the Book of Revelations there is a close affinity with the imagery of Jewish apocalyptic, as for instance the ten horned beast which also occurs in the vision of Daniel.

As with the Jews, these beliefs attained more to general acceptance or popularity in times of persecution. Perhaps the first Holy Spirit 'revival' was that of Montanus in A.D. 156 who preached that the New Jerusalem was about to descend in Phrygia. His followers were ascetic in the extreme and not only expected, but sought martyrdom. And Montanism spread rapidly with the wave of persecutions against the Christians; even the great early theologian Tertullian was a Montanist. However, a more moderate view is expressed in the Second Letter of Peter (c. A.D. 150) saying that:

> ... with the Lord one day is like a thousand years and a thousand years one day. It is not that the Lord is slow in fulfilling his promise, as some suppose, but that he is very patient with you, because it is not his will for any to be lost, but for all to come to repentance.

And by the third century A.D. we find the theologian Origen placing the emphasis, not on a physical coming of the Kingdom of God throughout the whole world, but on the experience of the individual soul as it progresses from this world to the next.

This was expanded by Augustine in the fifth century, who in *The City of God* considered the Revelation of John to be a spiritual allegory, not an historical prediction, and the now powerful and prosperous Christian church, in spite of the encroaching barbarian hordes, to be the New Jerusalem on Earth. And this became so much the accepted view of the Church that the parts of the great theological treatise of the second century by Irenaeus, *Against Heresies*, which had regarded the physical Second Coming as indispensable to orthodox belief, were suppressed — and only came to light in a rare manuscript that had escaped this expurgation, as late as 1575.

The changing orthodox view did not however prevent the continuation of a popular millennial belief, particularly in times of tribulation. And in times of universal social injustice and oppression, as the Church became wealthier and more institutionalised and a part of the fabric of the established ruling society, it was inevitable that from time to time comparisons would be made between the standard of life and morals of the contemporary clergy and those of the early disciples of Jesus. In this more direct attempt to return to basic religious fundamentals one finds an emphasis naturally being laid upon the Holy Spirit.

Within the Church this saw the foundation of the various monastic orders; and also the need for their reform from time to time through the centuries. Outside the Church, or at any rate on its fringes, or within the laity, (although only ordained ministers were supposed to preach), there was always a lively tradition of wandering lay preachers — as indeed Jesus himself had been. In some cases they developed messianic pretensions, particularly if they had charismatic healing or other gifts, and won enough temporary popular support to found 'churches' of their own — though such seldom survived the death of their founder.

Such movements have been always with us, and probably always will be, as long as social injustice remains and there is an archetypal pattern for the oppressed to pin their religious eschatological hopes upon. Professor Cohn cites as typical an example of its working in our own times in the Zulu Messiah, Isaiah Shembe (1870-1935):

> … a lay preacher of great eloquence and magnetic personality, who built up a church of his own in opposition to the white-sponsored Mission churches. At first he claimed only to be a prophet, and to the white authorities he would never admit to more. But to his followers he eventually divulged that he was

'the Promised One', a true successor and replacer of Jesus. What Jesus, in his day, had done for whites and their salvation, he was now doing for Zulus and their salvation. He claimed that the Lord had called him when still in his mother's womb. And he foretold that in due course he would stand at the gate of the Heavenly Jerusalem, when he would turn away the whites and those blacks who had followed the Mission churches, and admit only his own followers.

And Cohn sums up the general pattern as follows:

> For amongst the surplus population living on the margin of society there was always a strong tendency to take as leader a layman, or maybe an apostate friar or monk, who imposed himself not simply as a holy man but as a prophet and saviour or even as a living god. On the strength of inspirations or revelations for which he claimed divine origin the leader would decree for his followers a communal mission of vast dimensions and world shaking importance. The conviction of having such a mission, of being divinely appointed to carry out a prodigious task, provided the disorientated and frustrated with new hearings and new hope. It gave them not simply a place in the world but a unique and resplendent place. A fraternity of this kind felt itself an elite, set infinitely apart from and above ordinary mortals, sharing in the extraordinary merits of its leader, sharing also in his miraculous powers. Moreover the mission which most attracted these masses from the neediest strata of the population was — naturally enough — a mission which was intended to culminate in a total transformation of society. In the eschatological phantasies which they had inherited from the distant past, the forgotten world of early Christianity, these people found a social myth most perfectly adapted to their needs.

The prime mover of the early Christians was of course the Holy Spirit and therefore it is perhaps not surprising that we eventually find, in the twelfth century, an intellectual formulation of the work and power of the Holy Spirit, in the prophetic ideas of Joachim de Floris (1145-1202), whose system attained a world-wide influence that has since been rivalled only by Marxism in the twentieth century. In fact historico-philosophies like Marxism could almost be said to spring from it, through the influence of German idealist philosophers such as Hegel, whose dialectical philosophy was adopted by Marx but given a materialist bias.

Joachim was completely orthodox as far as the Church of his time went, and three Popes encouraged him, in turn, to publish the visions that he had received. These were to the effect that the history of the world can be split into three Ages: the Age of the Father (or of the law), the Age of the Son (or of the Gospels), and the Age of the Holy Spirit. The Age of the Father had existed up to the birth of Christ; the Age of the Son had existed up until the present time; and the Age of the Holy Spirit was about to dawn.

This was based on arithmetical calculations on the Bible, where 42 generations had taken place between Abraham and Christ, from which it was assumed that 42 generations would elapse until the Age of the Holy Spirit. With a generation calculated as being 30 years long this put the dawning of the Age of the Holy Spirit at between 1200 and 1260.

A period of incubation was assumed for each age, the incubation of the first being from Adam to Abraham, and that of the second from Elijah to Christ, whilst that of the third had begun with St. Benedict, the founder of the monastic system. The Age of the Holy Spirit would be characterised by love, joy, and freedom, and the whole world would be like one great monastery singing the praises of God in mystical ecstasy.

This doctrine was particularly enthusiastically received by more radically minded members of the newly formed Franciscan Order — who formed a pressure group striving to maintain St. Francis' original vision of poverty in imitation of Christ, an ideal increasingly made difficult as the Order became institutionalised and wealthy through popularity and size. They later formed a body outside the Order called the Spiritual Franciscans as opposed to the Conventual Franciscans who built monasteries in the accustomed manner. They went so far as to see themselves as the introductors of the New Age and thus destined to replace the Church of Rome. It is hardly surprising that some were eventually burned as heretics; and of course besides them there were many more sects and cults who embraced the Joachite ideas and cast themselves into key roles in their historical unfoldment.

We see something of the same phenomena happening today in speculations concerning the Age of Aquarius, stimulated by the phenomenon of the Precession of the Equinoxes, although not with such an ecclesiastical ambience for we live in a more secular society. In global terms, the millennial ideas of Marxism are an interesting reflection of the Joachite pattern, with the three ages of primitive communism, class society, and classless communism. It seems to be the kind of idea that appeals naturally to the human temperament — and particularly to the underprivileged.

It is interesting to speculate on whether the visionary Joachim simply got his calculations wrong, or whether his error was in putting spiritual principles into a temporal straitjacket. In the experience of all human beings there is the 'age of the father' (the submission to family law during childhood and adolescence) before the age of individual responsibility and relative freedom of adulthood, which becomes with advancing age more prone to personal eschatological hopes with the approach of old age and death.

Joachim's theories thus might tend to be a projection of the human life pattern onto the external world, in the same way that pagan god forms might be seen as projections of human personal characteristics. And just as the pagan myths of rebirth and a saviour god are thought by some to be glimmerings of the spiritual truth foreshadowing the Incarnation of the Logos, in Jesus, so Joachite (and Marxist for that matter) intuitions of a three phase history of society might also turn out to be reflections of a spiritual principle. If the fallout from the Incarnation is anything to go by, however, the temporal manifestation is not likely to be in quite the way that is expected or easily foretold.

In Joachite speculation we could say we have a mythology being engendered in a Christian form. This is a mythology which is very much alive with us today although it tends to take a secular turn.

To many, the Holy Roman Emperor Frederick II, in his protracted quarrels with the Papacy was seen as the forerunner of the New Age, who would strip the Church of its power. This was exacerbated, particularly in the North, by the Papacy placing all Germany under interdict, when the withdrawal of official church activities left the way open for wandering preachers to preach the iniquities of the Roman church. And with such questionable Popes as Innocent IV these alleged iniquities were by no means entire fabrication. But although some prophets hailed Frederick as a Messianic figure, others thought him more of the devil's party despite his correctly chastening the Church.

After his death a monk reported seeing him descending with his knights into the fiery crater of Mount Etna. Whether or not this was intended to brand him with the ignomony of descending into hell it was capable of another interpretation, in that Mount Etna, according to popular folklore, was the hollow hill of mythical heroes including King Arthur. As a result, ideas of a resurrected Frederick began to flow abroad, just as Arthur is credited with one day returning. In our more febrile times the preference seems to be for Jimi Hendrix or Elvis Presley!

Anyhow, such speculations played a part in German revolutionary history until at least 1510 and the dawn of the Reformation and the fragmentation of the Roman Church into splinter movements that have become the Protestant denominations of today.

In any case, the basic premises of Joachim were not entirely orthodox, for St. Augustine had laid down the line that the New Jerusalem had in fact already come. He saw it as the presence of the Church of Christ in the world — and that any more physical interpretation was as unreal as the militarist hopes of the early Jews. There are many, no doubt, who would take issue with Augustine over equating the Church with the New Jerusalem for the institutional church is obviously fallible, open to folly, even corruption, and in most respects only too human. However, we must remember that Augustine was writing at a time long before, when the church was a last bastion of civilised values against the encroaching barbarian hordes, and kept their flame alight throughout the subsequent Dark Ages.

Let us forget therefore, our own historical, personal and social prejudices about what we think the church to be, and look at it fundamentally as the body of human beings who have accepted the fact of the Incarnation of the Logos and are striving, however inadequately, to live their lives by that fact.

This is the Body of Christ that we have previously mentioned, the branches of the Vine which is the Christ. And if the Body of Christ seems at times to be stretched out on the gibbet of a human institution then in one sense this can be looked upon as a continuation of the Crucifixion. Similarly the achievement of the few genuine saints of remarkable closeness to God whilst in the flesh, are a continuation, however spasmodic, of the Transfiguration. Whilst the 'church that is not built with hands' remains unseen, with Christ, consisting of those who have died in faith.

The New Jerusalem is therefore with us all the time. Physically present in embryo in all who have conformed their will to God; and mystically present in those thousands who have died the physical death and whose souls live on united in Christ — as an aspect of the Godhead — or 'manhood taken up into God' as St. Athanasius put it.

When we speak of the powers of the Holy Spirit then, we should be careful therefore not to define things in too concrete a way. The movement of the Holy Spirit comes as a natural movement in the soul and the powers that it stimulates may be perfectly natural ones.

In the context of this book, however, we are aiming to consider those powers that relate to occult science and the 'inner side' of creation, and which may have the appearance of super-normality, but relate quite readily to the human psychic structure.

The psychic structure of the human being is built on a system of centres of force, known in the East as *chakras*, which broadly translated means 'wheels'. The idea intended is a kind of whirlpool or vortex of psychic matter of 'mind-stuff'. Those who are materialistically inclined can regard them as a kind of electromagnetic aura surrounding the physical mechanism — it makes no great difference at the level at which we now consider it. In point of fact, as with so much of the borderline material that we are intent to study, it can be a mistake to go either way in one's regard of these matters. It is just as much a source of error to 'spiritualise' and 'abstractify' such things as the *chakras* as it is to regard them simply as material adjuncts of the body.

In so far that they are not visible to physical perception some difference of opinion exists between schools of thought as to their precise detail, but there can be no doubt that they exist, for all schools of meditation testify to them — and in fact their presence can in some measure be felt by the most material of men. Not all may have experienced the unmistakable tingling sensation (at times almost painful) at brow or crown of head when in touch with certain inner powers, but the constricted or expansive feelings in throat, heart, solar plexus, genitals or anus will have been felt by most people in times of crisis or great emotion. These are not entirely physiological reactions.

In cataloguing them we are reminded of a point in Charles Williams' book on Dante, *The Figure of Beatrice*, that the body is an 'index' of the soul. Thus in our categorising of the psychic centres we are pointing at analogues of the existence of the soul at various degrees of existence.

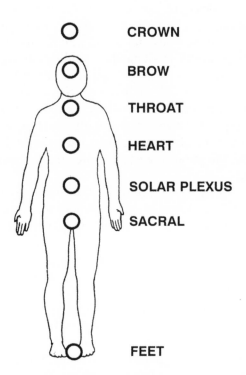

Figure 2

It is a mistake to chop man up, figuratively speaking, into a succession of bodies, peeling him like an onion, and seeing him slough off body after body in an ascent to higher worlds —first the physical body, then the emotions, then the mind, then various more abstract layers until one is left with a spiritual seed or Divine Spark which is the only 'reality'. This is a trap that has enough truth in it to make it easy to fall into.

Its error is to take complex and abstract matters somewhat too literally when they are described in a simplified way. As ridiculous, for instance, as to suppose that the higher man is in the head and the lower man in the trunk, and if we therefore cut off his head we could send him to heaven — presumably to be like one of those little cherubs with wings. However, at risk of over-simplifying things we shall proceed to examine a number of what we hope may be helpful diagrams.

The centres can be listed as in Figure 2. These are the major ones; there are many more, but they do not here concern us. These major ones are focal points of energy that relate to various levels of consciousness. The ones we are considering align with the spinal column. Or perhaps it might be more accurate to say that the spinal column aligns with them.

The chakras as 'index points' or 'indicators' of the whole man represent powers of the whole man because each relates to a focus of energy and life expression of man. It is best not to fall into the habit of calling these 'bodies' or 'planes'—useful to elementary understanding as these terms might be — because it can so easily lead to a misunderstanding of the realities of existence. To use alternative analogies we might regard man as a radio aerial (or centre of power — either for transmitting or receiving) capable of working upon various wavelengths and frequencies.

To aid the visual imagination we might see the analogy in terms of light — or to aid the aural imagination we could equally well use the analogy of sound.

By analogy with light we would see the higher frequency (that is, shorter wavelength) colours at one end (violet) and the lower frequency (or longer wavelength) at the other end (red), with the colours of the spectrum between.

Remember this is all analogy. The band of electro-magnetic wavelengths and frequencies extends a considerable distance either way through infrared and ultra-violet and we are simply choosing a handy picture from an arbitrary band of these vibratory rates and conditions to express a reality beyond normal human perception.

In the same way we might take sound waves (in the air or through any sound conducting substance) as examples of the same principle, with the higher-frequency/shorter-wavelength (higher pitch) at the top end and lower-frequency/longer wavelength (lower pitch) at the bottom. We can

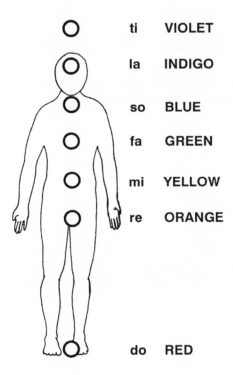

ti   VIOLET

la   INDIGO

so   BLUE

fa   GREEN

mi   YELLOW

re   ORANGE

do   RED

Figure 3

even fill in steps between by relating them to the musical intervals used in Western music. Thus we can introduce a colour and sound coding to our diagram of the chakras as in Figure 3. Again we stress, all is analogy, or at best, symbolism.

Symbols can be used in certain psychological techniques of magic and metaphysical speculation but we must beware of confusing symbols with realities. Here we should perhaps define the term *symbol*, and we are not likely to improve upon the definition of Samuel Taylor Coleridge, who said a symbol, to be a symbol, must have three characteristics:

i)   it must exist in itself,
ii) it must derive from something greater than itself,
iii) it must represent in itself that greatness from which it derives.

Because the word has tended to be misused in a way that plays down its reality as a thing in itself (for instance, mathematically, where x might mean some specific number, but have no great significance in itself, and could equally well be y or z) Charles Williams has suggested that the word *image* might be better used. Thus, according to the system we have chosen above, the colour yellow, or the note *mi* on the scale, and the solar plexus psychic centre (or chakra) are all related symbols. They are basically things in themselves, but because of their relative position in a scale of values, they can be made representative of states of reality or relationship in another dimension of being.

We must also avoid the tendency of taking symbols too rigidly which is a widespread error amongst elementary occult students. They accept one system of symbolism as a platform of inviolable truth from which to criticise the validity of any other symbol system. Yet in our diagram above, if we had introduced another centre (say the spleen), a different allocation of colours and notes could have been made, regarding the Crown as the higher octave (*do'*) of the lowest centre (*do*) and introducing the colour ruby-magenta, which falls between red and violet on the colour spectrum and completes it as a circular device, and giving this colour to the Crown centre. Or, instead of the spleen, we might have introduced another head centre, say the top of the spine, the *medulla oblongata*.

It is admittedly not easy to take a completely eclectic view of occult symbolism and any but the experienced student does best to stick to one system rather than try to cope with a number of different ones all at once. Which is why some esoteric groups discourage their neophytes from joining or studying with others.

The situation is rather like learning to play a musical instrument. The music you seek to express could be rendered by any one of a number of musical instruments, but you do best to learn the use of *one* instrument well before embarking upon others. Some instruments, as with symbol systems, are better at expressing some aspects of music than others; a flute is hardly best at martial airs, for instance, though its close relative the fife might be.

The various levels of consciousness that we are concerned with here, as analogues of the centres, are depicted in Figure 4. Each of these levels of consciousness is perceptive of a different 'level' or 'mode' of existence, a different wavelength or frequency of 'vibrations' if one wishes, though this useful term has been grossly overused and abused.

In the designation that we have used we may see how the Fall of Man, mythically expressed in the Garden of Eden story, and poetically expressed in Milton's *Paradise Lost*, is here symbolically expressed in that the soul of man has fallen from association with his *higher* self to association with his *lower* self. In actuality there is, of course, only one self, and this appearance of fragmentation is but one result of the Fall.

We must again avoid the fundamental error that regards the higher as good and the lower as bad. This is not so. Intrinsically all are good. It

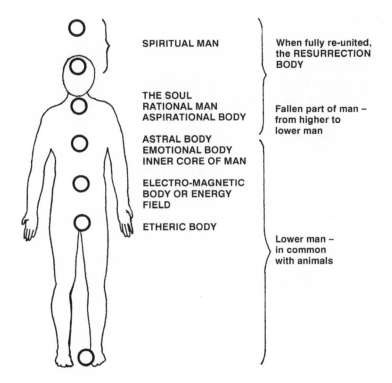

SPIRITUAL MAN

When fully re-united, the RESURRECTION BODY

THE SOUL
RATIONAL MAN
ASPIRATIONAL BODY

Fallen part of man – from higher to lower man

ASTRAL BODY
EMOTIONAL BODY
INNER CORE OF MAN

ELECTRO-MAGNETIC BODY OR ENERGY FIELD

ETHERIC BODY

Lower man – in common with animals

Figure 4

is how the soul expresses itself, on whatever level, that is good or evil. As Jesus said: 'nothing that goes into a man from outside can defile him; no, it is the things that come out of him that defile him'.

We *could* go so far as to say that the higher levels are more *dynamic* and *incorruptible*, and thus when man fell into evil ways (the elevation of the self at the expense of the whole) he was no longer able to function at the higher levels. Thus he became a dominating selfish influence on the lower levels and unable to perceive the higher levels — either of himself or objectively — except fitfully or 'in a glass darkly'.

When he is able to become conscious of the higher levels he is conscious of an overwhelming light (as a blind man might be on suddenly learning how to see physically) and of a force greater than himself, and yet in an indescribable way, also a part of himself — for the fragmented is becoming unified.

We have the subjective description of this in the writings of the mystics, or collected in such works as William James' *Varieties of Religious Experience* or Dr Richard Bucke's *Cosmic Consciousness*.

Bucke describes an illuminative experience of his own as follows:

> All at once, without warning of any kind, I found myself wrapped in a flame-coloured cloud. For an instant I thought of fire, an immense conflagration somewhere close by in that great city; the next, I knew that the fire was within myself. Directly afterwards there came upon me a sense of exultation, of immense joyousness, accompanied or immediately followed by an intellectual illumination impossible to describe. Among other things, I did not merely come to believe, but I saw that the universe is not composed of dead matter, but is, on the contrary, a Living Presence; I became conscious in myself of eternal life. It was not a conviction that I would have eternal life, but a consciousness that I possessed eternal life then ... The vision lasted a few seconds and was gone; but the memory of it and the sense of the reality of which it taught has remained during the quarter of a century which has since elapsed.

At another level we have the consciousness that becomes aware of an 'inner side' of creation — that is, the astral and etheric levels. This is not a *mystical* experience in the strict sense of the word but a *physical* experience, or if deliberately induced, a *magical* experience. The soul approaches (or should approach) such fields of experience (and their denizens of various kinds) from above. It is a mistake to take the attitude either of the back parlour table turner who assumes all who may be contacted in this way are 'great spirits'; or, on the other hand, the attitude of the medieval and renaissance sorcerer who attempted to bind and control them with mighty curses and conjurations.

Again we can represent this diagrammatically, and in a number of ways.

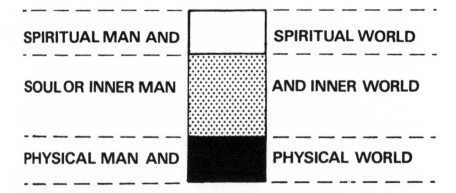

Figure 5

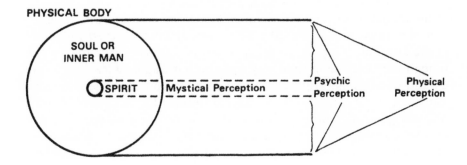

Figure 6

We can make a straight 'up and down' representation as we have with our examination of the chakras and the spine and this type of representation is commonly used in esoteric textbooks (Figure 5.)

This is a perfectly valid representation so far as it goes but has the disadvantage of instilling the idea of a world built in 'layers'. To avoid this problem we could use a circular mode of demonstration (Figure 6).

Physical perception is, of course, of the physical creation; psychic perception of the inner creation; mystical perception of the heavenly world which is of God. In the lower forms of perception God may be seen, heard or felt in his work; in mystical perception God is perceived direct.

To avoid the error that this figure might promulgate, of the spirit necessarily being buried deep within, we could turn the diagram round (as in Figure 7), which shows how 'outgoingness' is a way to 'inner experience' whether of a psychical or mystical nature.

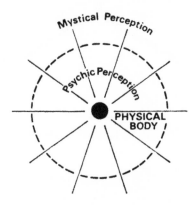

Figure 7

This form of diagram has been used frequently in describing the aura of the human body, and has the tendency to mislead one into thinking that the inner worlds are attenuated abstractions, or even radiations of the physical. The point to grasp is that *all* of these diagrams, helpful though they may be in their way, are also but fragmentary glimpses of a multi-dimensional truth and can also be misleading at the same time as being helpful. And this is the same with most forms of symbolism; it makes a good servant but a bad master. We must endeavour always to get at the reality represented and not to mould fanciful representations of the universe and God by casting them rigidly in the mould of our own symbol systems.

Let us attempt another mode of representation (Figure 8) using arcs of a circle to represent the different modes of reality. The advantage of this particular representation is that it gets away from the idea of the soul being a buffer between spirit and body and shows that each can link directly upon the other.

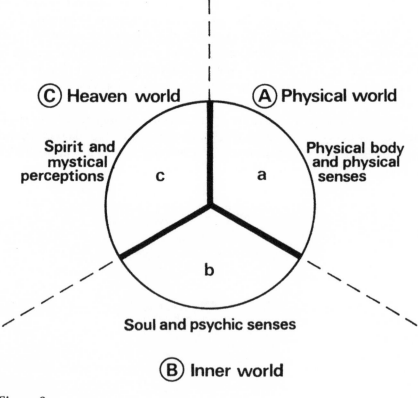

Figure 8

Here we have called the physical world about us A and our own physical constitution a, the links between the two being our physical activities and perceptions. All our senses, be they sight, hearing, taste or smell, are variations of the sense of touch — or contact or togetherness. All activities of communications are variations of movement; where there is no movement of anything there is no perception, whether the movement be of sound waves, photons, electrons or calories.

By the same token we may call the 'inner world' about us B and our own inner mentational processes b. The latter are not entirely subjective as is often supposed. They are either reactions to sensations coming via the body from the physical world, or reactions via the spirit to the 'heaven world' or God. The direct organs of perception are also evident however (more evident in some people than in others) in the psychic senses, be they evidenced as dowsing or healing ability, clairaudience, clairvoyance, telepathy, mediumship, or intuition — all of which correspond (though not necessarily directly and one for one) with the physical senses of sight, hearing, touch, taste and smell.

The presence of God is indicated by the area C and our direct mystical awareness of God by the area c. Here the means of perception manifest in love —a fact that is witnessed by all the true mystics of the world whether they be Christian or not — for the mystic forges a direct relationship to the One God that is not dependant upon formulations or creeds, although the wise mystic may choose to be guided by them as a check to his vision.

We may thus group human perceptions and experience into three categories, which we have arbitrarily labelled A, B and C. We may formulate and tabulate their nature as shown overleaf (page 68).

It is important not to fall into the trap that has beset some occult teachers in regarding mysticism as an emotional and inferior form of occultism. The truth is rather the reverse: mysticism is a higher form of occultism and the vitality and corrective orientation behind it.

We should also draw attention to the interaction that is possible between the categories we have tabulated (see Figure 9).

The ambience of God may flow over into the physical world and then we have Nature Mysticism, *God seen through his luminous garment* as someone has felicitously put it. This is not to be confused with pantheism or worship of nature, which is a distortion of this form of mysticism. Examples of true nature mysticism are to be found in the writings of Richard Jeffries or Thomas Traherne.

For instance, from Jeffries: "Through every grass-blade in the thousand, thousand grasses; through the million leaves, veined and edge-cut on bush and tree; through the song-notes and the marked feathers of the birds; through the insects' hum and the colour of the butterflies;

Objective	Subjective	Type of Experience
A. Physical World. The 'outer side' of Creation.	Physical body and senses. Taste, smell, touch, sight, hearing.	The meeting with other souls 'in the flesh', including non-human beings (e.g. animals) and also the inanimate structures of the creation, as well as lower forms of life such as vegetation. All that comes to us through the senses from our physical environment.
B. Psychic World. The 'inner side' of Creation. *Sheol.* The 'Inner planes'. The Summerland of the Spiritualists. Hades, in the pagan sense – not necessarily the diabolic or mediaeval hell – though conditions could be as unpleasant, as indeed they can be on the physical level, for example, in war, plague famine or other disaster.	Soul and inner structuring of the physical body. The psychic senses including the so called higher ones, of intuition, inspiration etc. all clairvoyance, clairaudience, mediumship, automatic writing, telepathy, divination etc.	The psychic world that is contacted in many and various aspects – by spiritualist mediums at one level, by occult intuitives at another. Human contacts which may, or may not be incarnate 'in the flesh'. Also non-human (elemental, demonic, possibly angelic). Human contacts could be 'spirit guides', teachers or *gurus,* possibly, but not necessarily better informed or wiser than their incarnate counterparts. Thus inner messages may vary considerably as to their factual and ethical content. Just as physical sensations may be illusory, so may psychic ones be or even mystical ones, particularly if these senses are relatively little used or if they are elevated to an undue importance, through lack of sense of proportion or commonsense.
C. God. Heaven.	The Spirit, Divine Spark. Resurrection Body or Body of Transfiguration.	Mystical union. Direct contact with God … whether in the sweetness of a love relationship or the awesomeness of a mighty vision and sense of mission. Or can be less spectacular and possibly unconscious in the dedicated soul … without the direct organs of perception being opened or developed.

through the soft warm air, the flecks of clouds dissolving — I used them all for prayer."

Or, from Traherne: "Oh what Art, what Order, what Curiosity hast thou shown in every Flower? How beautiful in Colours, how sweet in Odours, how rare in Substance, how curious in Form and Matter, how rich in Use, in all, how full of Pleasure? What a delicate sight it is also to behold the Corn in its first springing Verdure, in its increasing Growth, thick-bearded, strong-headed, and at last full-blown, and bending it self in its Fullness to us, and for us? Oh, how I hear it in its gentle Waverings and Whistlings, laugh and sound by Praise?"

Similarly the ambience of God may flow over into other facets of the physical world and heaven is seen to be reflected in some worldly thing. One may think of the poetry of Gerard Manley Hopkins. Or in Dante where heaven is seen in the city of Florence and in the girl Beatrice. It is this that is behind the whole cult of romantic love.

Just as the ambience of God may flow over into the physical creation so may it do so in the inner creation and here we have the strange visions of some of the mystics and the body of true prophecy. That is, the prophecy that we have spoken of before in relation to the Old Testament, which is not so much a matter of foretelling the future as of speaking *for* God. The direct relationship to God of the soul is tough love and is an at-one-ment or union that is devoid of images — but when God wishes to speak directly to man through a chosen human vehicle the interaction of two worlds or modes of being takes place and we have the divinely inspired action or utterance of a John, an Hosea or an Isaiah.

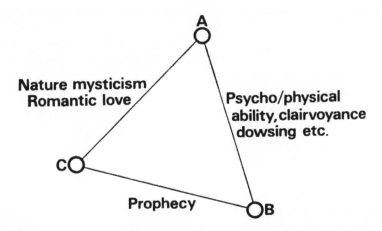

Figure 9

There are false modes of this too and all who feel themselves to be 'men of destiny' are not necessarily men of God — though they may do great physical deeds. There are other sources of 'inspiration' besides God, either in the pride of the isolated human spirit or in the power of higher spirits divorced from God. In this we have the whole cosmology of Satan and the Fall, and the need for the human will to be turned back to its proper source by acceptance of the 'crucified Saviour' — whose kingdom is not in conquering nations as a man of destiny, but whose example of sacrifice for others in spite of almighty power demonstrates a kingdom that 'is not of this world'.

There may also be an interaction of worlds, or modes of being, between the physical and the non-physical creation and here we have the evidence of so-called supernatural powers. Again, these may be of God or not of God. That is, works of the Holy Spirit or manipulations of the individual human being with or without the assistance of other beings of the inner creation, human or non-human.

We could produce another helpful diagram by turning Figure 9 round so that God is at the topmost point, as shown in the alchemical diagram (Figure 10) reproduced from the *Opus Medico-Chymicum* by Johann Daniel Mylius, published 1618.

Here, the world of God, or Heaven, takes up the top half of the diagram, showing the Holy Trinity in a representation of spiritual light. Below this is the twofold creation, the outer creation, or physical world, represented by the man, the lion, the sun, the phoenix; and the inner creation represented by the woman, the stag or unicorn, the moon, the eagle.

It is possible for these two symbol systems to be counterchanged, dependent upon whether one is looking at things from the inner or the outer creation.

Thus someone on the inner places would conceive themselves to be 'positive' to the 'negative' physical universe. To us on the physical plane, however, the physical universe is represented by the bright day and the inner world by the negative and twilight zone.

Each aspect of creation is, however, negative to the power of God.

Between the two worlds, however, stands the wise man, the mystical magician, *mystical* in that he works in harmony with the Will of God, and *magician* in that he is able to act as a link between them, and to work with the forces and modes of being of either side of creation. His spinal column acts as an axis for the whole picture. It is aligned also with the centre of the Hill of Vision behind him and the central essence of God. The powers represented by it are those that the 'wise man' seeks to develop.

Figure 10

EXERCISE FOR CHAPTER III

The Serpent-tongue of flame shall rise in you
And make you fit oblation for my Mysteries.

The exercise for this chapter is the building of a Rod of Power that is formed by a flame of fire rising from the base of the spine to fill the cranium with flame. There must be a realisation and intention that this is a dedication of the totality of all our human powers and faculties to the service of Almighty God. Otherwise this exercise could bring considerable disturbance. In the East, where a similar exercise is practised under the discipline of Kundalini Yoga, many precautions are taken and close supervision made of those who assay it.

However, it is perfectly safe if divorced from particular detailed breathing techniques and postures that characterise its use in the East; and if it is used in the context and order in which we have placed it here — *after* the Sphere of Light and the fiery Spear of Divine Love have been firmly built within the aura and the psyche.

Even so, the practice of this exercise may well bring some emotional disturbance into the daily life in the beginning — unlike the perfectly placid and soothing previous two exercises. This is quite normal and this type of occurrence comes to be expected by the seasoned occult student when inner forces are stirred. It denotes that things are happening, and even though there may appear to be no rhyme nor reason in any such disturbance accompanying such seemingly subjective and arbitrary exercises, the beginner may at least, until powers of intuition and discernment are better developed, take heart that the work is taking effect, even if the results are temporarily not too comfortable!

Figuratively speaking, it marks an advance through the thorn bushes that surround the castle of the sleeping beauty — and any step forward in a briar patch brings an automatic reaction of branches occasionally painfully swinging back after their disturbance. But with the faith and dedication that are symbolised by the Sphere and Spear, the powers of the Rod need cause no concern. But this is the truth that lies behind the traditional cry of the Guardian of the sacred Mysteries — *Hekas, hekas, este bebeloi!* — Begone, profane ones!

CHAPTER IV

The Holy Grail

In the Quest of the Holy Grail we are concerned with poetic truth. And we are also concerned with the imagination — in the Coleridgean sense — for it is through the imagination that the soul comes nearest to fundamental truth. The imagination is not merely an agent of fantasy but an organ for the perception of real things.

As William Blake put it, when he saw the sun he saw not 'a round disc of fire, something like a guinea', but 'an innumerable company of the heavenly host crying — Holy, holy, holy is the Lord God Almighty'. He likened the physical things of this world to the physical organ of the human eye — a window that one sees through. 'I look through it, not with it.' The things of the physical world are as indicators of a higher reality.

This philosophy stems from Plato and from its pagan beginnings runs through Plotinus and subsequently to the Christian Church through St. Augustine. It is a stream that has continued to the present day when, over the last two centuries, we might trace it through the romantic tradition of English poetry, from Blake, Coleridge, Shelley and Wordsworth up to the modern poetry of Edwin Muir, Vernon Watkins, David Gascoyne or Kathleen Raine.

It is interesting to trace back this line of thought, which is intimately connected with theology on the one hand and creative art on the other. Christian Platonism is found in the works of Charles Williams and C.S. Lewis. Lewis, Williams and Tolkien were all well acquainted with each other at Oxford, where they formed a small creative writers' circle called 'The Inklings' and used to read their work in progress to each other.

C.S. Lewis confesses a great debt to George Macdonald, has edited an anthology of Macdonald's thought and featured him as a major protagonist in his book on heaven and hell, *The Great Divorce*. George Macdonald in one of his few poems dedicated to another actual person, writes no less than nine stanzas entitled *A Thanksgiving for F. D. Maurice*.

F. D. Maurice is described in B. M. G. Reardon's survey of nineteenth-century theology *From Coleridge to Gore* as 'arguably the most original theological thinker that the nineteenth century produced in this country. His originality was, in fact, too much for the majority of his contemporaries.' Maurice was indeed dismissed from a professorial chair at Kings College,

London, and it is interesting to note that George Macdonald in his early years was forced to resign as a chapel minister on grounds of heresy, in that 'he had expressed belief in a future state of probation for heathens and was tainted with German theology'. Maurice himself was stigmatised as 'Platonism in gown and cassock' by some of his contemporaries and was directly and considerably influenced by the poet S. T. Coleridge who, according to Reardon, influenced also Thomas Arnold, Julius Hare, F. W. Robertson and possibly even John Henry Newman.

Coleridge was thus one of the great seminal thinkers of the nineteenth century. His literary reputation has outweighed his value as a theological philosopher, although both functions were marred in their expression by a lack of sustained coherent application to the task of writing, aggravated by addiction to opium as a result of taking it medicinally for the relief of pain. Reardon describes him thus:

> The significance of Coleridge's genius rests in its many-sidedness. As a philosophical thinker he is always stimulating and often profound, even though his place in the textbooks of modern philosophy is not prominent. Insatiable in the pursuit of truth, his mind was perhaps too eclectic. He has aptly been called *the first of the great nineteenth century 'thinkers'* rather than a philosopher in the strict technical sense. His concern was with the spiritual life of man in its widest range, so that theology, philosophy, politics, social theory and aesthetics are severally viewed by him as the intellectual aspects of a single existential reality ... Coleridge's thinking struck out new paths, which he followed with a degree of spiritual concentration, an awareness of essential problems and a personal if idiosyncratic self-dedication for which his times, in this country at least, afford no parallel ... had he possessed a more sustained architectonic gift, a more evident ability to control and direct the flood of his often paradoxical thought, he might have been the greatest original theologian this country has ever produced, as well as one of its foremost philosophers. As it is his very failures are such that beside them other men's successes look meagre.

Coleridge marks a peak in a mountain range of the creative imagination that included Wordsworth and Blake, Thomas Taylor the Platonist, and indeed the whole romantic tradition. There has been much learned controversy over the *origin* of the romantic tradition, from Denis de Rougement's celebrated *Passion and Society* to C.S. Lewis' equally authoritative, and different, *Allegory of Love*. But we are not so much concerned with learned arguments as to how it started, as with a general survey as to what it is — for it is very germane to our investigation of the 'inner side' of creation.

We need first of all to pay attention to the religious and mystical ideas of a very significant two hundred years of Western history that starts with the preaching of the First Crusade (1095) and ends with the publication of Dante's *Divine Comedy* (commenced in 1308). In the middle of this period in the couple of decades before and after 1200 came the birth, in writing at any rate, of that strangely moving cycle of legends of the Holy Grail. The period also saw the development of the Troubadour tradition and the elevation of the feminine to a pinnacle of worship and love, much as the relief of Jerusalem by the early crusaders had almost the intensity of a love affair.

All this was subsequently summed up by Dante, in the framework of Aquinan theology, in the mystical significance of the image of *(a)* the young girl, and *(b)* the city. In his case he used Beatrice and the city of Florence. The meaning also extended to the Blessed Virgin and the New Jerusalem. At another level it meant the individual Divine Spark of immortality and the whole human and angelic concourse of such 'sparks'. And ultimately both stood in daring analogy for God, as lover and encompassing civic setting for the human soul.

All this of course was mixed up with crosscurrents of other influences, the impact of Islamic culture for instance, and the social and political conditions of the West at that time. In 1095, when the First Crusade was preached by Pope Urban II, the response to his preaching was universal. Not only did the Norman aristocracy respond but the serfs and peasants too. Within a year great bodies of people, for the most part ill-armed mobs, went marching off towards the East to relieve the city of Jerusalem.

There were other motives on the part of the Pope for preaching the Crusade, just as there was a mixture of motives in those who responded to his preaching. Jerusalem had in fact been in the hands of Islam for hundreds of years without any Christians in the West worrying very much about it. It had fallen to the Caliph Omar as far back as 638!

Geographically situated as it is, in the narrow corridor of the fertile crescent between two continents, it has always been a town that saw more years of war and marching armies than of peace. It was so as far back as the patriarch Abraham's time. There were, then, powerful hidden motives for such a concern for Jerusalem suddenly to arise in 1095.

Some of these motives were political. The great breach between the Eastern and Western churches, centred on Rome and Constantinople, that were to resolve into the twin arms of Catholicism and Orthodox Christianity, had occurred not long before, in 1054. Since then, a revival of Islam had occurred under a newly arising horde, the Seljuk Turks, who were pressing upon Constantinople (or Byzantium) and threatening to overrun it, and all Eastern Christianity to boot.

In extreme peril, the Emperor of the East, Michael Comnenis, appealed to Rome for assistance. Such an opportunity to take advantage of one's opponent's difficulties could hardly be rejected — and it was readily seized upon by the Pope, who, no doubt, was not without the genuine conviction that God was pulling the strings of history to renew the unity of the Church in Rome's favour. Thus the Church's vested interest in the Crusade.

The Norman aristocracy, who not many generations before had been Norsemen, and who had even more recently developed their own form of social government (the feudal system) based on violence and protection (a kind of class protection racket), had, by their system of primogeniture, of handing a dead father's lands down to his eldest son, produced a sub-class of land-hungry younger sons. Even a King of England found himself in this predicament — John, Richard the Lionheart's younger brother — nicknamed Lackland. For men such as these, the colonising opportunity to go and hew out new lands for themselves at point of the sword, and with secular and religious backing, was a temptation indeed. Thus many knights enrolled to go — although of course there were also a number who went through genuine religious conviction.

Such religious conviction was amplified by the indulgences given by the Church to any who went upon the Crusade. Sins would be forgiven, property and dependents of any who fell would be protected, and they themselves would be assured a place in Paradise. The Church itself, in spite of apparent political machinations, was also glad of the opportunity to channel the war-like energies of these Norman knights into some constructive united effort.

The Church had steadily tried to induce peace among the warring barons and kings, mostly by the device of introducing truces on holy days, and then by trying to extend these, so that some principle of law and limitation should be introduced into the popular custom of war.

Also, the Church sought to reduce the incidence of tournaments and joustings, which in the early days were far from the edifying and noble picture that has come down to us in the tales of romance. It was done for money if not for pride, and knights errant (landless younger sons) hired themselves out as bully boys to any local lord. A tournament would take place between villages or towns, a posse of knights setting out from each town towards the other, unhorsing and capturing, by fair means or foul, any knight of the opposite party he met on the way. The winner kept the horse and mail of the vanquished — a lucrative prize by which a professional could make a living of sorts until possibly he managed to acquire some land by marriage or conquest. One of the most skilful of knights of his time was William the Marshall, who indeed led an honourable career, and was the sought after champion of princes.

The Church, in the years before such barbarous customs gave way to less dangerous, more regulated forms of the tournament field (with plate armour and tilting yards) tried to restrict such rowdy pastimes where men were licensed robbers by violence, and women merely chattels who could be captured along with horse and armour.

As for the lower classes, their lot was miserable in the extreme, and the chance to go on the Crusade, freed from their serfdom to a narrow plot of land and cold damp hovel, with all sins forgiven, the Church's blessing, and the prospect of eternal bliss guaranteed in Paradise was not to be foregone. Though there was more to it than this.

None, such were the limitations of their circumstances and upbringing, had any idea of what Jerusalem was like, or how far it was. Still less did they know anything of who the Turks were, or the politics of the situation. To them, Jerusalem meant the holy place where God was crucified and buried; and the whole place was invested with a mystical aura. They saw themselves as great Christian soldiers going to save their Lord. The Turks they equated with devils, and the liberated Jerusalem would be the New Jerusalem of Revelations descending from on high studded with jewels, with the Lamb of God in the centre, and they themselves as the Elect.

Popular preachers such as Peter the Hermit whipped thousands of common folk into a hysteria of popular frenzy to go off on the crusade. Thousands of them did, a vast rabble streaming across Europe towards Constantinople.

The reality fell far short of the vision. On the way they massacred Jews as part of their supposed divine mission, and mistaking Christian Bulgars for Moslems massacred them as well. The Emperor of Byzantium, horrified at what had appeared as a result of his request for military aid — no properly organised knightly crusade got under way until a year later — shipped them as hastily as he could across the Bosphoros.

Although they had suffered many privations on the long journey they continued on their way, singing hymns, intent on the sacredness of the divine mission — to be cut to pieces by the Turks in Asia Minor, every man, woman and child being massacred or sold into slavery.

The debacle had some slight military significance in that a year later when the main body of properly armed and organised crusaders arrived, the Turks underestimated their fighting capabilities, and through overconfidence suffered a major initial setback — although it took three years for the crusaders to fight their way to Jerusalem.

There were, alas, other popular crusades, such was the power of the millennial vision, including one of children. All came to an unedifying and bloody end.

The actual crusaders, for the most part little more experienced as fighting men than those on the popular 'people's crusades', but under military discipline, were also not without their visions of mystical grandeur. At times it saved their lives, as when besieged in Antioch and at their last extremity, they discovered what they genuinely believed to be the Holy Lance with which the centurion Longinus had pierced the side of the Christ. Such was their faith in a miracle that they flung open the gates of the beleaguered city and marched out. The amazed Turks, fearing some kind of ingenious trap, fled!

However, human nature soon reduced the united religious fervour to political bickering about the status of those knightly leaders whose followers had found the lance. But fervour returned with the sight of Jerusalem. They marched ceremoniously round and round it, and once inside carried out a wholesale butchery so merciless that their horses were wading knee deep in blood — the whole inhuman ferocity accompanied by tearful piety at having attained the holy of holies!

They held Jerusalem for almost a hundred years and established a clutch of small Frankish kingdoms, counties and principalities in the Holy land, the last remnant of which fell two hundred years later. During this period there was ample opportunity for Moslems and Christians to culturally cross-fertilise even though they were implacable enemies. Yet they never got to understand each other's religion, even though both were founded in the Old Testament. The Turks could never understand how the doctrine of the Holy Trinity was not polytheism; the parading of images such as the cross was anathema to them, and smacked of pagan idolatry.

The Saracens were in fact more civilised than the rough Frankish crusaders, although some Franks did study Arab culture in some depth. There were frequent opportunities to do so in that nobles taken prisoner were seldom killed, but held captive for ransom, and sometimes it took years for a ransom to be paid.

Knights such as Balian of Ibelin (who negotiated terms when Jerusalem finally fell to Saladin), Humphrey IV of Toron (later translator for Richard the Lionheart on the Third Crusade), and Raymond III of Tripoli, were better known men of the two cultures — but there were many more in lesser degree — and Saracen ideas penetrated Europe through the tales of returning crusaders and pilgrims. This reinforced a trend which was also present through the action of trade, not only through the fleets of the Italian city states, but through cosmopolitan centres such as Toledo or the Norman Kingdom of Sicily — which stretched as far North as the environs of Naples on the mainland of what is now Italy.

The lands that formed the Kingdom of Sicily had been part of the Byzantine Empire and thus under the sway of Eastern Orthodox

Christianity — with its more mystical approach. They had then fallen to the Turks, who were themselves then ousted by the Roman Catholic but still semi-barbarous Normans. When King Roger took the throne in 1130 a most accommodating multi-racial, multi-religious compromise had been reached, with Christians holding the rank of Emir, and Turks holding Christian offices. It did not last more than a hundred years but indicates the amount of interchange that was possible.

The establishment of Frankish kingdoms in Palestine, holding established ports such as Acre and Jaffa, encouraged more international trade, particularly under the enterprise of such maritime city states as Venice. And the actual population of these Frankish kingdoms was a cosmopolitan mixture of Turks, Jews, and Eastern and Western Christians. The Franks were but one new army of temporary conquerors in an area which was familiar with a constant historical succession of conquering armies.

The signs of strange ideas floating about in Western Europe can be seen by various events during the two-hundred-year period 1100 to 1300. The time-scale we give in Figure 11 has on it a number of events which may give fruit to speculative thought.

For one thing there was that glory that is still very much with us, the flowering of gothic architecture. As Louis Charpentier remarks in *The Mysteries of Chartres Cathedral:*

> ...the gothic has always eluded attempts to fix its origin. The historic question remains posed. It appears suddenly, without preamble, toward 1130. In a few years it reaches its apogee, born whole and entire without experiment or miscarriage. And the extraordinary thing is that all at once it has at its disposal master-craftsmen, artisans, builders, enough of them to undertake the construction of eighty huge monuments in less than a hundred years.

In engineering terms it was a matter of discovery of the arch based upon the ellipse rather than flying buttresses. It may well be that the origins of Freemasonry stem from this period as there were indeed guilds of 'free masons', bound to no lord, whose new lore made such constructions possible. Charpentier feels that the gothic style is intimately linked with the Templars.

These knightly religious fraternities gained enormous power very quickly and became virtually a power unto themselves, playing a major and unpredictable part in the troubled local politics of the Kingdom of Jerusalem.

The Order of the Temple was formed in 1118 as a body of warrior monks — a combined ideal that carried particular emotional force to the

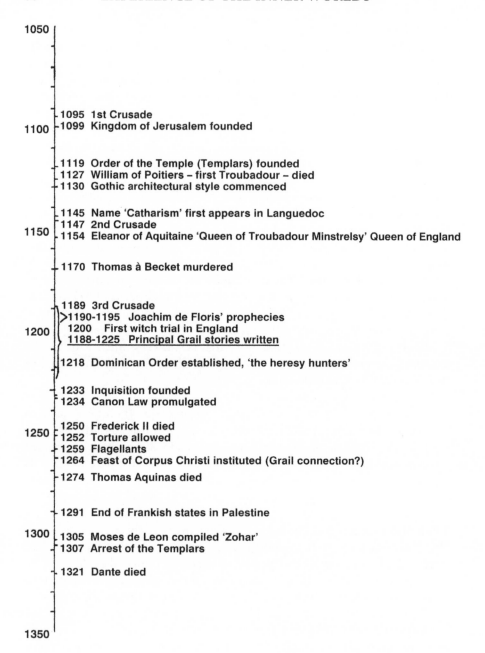

1050

1095 1st Crusade
1100 1099 Kingdom of Jerusalem founded

1119 Order of the Temple (Templars) founded
1127 William of Poitiers – first Troubadour – died
1130 Gothic architectural style commenced

1145 Name 'Catharism' first appears in Languedoc
1147 2nd Crusade
1150 1154 Eleanor of Aquitaine 'Queen of Troubadour Minstrelsy' Queen of England

1170 Thomas à Becket murdered

1189 3rd Crusade
1190-1195 Joachim de Floris' prophecies
1200   First witch trial in England
1200 1188-1225 Principal Grail stories written

1218 Dominican Order established, 'the heresy hunters'

1233 Inquisition founded
1234 Canon Law promulgated

1250 Frederick II died
1250 1252 Torture allowed
1259 Flagellants
1264 Feast of Corpus Christi instituted (Grail connection?)

1274 Thomas Aquinas died

1291 End of Frankish states in Palestine

1300 1305 Moses de Leon compiled 'Zohar'
1307 Arrest of the Templars

1321 Dante died

1350

Figure 11

medieval mind. Their self-appointed task was to keep open the pilgrim routes and they were similar to the Knights Hospitaller and the Knights of St. John who carried out a similar function.

A para-military religious organisation develops tremendous thrust and they were respected and feared and eventually distrusted in much the same way that the Jesuits later became. Like the Jesuits they were eventually suppressed, though the Jesuits did rise again, their military idealism being more subtle and intellectual than the more physical soldierly function of the Templars. (The Salvation Army in our own day, perhaps the most respected religious organisation by the ordinary man of the world, shows how the archetypal military/religious combination survives.)

The Templars got their name from their headquarters being on the site of Solomon's Temple in Jerusalem, though one doubts if this were mere coincidence. They were suppressed in 1307, partly for political reasons, to curb their immense power and wealth, but also because of alleged heresy. They were accused of practising strange rites involving a being called Baphomet with a goat-like head, of trampling and spitting on the Cross, and of certain obscene ritual gestures possibly involving homosexual practices.

The possible reasons for the strange rites and their probable significance are all part of the strange pattern of mystical heresies that came to the fore when (oddly enough) the Roman church was at its period of greatest influence.

In 1127 William of Poitiers died. He is remarkable for being accredited as the first Troubadour. The Troubadour tradition is associated with the cult of Courtly Love. This was in part a poetic convention, and in part a diversion of aristocratic ladies. Its effects, however, are with us to this day in our attitude to many things — not least of all the romantic novel and the whole convention of the 'eternal triangle' cast into sentimental terms.

A full analysis of this is made in Denis de Rougement's *Passion and Society*, though he probably does not have the whole truth. But we are in fact still living in a literary and psychological epoch which began in the early twelfth century with the conventions of Courtly Love, which considered passionate love to be, not a folly or indiscretion, as the ancients would have regarded it, but as an ennobling experience. (In one sense Joachim de Fiore was right about the coming to birth of a new age, though it was not quite so drastic and millennial as had been expected.)

The movement centred in Southern France, in Provence, and an early patron of it was Eleanor of Aquitaine, a remarkable woman, who became Queen of France and subsequently Queen of England. Having been divorced from Louis VII of France she married Henry Plantagenet, who became Henry II of England. She was mother of Richard the Lionheart and of John, future kings of England, and her daughter, Marie of Champagne, in her turn became a leading patron of Troubadour Minstrelsy.

The principle feature of the cult was the elevation of the regard for womanhood. From being a chattel in the eyes of a husband she became a goddess in the eyes of a lover. Its implicit philosophical basis was therefore one of adultery, although the institution of marriage in those days, at aristocratic level anyway, was principally a matter of political or economic convenience, extending even to the betrothal of infants. Thus apart from the necessary function of siring legitimate children to continue the family line a wife was as often as not neglected in favour of a mistress. Husbands faithful to their wives were exceptional enough to merit comment.

There is some doubt as to how far the cult actually encouraged physical adultery. Most of the emphasis was placed on the pangs of unrequited love, and placing the beloved upon a remote and lofty pedestal in adoration of her exquisite nature and beauty. So much so that any physical embrace would seem to be something of an anticlimax!

The speed and extent to which Courtly Love caught on, however, leads one to suspect that there was more to this movement than appears on the surface. Granted, the social justifications were there, and in the majority of instances it perhaps was little deeper in content than a parlour diversion on a par with backgammon and needlework, but the hold it took and the influence it had speak of hidden archetypal stirrings of a psychic or religious nature.

The deification of the lady love, and the division of the lover's approach to her into seven set stages, have parallels with pagan mystery cults of the Queen Venus. Once again, as in the Song of Solomon, we feel the influence of Ishtar, behind a veil of mystery. Purporting to be conventional religious or social belief and custom under slightly unusual imagery, there is the feeling that something more is there, waiting to burst out upon us.

This is another thread in our fabric of mystical 'heresies'. A further one is a more ostensibly heretical movement, the Church of the Cathars, also centred in Provence, particularly about the town of Albi, so that they were also known as the Albigensians.

Subsequently they had a crusade preached against them which resulted in massacres and tortures on a genocidal scale, and the heresy was wiped out in 1209. Heretical they no doubt were, because they had become strongly influenced by Eastern ideas of the intrinsic evil of matter. In their belief there was not one God who created the world but who permitted the possibility of sin and evil in order that his creation should enjoy and responsibly use free will. They saw the opposing creative principles as of equal rank — the one good, the other evil. The good was equated with spiritual abstraction, the evil with concrete materiality.

Apart from the diminution of reverence to the One God that such a belief implied, it also logically demanded a highly ascetic regime from the righteous. Any co-operation with the natural processes was indeed seen as a co-operation with evil. Thus it was a sin to produce children. Ideally the human race should become extinct through voluntary refusal to procreate and thus finally be free from the toils of the flesh. Until such time those who were unable spiritually to live up to this rule would reincarnate again and again until they learned wisdom.

In practice it tended to develop, by ill-considered repression of the natural instincts, some morbid elements, and homosexuality was a commonly accepted compromise. However, this does not detract from the fact that the heresy was, of its type, and in its ideal purity, a highly spiritual one.

It had very ancient antecedents. The theology of dual principles was of Persian origin and it has come back to haunt Western Christianity with remarkable persistence through the ages. We have already looked at this in regard to Mithraism. No doubt there is truth in it — there are good and evil in the world in opposition one to the other — although giving evil the privilege of an equal standing with good is another matter. One sees how important it is to get these basic theological propositions right. Although it has to be said that Church teaching has from time to time come pretty close to the heretical position with the concept of the Devil being promoted to the level of an anti-Christ. Strictly speaking he is traditionally but a fallen angel, and like us, one of the created.

The Plantagenet kings play an important part in this interesting period, and were popularly regarded as descended from an infernal being. They were indeed called The Devil's Brood and Alfred Duggan has written an interesting book about them with this title, whilst Hugh Ross Williamson in *The Arrow and the Sword* considers both Henry II and Thomas à Becket to have been members of the Cathar church.

Henry II and Eleanor of Aquitaine were the parents of Richard the Lionheart whose troubadour connections are enshrined in the legend of Blondel travelling through Europe seeking his imprisoned master by singing beneath every prison tower.

Richard's period as King of England (a matter of ten years in which he spent barely five months in the country) was the traditional setting for the strange ballad cycle of Robin Hood and his Merry Men. There is more to this outlaw community than the literal social level of rural guerrilla warfare. They included a man of God, a most unlikely but very loveable one, Friar Tuck (who is also anachronistic as there were no friars in those days). There was also a maid, Maid Marian, though what kind of a maid she could have been in such rude and rough outlaw company is open to conjecture. In one way she is a forerunner of Joan of Arc, who inspired a beaten nation to victory.

In many characters of this period there is a kind of mystical ambiance surrounding them as if they carry more significance than at surface level meets the eye.

Richard I was, for instance, a very poor king, an absentee and forever fighting in foreign wars. Yet he has come down as a romantic hero of history books, and indeed he was a very popular and charismatic figure in his own day. Admittedly he was handsome, strong, and a good fighting man, but as well as his mother's good looks he inherited her petulance and obstinacy.

Thomas à Becket, at first drinking companion of Henry II, became a martyr, and, as such, founder of a seat of pilgrimage for the entire nation for centuries to come. Queen Eleanor was such a dominating and fascinating woman, with her high political and social connections as well as the tenuous heretical connections, that she is the subject of popular cinema entertainment to this day.

It was indeed a period when something new seemed to be loosed abroad. Something that had long been pent up and whose release covered those through whom it came with a kind of reflected radiance that has lasted well into our own day.

In one way it could be looked upon as a release of the feminine, for the religious traditions of the Jews, which are the foundation of the faith of the West, grew with a pronounced masculine bias in their religious imagery.

There are three ways of trying to describe God for those who seek to do so by one of the three pronouns that language allows us — He, She or It.

To the Hebrew *She* was absolutely unthinkable. The whole social structure of their society militated against it, and in any case it was redolent of the surrounding scandalous pagan practices of Ishtar. In so far as the pagan nations were political rivals for territory also, an element of patriotism also entered into religion.

Neither was *It* acceptable. God was above all a personal God and *It* was only attractive to the philosophical Greek mind. It reached its highest point in the philosophical system of Plotinus but though it has much to commend it (and it may well seem the most 'reasonable' to our impersonal scientific age) it tends to deny by implication the personal concern of God for the act of creation.

Therefore *He* it had to be. There is, however, another alternative, which the very earliest Hebrew scripture uses, and that is *They*. The Hebrew language achieved a remarkable compromise here in putting together a feminine noun and masculine plural ending to get the name for God in the first verse of Genesis — *Elohim*. But here the difficulty is that one runs into the danger of polytheism, and visualises not one God but a swarm of godlings.

So *He* it became, with the attendant dangers of making Paradise patriarchal and repressing the feminine element.

In point of fact God announced his name to Moses as I AM — which neatly avoids the philological trap. And indeed if man bends his attention *to* God, instead of talking *about* God, then *You* (or the more intimate *Thou*, which has regrettably become an archaism in the English language except for some local dialects) avoids the semantic problem of He, She or It.

Regrettably on such tiny problems many have gone to fire and the sword, the torment and the dungeon. One sees the wisdom of Meister Eckhart's injunction: 'Why dost thou prate of God? Whatever thou sayest of him is untrue.' Indeed as soon as the soul turns from God — even to speak of God — then the deadly consequences of original sin begin to manifest themselves.

However, we inherit the Judaic conception of God being He, which in its higher understanding, as exemplified in the teaching of Jesus of the fatherhood of God, is full of wisdom. Though in its debased form it can degenerate into the wrathful old man — a thinly disguised aggressive tribal deity, and not a very pleasant one at that.

But God, as Creator of All, can hardly be confined to the sense of a masculine pronoun. Valid though this approach to God may be, it cannot but be a one-sided one, and the necessity to fill a psychological vacuum was felt from quite early times in the Church, and was catered for to some extent by the veneration of saints (*dulia*) and in particular the special veneration for the Mother of God, the Blessed Virgin Mary (*hyperdulia*), as opposed to the worship (*latria*) due only to God.

The early Church borrowed quite freely from pagan worship and this is not necessarily a dilution or corruption. Innovation is necessary in all things that are to survive and without it Christianity would have remained a minor sect within Judaism, open to none but to born Jews, or to Gentile proselytes willing to undergo circumcision and obey the Levitical code.

In religions, particularly to the outsider, the superficial frequently appears as the essential, and the essential as the superficial. Superficialities are the outward form, the style of worship, the organisation of the institution, the payment of ministers and Church servants. Essentials are the root principles of belief. The early fathers spent time and energy on essentials, even though the modern mind (which takes for granted much that was hard fought for) tends to regard them as logic chopping contentious disputers of minor points of doctrine.

Even the first Christian Roman Emperor, Constantine, had difficulty in realising this. And later, another Roman Emperor, Julian the Apostate, considered the cult of relics of saints, the exaltation of Mary, and the divinity of Christ, as innovations and corruptions of original primitive Christian belief.

But whether relics of saints were introduced, or Mary exalted to Queen of Heaven, as a counter attraction to the Mystery goddesses such as Isis, Queen of Heaven; or candles, robes and incense introduced together with the retention, or taking over, of pagan feast days such as Christmas (formerly birth date of Mithra, and the Winter Solstice); or the Assumption of the Blessed Virgin Mary instituted on the date marking the rise of the star Sirius, or Sothis, which heralded the annual Inundation of the Nile, essential to Egyptian life and prosperity; these were superficialities, making it easier for pagans to believe the essential point of the Gospel or 'good news' of man's redemption.

However, the balance was still not achieved of realising God to be approachable through the image of the feminine as well as through the masculine. Hence one reason for the somewhat heretical nature of such cults as Courtly Love. This was finally resolved into orthodoxy however, by the great poetic portrayer of the vision of the high Middle Ages, Dante (1265-1321), who saw in Beatrice the image of God. Even so, Dante's early work, the *Vita Nuova*, a treatise on poetry, in which he describes his first experiences in love in terms that spill over into the theological, was censored by the Church authorities.

Indeed, the realistic modern mind, particularly in the anti-romantic phase it has been going through in the twentieth century and beyond, may well feel that Dante is over-egging the pudding somewhat. But he was young, medieval and Italian, which may explain a lot to our less passionate world view. To him, the first sight of Beatrice (meaning 'joy') had a stupefying effect. It was love at first sight at its most romantically devastating.

Subsequently the real Beatrice died, and Dante's acquaintance with her was never much more than adoration from afar. No doubt the real Florentine girl, Bea Portinari, was no more divine than the rest of us, but to Dante she represented deity and perfection incarnate. It was from this that his great poetic cycle *The Divine Comedy* sprang. For if the divine can be seen in one girl like this, then this is not necessarily a subjective illusion, but a glimpse of the perfection that that person could be — and indeed *is* — in an unfallen state. This can be applied to all such glimpses of perfection or eternity in others.

Love was considered by the pagans to be something of a madness. Possibly it is. It is written down as 'infatuation' or 'calf love' by the wordly wise and no doubt they are right — because marriage or any close relationship based on this impossible image of perfection is bound to fail if the subsequent readjustment of vision to material reality is not experienced maturely. In modern times we have even psychologised it — in Jungian terms it is a projection onto another of an archetype of the unconscious.

It may be all of these things — in part. But this still does not invalidate it or the soul's inherent knowledge of pristine divine perfection, and this has been enshrined for all time in Dante's poetry, which, as he took pains to point out, is written to be understood on at least four levels of meaning.

Thus passionate love has something of the divine in it, in that it has been assumed, despite all evidence to the contrary, to have an ennobling effect. And as de Rougement has pointed out in *Passion and Society*, it has certainly affected Western literature and society to a marked extent.

The ideal fashion for passionate love to develop is in a gradual realisation of its essential truth tempered with compassion to the existential reality. In terms of human love this is the basis of a happy marriage — or as happy as can be in a fallen world. The danger of the naked passion is its otherworldliness — the apparent 'unreality' of its vision of perfection.

However, this searing flame, if kept alive and not allowed to be quenched in disillusion — the idol loved the more for its feet of clay — can become realisation of the love that moves the stars in their courses and directs the universe. Something of this realisation is expressed by Teilhard de Chardin in *The Divine Milieu*:

> Throughout my life, by means of my life, the world has little by little caught fire in my sight until, aflame all around me, it has become almost completely luminous from within ... such has been my experience in contact with the earth — the diaphony of the Divine at the heart of the universe on fire ... Christ: his heart; a fire; capable of penetrating everywhere and, gradually, spreading everywhere.

The Dantesque passion for a fair lady is thus one aspect of a diffused passion for God, the whole human race, the whole creation — animate and inanimate, worldly or heavenly. This 'light in extension' is 'the light which lighteth every man that cometh into the world'. This light has been likened to Christ, the Word, the Creator, and its realisation and extension are the fulfilment of the supreme commandment of the New Testament: 'To love the Lord thy God with all thy heart, with all thy soul and with all thy strength: and thy neighbour as thyself.'

This is the realisation that comes from true belief as a grace of God. It is a far cry from the approach from the other pole, of regarding such an ethic as desirable on social or humanitarian grounds and then trying to live up to it. This is to follow the good example of a dead rabbi rather than to realise the overflowing loving kindness of an incarnate, living God. It may be commendable effort of fallen human nature doing its best — but it misses so much.

This vision of perfection applies then, not only to the sexual sphere (lest anyone confuse 'joy' with 'Freud')! Dante also used the image of the city — his beloved Florence — from which he was exiled. And in this he followed in the path of St. Augustine and his seminal *Civitas Dei*, and before that to the awesome imagery in the Revelation of St. John in the New Jerusalem:

> Then I saw the holy city, New Jerusalem, coming down out of heaven from God, made ready like a bride adorned for her husband. I heard a loud voice proclaiming from the throne: "Now at last God has his dwelling among men! He will dwell among them and they shall be his people, and be an end to death, and the mourning and crying and pain; for the old order has passed away!"

The old Jerusalem, to the medieval pious mind, had something of the mystical quality of the New, as is witnessed by the vast and tragic popular impulses to go on the Crusades. And a like tremor ran through the Christian world when, almost a hundred years later, Jerusalem fell to Saladin — an event that crystallised in consciousness the image of the Holy Grail.

In 1187, at the Battle of Hattin, the crusaders' army, through mismanagement and long internal feuding, was virtually wiped out in a nightmarish battle — trapped in full armour without water in a sun-baked plain. And when Jerusalem fell a few months later a shock wave ran through the whole of Christendom.

It caused the mounting of the Third Crusade — in which Richard the Lionheart played a leading role — but Jerusalem was never recaptured. This was the last of the true Crusades; the ones that followed were an assault against Eastern Christendom (the Fourth, in 1202); a bloody purge of the heretic Cathar church in the South of France (the Fifth, in 1213); and a cynical piece of politicking by Emperor Frederick II in defiance of the papacy (the Sixth, in 1218).

In addition to sparking off the Third Crusade, the fall of Christian Jerusalem sparked a kind of literary movement that produced the legends of the Holy Grail. The grounds for linking this legendary cycle to the historical events of the time are interestingly pursued by Helen Adolf in her *Viseo Pacis, Holy City and Grail.*

The legend appears in several versions, but all within a period between the last two decades of the twelfth century and the first two decades of the thirteenth.

These were: the *Conte du Graal* by Chrétien de Troyes, the *Grand St. Graal* and *Romanz de lèstoire du Graal* by Robert de Boron, the *Queste del San Graal* attributed to Walter Map, the *Perlesvaus* probably written at Glastonbury, and the German *Parzival* by Wolfram von Eschenbach.

From this, there followed, as with all literary or artistic successes, a whole host of imitators, of which we should mention two, which stand in a class of their own.

The first is *Le Morte d'Arthur* by Sir Thomas Malory, the means by which most of us today know about the Grail Legends. Malory, a knight in the Wars of the Roses, collected together the legends of the Matter of Britain (Merlin, King Arthur, the Round Table, the Holy Grail, etc.) contained in old French manuscripts and made them into a more or less coherent narrative. It was completed in 1469/70 and was one of the first books to be put into print, by Caxton, who with a rare publisher's eye for a best seller, issued it in 1485.

The other important version was in the *The Mabinogion,* translated by Lady Gregory from Welsh sources, containing stories in somewhat primitive form, suggesting that Arthurian and Grail material had been around for some considerable time even though the earliest MSS surviving date only from the 1300s.

So what we have in the period 1180-1220 is a sudden crystallisation of a body of legend into meaningful structure. And this is a mid-point of a two hundred year period wherein, in our view, there was a re-efflorescence of the Way of Affirmation — the *via positiva.* There was a mystical realisation of the relevance of the image of God in the feminine, and also in the corporate organisation (or city), and also, as we shall discuss in our next chapter, in substance itself, in the work of alchemy.

The Grail stories vary somewhat, and much paper and ink have been devoted to theories as to what the Grail really was and what it meant. Certainly a number of traditional streams unite in the Holy Grail stories so that any number of theories can be aired with a fair degree of plausibility. There are elements of Christian doctrine, fairy-tale material, ritual symbolism possibly of Templar or Cathar origin; alchemy, and ancient Celtic and Oriental legend and myth.

The stories are generally known as the Matter of Britain, probably because they were circulated by Breton, British (i.e. Welsh), and Anglo-Norman singers and story tellers at the courts of France and England. The close links, through conquest and marriage, between England and France, had something to do with its spread, and it sprang into high fashion in the twelfth century, more or less contemporaneously with the Plantagenet line.

The Courts of Love, as we have said, were at their peak, instituting a code of behaviour towards women quite uncharacteristic of ages before or since; and in addition to this, tales of King Arthur's Round Table laid down ideals of chivalry and knighthood even if these were, as often as not, honoured more in the breach than the observance.

Arthur is first mentioned in history in the *Historia Britonicus* of Nennius towards the end of the ninth century where it is recorded that he was a *dux bellorum*, a leader of a resistance movement of the old Celtic civilisation against the invading Saxons in a series of twelve battles, the last of which was in 516. The panoply of high chivalry and plate armour with which he is attributed in popular legend to this day is an interpolation of the fifteenth century when first these legends became printed literature. The original Arthur would have been a rougher, ruder figure with little concern for the niceties of chivalry.

The Round Table is mentioned for the first time in Wace's *Roman de Brut*, a free Anglo-Norman translation of Geoffrey of Monmouth's *Historia regum Britanniae* (c.1135). Stories of Arthur must have been already popular at this time. Geoffrey does not mention the Grail but it was this that sparked off the great body of literature when it was used by Chrétien de Troyes. Chrétien did not get beyond line 9004 of his *Conte du Graal* but others carried on the theme, completing 60,000 lines in all. Chrétien was writing between 1180 and 1190 and the last of his continuators were active until 1230.

Perhaps contemporaneously with Chrétien, Robert de Boron appears to have been writing *Romanz de lèstoire du Graal,* making it much more of a Christian legend, though with some daring near-heretical speculations on the Holy Trinity that indicate him to have been a pious layman, theologically naïve, rather than a cleric well versed in orthodoxy. He bases it on the Apocryphal *Gospel of Nicodemus* or *Acts of Pilate* which treats at some length the role of Joseph of Arimathea — who is mentioned briefly in the Gospels as getting permission for custody of the body of Jesus from Pontius Pilate and burying it in his own sepulchre.

There does in fact seem to be strangely little written or thought about Joseph of Arimathea, apart from later stories of receiving the blood of Christ in the Cup of the Last Supper, which we owe to Robert de Boron.

Even going by the bare bones of the Gospel narratives, if it had not been for Joseph of Arimathea there would have been no empty tomb, and no traditional story of the Resurrection! He plays a crucial role in the drama of the Passion. Again we can see how neglected aspects of orthodoxy tend to spring up with many accretions about them.

The other principle Grail writer, Wolfram von Eschenbach, wrote his *Parzival* (upon which the Wagnerian opera cycle is based) between 1200 and 1207. His version is similar to that of Chrétien though he claims Chrétien has got the story wrong and gives his own slant to it. His version more clearly shows oriental influences, and by calling the Grail a stone rather than a cup, and by other parallels, he connects the Grail with alchemy.

As with alchemy itself, there tend to be as many Grails as there are writers about it — but there is a discernible connecting thread.

Other versions which deserve mention are the *Lancelot Graal* (1200-10) allegedly by Walter Map which was the basis used by Malory for his *Le Morte d'Arthur* and thus has a considerable modern influence because of this. Walter Map is also credited with the *Queste del Saint Graal* (c.1200) which has a pronounced Christian flavour. So also does the *Perlesvaux* (1191-1212) associated with Glastonbury, which is also highly allegorical and symbolical and has been translated by Sebastian Evans as *The High History of the Holy Grail*.

The English *Sir Percyvelle* contains no Holy Grail but is so artless as to suggest that it may be close to original sources, although the extant MSS is late (c.1370). *The Mabinogion's Peredur* contains early Celtic material but may be no earlier than Chrétien's version, perhaps sharing a common, now lost, original. Whilst *Diu Crône* by Heinrich von dem Türlin is a somewhat confused version but with interesting features such as alluding the Grail to the Eucharist.

There has been much speculation about the original source of the Grail legend. The main writers, Chrétien, Robert de Boron and Wolfram, amongst others, contain fascinating hints that suggest it not impossible that the legend may have been around in written form in the eighth century — but this is unproven.

The other element in the Matter of Britain besides the Round Table and the Holy Grail is the figure of Merlin, the magician or wise-man, something after the Judeo-Christian-Islamic tradition of Elijah, who first appears in Geoffrey of Monmouth's history of c.1134. Though a similar figure, called Ambrosius, does appear much earlier in the anonymous *Historium Britonicus* (seventh to ninth century).

Merlin also became the focus of a whole body of 'prophetic' literature particularly emanating from the various millennial and Holy Ghost movements, of which the most important figure is that of Joachim de Fiore (or de Floris). His ideas, which we have already discussed, about the coming of the Anti-Christ were published by his followers as the *Verba Merlin*. There were also quite orthodox but reforming works such as *Les Propheties de Merlin* critical of Church abuses. The general efflorescence of this literature coincided with the spread of alchemy. Eventually such writings began to be a cloak for all kinds of political pamphleteering and many were criticised and even prohibited by the time of the Council of Trent (1545-63).

There is also an interesting parallel between religious millennialism and Utopian socialism and communism, which can be traced right up to the nineteenth century when many occult societies and sages (including the famous Eliphas Levi) had political as well as religiously revolutionary ideas. Their lack of practicality carried little real threat, however, to the *status quo*.

As we have mentioned, there is some mystery as to what the Holy Grail actually is, as well as to what it actually does. It is commonly assumed to be a cup, just as the forbidden fruit of Adam and Eve is commonly assumed to be an apple, though there is no mention of apple trees in Genesis. Similarly there is no specific consistent description of the Grail within the Grail literature. To some it is a dish or tray, to others it is the Cup of the Last Supper, and to yet others, a stone. As a cup it is considered to have been used to catch some drops of Christ's blood from the Cross — and in this connection one finds the Lance of Longinus equally revered and connected with the Grail so as almost to become an integral part of it. And it is a moot point which is the most central to the significance of the legend, the blood of God (the *sang real*), or the objects themselves.

It is plain that the whole Mystery is much concerned with the central Mystery of the Christian belief, the Passion of Christ and its significance for man and the world.

There was, at this time, considerable speculation within the Church on what was to become a major article of discord — the real presence of Christ in the bread and wine at the Mass. And it was in the twelfth century that the practice of elevating the sacraments during the liturgy of the Mass was first introduced. Rather than become involved in what is still a vexed question of interdenominational theology it will suffice for us to note that the problem was obviously coming up to the conscious preoccupation of Christians at the time of the Grail stories' formulation. And this supports our contention that troubled doctrinal waters point to a truth which has not or cannot be readily assimilated by the Church.

Such a point of infection (or inoculation, if one likes to put it the other way) attracts similarly 'charged' symbolism about it — some of it from other traditions, some of it of archaic origin. Thus we have the oriental and fairytale elements in the Grail stories as well as primitive material to such an extent that scholars such as Jessie Weston (in *From Ritual to Romance*) have argued that the Grail is the remains of a primitive fertility ritual. Certainly the most ancient four key symbols of Celtic mythology — the spear, the cauldron, the sword and the stone — have their parallels in the Grail and Arthurian stories wherein important messages seem to come to Camelot via floating stones, and the true kingship of Arthur is revealed by a test of pulling a sword from a stone.

The fiery spear of Lugh, the God of Light, becomes the Lance of Longinus which pierced the side of Jesus, with the intention of entering his heart to kill him, and this becomes a holy relic guarded at the Grail Castle and the weapon that deals the Dolorous Stroke. A knight, Balin, though admittedly in extreme physical danger, seizes it and defends himself with it to his own ends. This wounds the King, significantly in the generative organs, and the country is at the same time all laid waste. The King does not die but lies to a great age until the Grail Winner shall come and cure his wound and release him from this life, whilst at the same time restoring the surrounding land of Logres from its enchantment.

The Grail side of things has an even more primitively rich origin. An old Celtic deity, Bran the Blessed, whose head is supposed to be buried at the White Mount, on which stands the Tower of London, ready to warn of invasion, had a large cauldron of miraculous properties. Not only would it — like the classical Cornucopia — provide food for as many as were present — but it would restore the dead to life if they were boiled up in it. Obviously this was a very useful acquisition for any warring, hunting community. And like most useful acquisitions it became the cause of as much strife as it did benefits. One might be tempted to say the same of the Holy Eucharist — the most holy and central Christian rite which yet has been the centre of so much Christian discord.

The miraculous appurtenances of the Holy Grail are similar. When it appears and processes round the company each one finds before him the food he most likes to eat. And it is of course intimately associated with the cure of the enchanted land and remedying the sin of the Dolorous Stroke, in so far that the Grail Seeker must ask three key questions about it.

These are: What is the Grail? What is the purpose of the Grail? Who is served by the Grail?

As has been discovered in many a modern context, it is not enough to be able to answer difficult questions that solve a problem, but the ability to discern the right questions that need to be answered.

The Grail Stories tell of what happens when a Grail Seeker wins through to a revelation of the Grail but fails in his wonder to ask the right questions. All disappears as a phantasm and he finds himself back in the enchanted Wasteland (for which read the normal condition of this world and human consciousness), with castigation heaped upon him for his lost opportunity.

It can be helpful to regard the whole story of the Matter of Britain as a drama of the soul, with the various characters as aspects of the soul. This method is suggestive only, because as there is such a cross-fertilisation and mixing of traditions in the stories, no one tradition has emerged in a fully coherent form. But this may make it more like life as we know it.

There are, for instance, two centres of influence, the Castle of Camelot and the Castle of Carbonek, which are representative of the interests of the outer life and of the inner life — the former that of the Court of Arthur and the Company of the Round Table, the flower of chivalry — and the latter the Grail Castle, where deep and holy Mysteries are contained.

All is not well, however, for the flower of chivalry has its internal canker in the bud. Lancelot, the fairest and best knight in the world, loves the Queen, who returns his love. All this stems in some way basically from Arthur himself, who, preoccupied with affairs of state, sent Lancelot to meet Guinevere his betrothed. This slight tip of unbalance, seemingly insignificant, being enough for evil to come into the Camelot world.

The Round Table was part of the dowry of Guinevere, and when the forces of evil finally break out the Table is destroyed, Arthur killed, and Guinevere and Lancelot repent and spend their last days in the religious life. The prime instigator of evil, Mordred (who was present at the institution of the Table, in the womb of his mother Morgawse, fruit of an incestuous relationship) uses, as evil does, the apparent upholding of good to work evil. It is by denunciation of Lancelot and Guinevere that the rot really sets in, and bloody feud breaks out as Lancelot inadvertently kills the other Orkney brothers, Gareth and Gaheris, when rescuing Guinevere from the stake. This incites their brothers Gawain and Agravain to become sworn enemies of Lancelot and civil war breaks out which finally destroys all.

Again, at Castle Carbonek all is far from well. For the King of the Castle, Pelles, lies stricken with the Dolorous Stroke, struck when an early knight, Balin, sacrilegiously seized one of the hallows, the Lance of Longinus, to defend himself against Gorlon, evil brother of Pelles the Grail King, who usually when abroad in the world was invisible, striking people down without warning; a figure of disease, sin, and death. Since then, as we have said, the King has lain wounded in the generative organs, with the land laid waste under enchantment until the Grail Winner comes.

The Grail Winners are three in number. The fully dedicated Grail Winner, born to the task, is Galahad, and by a great Mystery of Atonement and of good and evil he is Lancelot's son, begot by enchantment on the Grail Maiden, and this unfaithfulness to the Queen causes him to go mad. We are in deep waters here. The other two Grail Winners are Percivale, the dedicated religious, and Bors, the man of the world, with wife and family, who returns to the world after winning the Grail, and leads a life of valour and honour.

Behind all this are the figures of Merlin and Nimuë, the Lady of the Lake, strange, half-human, half-faery creatures, influencing the humans to do their work of destiny — yet prey to error themselves.

It is a tangled skein and the literature is vast, but this simple structuring outlined above may help in the reading of the great tapestry that is Malory's *Le Morte d'Arthur*. If it can be obtained, *Le Morte d'Arthur of Sir Thomas Malory and its Sources* by Vida Scudder is a helpful guide through its prolixities. Other versions of the tales, from the early romance texts to the re-workings of Victorian poets, are all worth reading, but lack the great synthesising mythological grasp of Malory, and tend to emphasise just one fact or other of the great body of stories even though they may be possibly more coherent.

Tennyson has, for instance, used the material to construct his own allegory. But we do better, if we wish to get all we can out of the Matter of Britain, to use our own allegorical faculties and see the drama as a part of ourselves. Lancelot as our noblest but all too human aspirations, Galahad as the part of the direct relationship to the Christ within us, Arthur and Guinevere as the centre or 'throne' of our being, Mordred as our evil side, and the other characters in a general mixture of good and evil, masculine and feminine; a complex story but — as Walt Whitman has said —we are big enough to contain thousands!

To find the Grail it is needful that we go and seek it. It is not necessarily to be found in analysis of the old Grail stories, helpful and inspiring though these may be, but in seeking it in our own hearts. By finding it *there* we can then discover its meaning and purpose. The search for the Grail is thus not a literary, but a practical Quest.

EXERCISE FOR CHAPTER IV

A Chalice shall you be, a Holy Grail
All emptied and receptive to my filling.

In the practical work that we have before us we shall regard the Grail as the receptivity of ourselves to the divine vocation that we are called to perform. In some Eastern systems of yoga a small picture of the 'master' or *guru* is visualised in the heart centre. For our purpose we visualise the Grail. We may see it as a cup or dish or any form of receptacle that imagination suggests. And a stone is a receptacle of forces and light.

It is to us the heart's desire — either for the lost Heavenly City or for the lost heavenly Beloved. It holds within it all the power that goes with the Jungian contra-sexual archetype — the *animus* or *anima*. For this contra-sexual image is often that of the higher part of the soul. And in so far as the higher part of the soul is 'with God' or 'in Christ', so is it at the same time beloved partner and beloved city: perfect personal relationship in the milieu of a perfect place, or corporate relationship.

Visualise, then, the Grail, before your heart. You may well find that it tends to coalesce with your physical heart inside your breast and that when it does, your heart burns within you. This is a subjective test of the validity of the candidate's suitability in Mystery tradition and a sign that he is accepted by the inner teachers.

The building of this symbol aligns one with the whole Eucharistic tradition, going back to pre-Christian days of the sacrament of bread and wine. In written tradition this goes back to the strange being Melchizedek, whose effigy is to be found in Chartres Cathedral, to whom Christ was likened in the Epistle to the Hebrews, written by an unknown Christian hand under Paul's name.

> This Melchizedek, King of Salem, priest of God Most High, met Abraham returning from the rout of the kings and blessed him; and Abraham gave him a tithe of everything as his portion. His name, in the first place, means "king of righteousness"; next he is King of Salem, that is, "king of peace". He has no father, no mother, no lineage; his years have no beginning, his life no end. He is like the Son of God; he remains a priest for all time. Consider now how great he must be for Abraham the patriarch to give him a tithe of the finest of the spoil.

So far, Hebrews Chapter 7. The original reference to Melchizedek is to be found in Genesis 14.

The use of this symbol of the Grail is in itself an act of consecration and one's readiness to become aware of the Will of God in one's own life and destiny. And in this consecration to destiny, one does well to realise that one is never alone, however lone or long the furrow one has to plough may seem.

One has to become part of a great Universal Church, invisible in the Heavens, not built with hands — and like an army with banners, stretched out into all Eternity, only the small minority being at present incarnate on Earth. One forges one's links with the Infinite as a temporal part, and priest, of the Infinite — an agent of God, helped and sustained by many other agents, visible and invisible, human, elemental or angelic.

And to attempt to use such symbolism outside such a contest is akin to the blasphemy of striking the Dolorous Stroke, or the ignorance of failing to ask the essential Grail Questions.

CHAPTER V

The Sea of Light

For any real advance into the deeper reaches of occult science it is essential to realise that God is he 'in whom we live and move and have our being'. This does not mean that God is an impersonal attenuated gas. It does mean that he is an omnipresent being, whose reality has been summed up as *'the circle whose circumference is nowhere and whose centre is everywhere'*. Just as the sun illuminates all upon which it shines, so is God present and revealed in all his creation.

There is something of this in the doctrine of the alchemists of the precious *first matter* being everywhere and thought valueless and commonplace. The Western study of alchemy grew alongside the events that we have already described pertaining to the various doctrines and movements that contributed to the legends of the Holy Grail. It may be regarded as another symptom of the influence of the rest of the world upon Christian Europe, principally through Islam. The very word *alchemy* is of Arabic derivation.

Alchemy, as properly understood, has little to do with primitive chemistry. Though primitive chemists there were in plenty, known as 'puffers', searching for *gold*, or the *elixir of life*, these terms are really to be understood in a mystical sense. Having said this, we should add that this does not necessarily imply that alchemy has no basis in physical fact — but rather that a mystical rather than a materialistic approach needs to be the basis of any physical operations. Still less is it a matter entirely of the mind, capable of being circumscribed by psychology.

In general the alchemical process starts with a *prima materia* or *first matter*, substance which is everywhere and nowhere, which is common and also rare, which is spurned as worthless and yet also sought after as priceless. This material is then put through the alchemical process of being dissolved and distilled — to reduce the process to its absolutely simplest terms.

The distillation of the *prima materia* or *massa confusa* — heating in a rotund flask — produces from the blackening of the first dissolving (*melanosis* or *nigredo*) a whitening (*leukesis* or *albedo*), preceded, according to some early alchemists, by a greening (*viriditas*), an indication of the process of organic change starting to occur. The whitening process marks the end of the first stage, which many may be content to regard as the final one. However, alchemical gold has not yet been achieved. There now should come about the marvellous principle of the divine conjunction (*mysterium coniunctionis*). This is marked by a yellowing (*xanthosis* or *citrinitas*) though some alchemists here describe a quick running through all the colours, called the peacock's tail (*cauda pavonis*). This becomes a reddening, with a final end of bright, light coloured gold, more pure and precious than any gold found on earth.

It may help if we lay out the process in diagrammatic form according to the traditional symbols for the metals, which placed in a certain order, give a visual indication of the process in simple terms (Figure 12).

(Mercury)	Lead	Tin	Silver	Iron	Copper	Gold

Figure 12

There are three ideographic elements composing these symbols: the **Cross** — which symbolises the four elements of the flesh; the **Crescent** — which symbolises the achievement of the first stage, a perfected reflective instrument for the higher life, natural man at his highest possibility; the **Circle** — which represents the spiritual life.

These three aspects of man are represented in the sign for Mercury, which, somewhat in keeping with the physical nature of quicksilver, takes on many forms. Mercury at normal temperature and pressure is a metal that is liquid, though it can easily be frozen, when it acts like a solid metal (it can be frozen, for instance, into the shape of a hook and made to lift objects), or it can be heated to form a gas, where in practical usage we have the mercury vapour lamp. Its most commonly known use is its rapid expansion under heat which, together with its liquid property, enables it to be used as a measure of temperature in thermometers. Of considerable fascination is the aptness of the name *quick-silver* in the way it runs about on any surface. Its density allows heavy objects to be floated in it. It is also very reflective and is used in the making of mirrors. Again, it easily becomes dirty, yet can be used as a purifying agent of other metals in that it easily forms amalgams with other metals and can then be separated from them.

All these physical qualities make it an appropriate symbol of consciousness, and the sign for Mercury shows the three states of consciousness fixed in animal form (the Cross), self-conscious and reflective (the Crescent), or as a radiating centre of influence (the Circle).

Consciousness in its 'raw' state is similar to the 'collective unconscious' postulated by Jungian psychology, but should not be confused with it. A better image for it is the still waters of the Great Sea over the face of which the Spirit flew in the description of the fount of creation in Genesis. In some Rosicrucian and alchemical texts it is symbolised as a naked sleeping virgin — the Lady Venus.

It is certainly not the teeming jungeloid nature of myths, dreams, and psychoanalytic fantasies. This is a particular aspect it can take when the waters are troubled, as it were. But the patterned fantasies of psychotics and neurotics are not necessarily the same thing as the visions of the spiritual life — although it is possibly a symptom of our times that they should be so confused.

In viewing the transformation of consciousness through the mystical alchemical process, the **Mercury** may be seen in its first stages as being the *prima materia*, or first matter, and ending as the Stone of the Philosophers. (Precise terminology varies from alchemist to alchemist, in keeping with the fluid nature of the mercuric consciousness they are trying to describe.) The process can be regarded as being a way between two principles — the Passive and the Active — which are symbolised very often as **Salt** and **Sulphur** (Figure 13).

Ideographically these can be interpreted as the radiating principle (Circle) fixed in an inert state (Cross-bar), and at the other end, as the triune spirituality (Triangle), acting freely in the animal sphere (Cross).

The relative positions of the basic signs that occur in the sign of consciousness, Mercury, (Crescent, Circle and Cross), signify stages in the process which are marked by the symbols for the traditional alchemical metals.

(In passing we should note that the sign for Mercury, when being specifically acted upon by the two active and passive principles of Sulphur and Salt, is sometimes drawn slightly differently with two straight lines converging at an angle from above in place of the Crescent.)

Thus the first stage of consciousness, of ordinary man, is represented by **Lead** (Cross over Crescent), in which the reflective perceiving nature of consciousness is dominated entirely by the world of the physical senses and instincts.

The initial result of the alchemical process shows the reflective consciousness rising up onto and above a level with the ordinary 'natural' level, giving us the stage represented by **Tin** (Crescent rising above Cross).

This culminates in **Silver**, which could have been expressed as the Crescent on the top arm of the Cross, but in so far as the reflective process

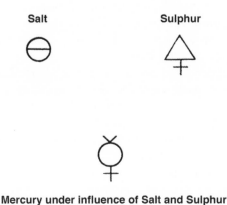

Mercury under influence of Salt and Sulphur

Figure 13

is now free to operate on its own — though some might prefer to see
it as a double Crescent, the reflective lower man being attuned to true
reflection in *all* its hitherto 'cross-wise' elements, rather as an iron bar
becomes a magnet because all its constituent atoms have been induced to
face the same way.

Silver, in the alchemical process, may thus be considered to mean the
purified personality, or 'natural man'. St. Paul called this 'the flesh' and
has been misunderstood by many people ever since, particularly by those
who have not read his remarks in their whole context. He was not simply
talking about sex.

To some, the stage represented by Silver is achievement enough
although it is but the end of the first stage of the complete process, for
what is purified can easily be sullied once more, particularly by reason of
its naturally reflective nature.

The next stage is the introduction of the spiritual radiating principle
(the Circle) into the natural man, and this is represented by **Iron** (a Circle
under a Cross), showing the spiritual principle coming down to the very
base of physical nature. In Christian symbolism this corresponds to the
baby Jesus born in a cave or stable among the cattle.

And the stage after that is marked by the spiritual radiating centre
dominating the physical and natural man, in the sign of **Copper** (a Circle
over a Cross), whilst in the final stage this spiritual principle infuses and
transfigures all in the symbol of **Gold** — represented by the Circle with a
small but important Central Point within it.

The whole process takes place in an alembic, or retort. The descriptions
of this container in alchemical treatises, as with their descriptions of the

First Matter or Stone, give the impression of some confusion allied with a considerable numinous importance. This is because the 'material' of the process itself, and the 'container' of it, are very closely allied — each being aspects of consciousness and itself.

Just as the 'matter' worked upon in the alchemical process is not easily definable as 'consciousness' or the 'subconscious' or 'the collective unconscious' (it can be any of these things but is not united by them) — so the alembic might be defined as 'the self' or 'consciousness' or 'the psyche' but is not properly defined by any of these more modern attempts at scientific psychological definition.

It will serve little purpose in trying to become involved in precise philosophical, psychological or even theological definitions, for none will be adequate. The matter of alchemy covers all three subjects but in such a way that one can hardly be used without reference to the other two. We will do better to try to come to some understanding of the actualities involved by a use of the alchemical symbols themselves — however bizarre they might at first appear. To attempt to do otherwise will be like trying to describe the perfume of a flower in terms of botany, chemistry and physics.

Let us then see the alembic, or retort, as ourselves, in which our own consciousness (or Mercury) is processed from a state of a partly congealed, confused mass of preconceptions and ideas (impure Lead), to a radiating, integrated, spiritual awareness (pure Gold).

This is not an entirely subjective process, for the first matter, or consciousness, is not confined entirely to ourselves. We are as fish swimming in an ocean of it, to follow an alternative line of alchemical symbolism. And our conscious reaction to it will modify us, and the consciousness we process, very profoundly.

We are not creatures in isolation. But in so far as we are each a unit of consciousness—or of 'being' which is a nucleus of consciousness—that being, consciousness, and its psycho/physical envelope, can be regarded as a glass retort, containing the *prima materia*, the Philosophical Mercury.

We now proceed to apply a gentle heat to our flask, hermetically sealed. But what is the nature of the heat?

Traditional alchemy is very good at providing stimulating symbols for actual stages in the process, but tends not to be so clear on the actual process itself. For this we might do well to turn to a mystical treatise of unknown authorship but of considerable reputation amongst discerning contemplatives since it first appeared in the fourteenth century.

This is *The Cloud of Unknowing* which, although quite theologically orthodox, starts off with the kind of dark provisos that one comes to associate only with alchemical and similar hermetic works. Thus:

In the Name of the Father and of the Son and of the Holy Ghost I charge and beg you, with all the strength and power that love can bring to bear, that whoever you may be who possess this book (perhaps you own it, or are keeping it, carrying it, or borrowing it), you should, quite freely and of set purpose, neither read, write, or mention it to anyone, nor allow it to be read, written or mentioned by anyone unless that person is in your judgement really and wholly determined to follow Christ perfectly. And to follow him not only in the active life, but to the utmost height of the contemplative life that is possible for a perfect soul in a mortal body to attain by the grace of God. And he should be, in your estimation, one who has for a long time been doing all that he can to come to the contemplative life by virtue of his active life. Otherwise the book will mean nothing to him.

And further —

I do not mind at all if the loud-mouthed, or flatterers, or the mock-modest, or fault-finders, gossips, tittle-tattlers, talebearers, or any sort of grumbler, never see this book. I have never meant to write for them. So they can keep out of it. And so can all those learned men (and unlearned too) who are merely curious. Even if they are good men judged from the "active" standpoint, all this will mean nothing to them. But it will mean something to those who, though "active" according to their outward mode of life, are, by the inner working of the Spirit of God — his judgements are unsearchable — disposed towards contemplation. Not continually, maybe, as in the case of true contemplatives, but now and then willing to share in the deep things of contemplation. If such people see this book, by the grace of God they should be much inspired by it.

The Cloud (whose full title is *A Book on Contemplation called The Cloud of Unknowing in which Cloud a Soul is United with God*) is a treatise on a mystical process that is strangely neglected in the West. In mysticism there are two ways by which the devout soul may approach God — the positive way (*via positiva*) and the negative way (*via negativa*).

The Positive Way attempts to describe God and his ways in whatever terms, symbolic or otherwise, that imagination and intuition can together devise; whether this be in terms of an old man in a white nightshirt, or as a geometrical figure, or in the extended poetry of Dante.

The Negative Way tends rather to say that God is in any case indescribable and therefore it is useless trying to define what he is — it is perhaps better to define what he is *not*. He is plainly not an old man in a white nightshirt, nor a geometrical figure, nor any other symbolic rendering, however well such imaginative attempts might give an intuitive glimpse of one particular small viewpoint of God. By rejecting all images one comes finally to a Dark Cloud — the Cloud of Unknowing. This may seem a very rigorous and unrewarding process but it is in fact far from this.

In so far that the way of the Cloud of Unknowing may be adequately described in a paragraph or two, it discards all intellectual preconceptions about God and simply fills the soul with longing for God. Its only prayer will be of one word, preferably of only one syllable, that sums up the desire of the soul for God. Such a word can be chosen by the individual. It might, for instance, be 'God', or even 'Help'. It acts simply as a focus for the mind to keep one-pointed and prevent it from clouding the emotional one-pointedness by intellectual speculations and imaginative visions.

This is not a matter of self-hypnosis. Such would be a degradation or perversion of the method — as meditation systems centred on technique, or the self, instead of on God, may well become. The quality of God is Love and it is by love, in full consciousness, that the soul makes real experiential contact with God.

The process is also, in different terms, the alchemical process. The one-pointed emotional direction towards God is the heat applied to the hermetically sealed retort. The contents of ordinary consciousness are dissolved and vapourised by this steady heat and pressure. A purification sets in by this distillation of consciousness (the first stage of the way), and the later stages are the contact of the soul with God and the transfiguration and transmutation of consciousness and being that this entails. This final gold making process, based upon love, which is the source of heat for the operation, is the *mysterium coniunctionem*, in some alchemical Rosicrucian documents quaintly known as 'the Chemical Marriage'.

We should say, however, that the alchemical process in its fullness contains rather more than this, and has quite remarkable physical applications, although beyond the scope of our immediate concern, which is simply to lay down some elementary general principles. But by mastery of these the dedicated student will in time make his or her own discoveries.

In the topics that we have been discussing Islamic mysticism constitutes a major force. The mysticism of Islam is *Sufism*.

This developed within Islam, not particularly as a result of Islamic theology, but as a force to give mystical flesh to the bare bones of it. It never set out to formulate a theology of its own but was content to allow itself to form in the interstices of Islamic orthodoxy — and indeed it found itself capable of a similar function in Christian orthodoxy — though in a rather different fashion.

It could do this because its prime moving force was of the feelings rather than of the intellect. Deep feeling is not expressed or even experienced readily by a predominantly white, Anglo-Saxon, Protestant civilisation of the West, and even tends to be mistrusted. We tend to pin our faith on the intellect and then to try to use the intellect for problems and realms that the intellect is hardly well fitted for.

Things are not made the easier by the psychological fact demonstrated by Jung, that any individual or race that unduly elevates or identifies with the thinking function, does so at the expense of the feeling function, which is its psychological polar opposite, and which will then tend to seek expression in uncontrolled and distorted ways.

However, sloppy feeling is no more to be encouraged than sloppy thinking. But controlled and deep feeling that is a true expression of the deeper movements of the soul and spirit is certainly on a par with, and in many ways superior to, a controlled and disciplined intellect.

Feeling (and its subjective expression, emotion), under discipline, is found most readily in art forms. And thus it was no accident that, as the depiction of images offended against Islamic orthodoxy, poetry became a vehicle of communication of the religion of love, rather than the legalistic prose of the institutionalised religion of the West.

Thus the Sufi mystic Rumi can write in religious vein:

Love came and like blood filled my veins and tissues,
Emptied me of myself and filled me with the Friend,
The friend has taken possession of every atom of my being.
The name is all that I have left now — all the rest is He.

Or, at an earlier period, Attar writes:

Fiercer than thine the fire within his breast,
His Heart beats faster than that heart of thine.
Stay within that burning Heart of his
And thou'lt learn His Love is infinite.

This might well have been written by a devotee of the Christian Sacred Heart, and the parallel is noted in a useful little book *The Persian Sufis* by Cyprian Rice O.P.

The Sufi path of mysticism has, like alchemy, certain well defined stages, and also certain well defined states — the two are not necessarily synonymous.

There is a constant danger, when we deal with such matters, of trying to over-codify and classify. This is the intellect trying to establish its terms of reference in a field that is basically foreign to it. The spirit *bloweth where it listeth* and the Grace of God is not confined to rules and regulations, whether they be psychological, theological, philosophical or ecclesiastical.

As with alchemy, the precise steps will vary to a fair degree from one practitioner to another, but a broad empirical framework can be discerned.

In Sufi mysticism the mystical stages are seven in number:

1. *Repentance, or Conversion* — the realisation that one is in a state of sin, that one is not anywhere near the grand person one would like to take oneself for.
2. *Filial Respect of the Lord* — what used to be called Fear of the Lord, but which can be misunderstood by modern ears. It is a recognition of the existence of God as a real being, and of the soul's relationship to Him.
3. *Detachment* — a realisation that the affairs of God are more important than the affairs of this world.
4. *Poverty* — a cessation of preoccupation with material possessions. This does not necessarily mean dispersing all one's goods and responsibilities and throwing oneself on the charity of the world or to chance. It is a following of the logical conclusions of detachment. One can *take* the things of this world or *leave* them. One is *in* the world but not necessarily *of* it. In this stage is the meaning of Christ's much misunderstood statement, "It is easier for a camel to pass through the eye of a needle than for a rich man to enter the Kingdom of Heaven." The accent is on material *desires* rather than possessions.
5. *Patience* — again logically following on from the above — an acceptance of what circumstances bring in the belief that they are brought from God. This is very much the lesson of the prophets of Israel in the Old Testament — that all things are the dealings of the soul with God.
6. *Self-surrender* — this is an extension of what has gone before into the very structure of the soul itself. A forgetfulness of the soul — a cessation of any tendency to keep on taking one's spiritual temperature, for there can be spiritual ambition as well as material ambition. It is a genuine forgetfulness of the self in greater concern for the beloved, in this case God, with whom one is content to identify.
7. *Contentment* — this is the state of Union with God, or Divine Grace.

One could relate to this ladder of the soul the several stages of alchemy. Repentance being the beginning of the operation, a recognition of the **Leaden** state. Fear of the Lord, Detachment and Poverty are a gradual transition from the **Tin** to the **Silver** stages. Patience corresponds to **Iron**, Self-surrender to **Copper** and the final **Gold** represents Contentment.

We see that we have constructed a kind of ascending scale of mysticism, and valid though this may be, we must be very careful not to fall into the common error of the intellectualised occultist or the mystagogue, and make it into a rigid '-*ism*' or place ourselves and others upon it in a kind of transcendent 'keeping up with the Jones'. Both errors betray rather shallow preoccupation with intellectual analysis in what should be a living and loving relationship.

One would not for instance wish to award grades for marital bliss, or personal friendship. No doubt it could be done but it would serve no real purpose in making a happy successful marriage or a lasting and deepening friendship. Rather the reverse. Life does not allow itself to be cut up into neat intellectual departments in spite of man's frequent attempts to do so. The psychologist, striving to emulate the scientific method of the physical sciences and technology may construct his measurements of intelligence, or creativity, or what he wills — it is rather like trying to catch the moon in a bucket.

And what goes for human relationships goes also for relationships either with God or with beings on the inner side of Creation. It may be convenient in certain contexts to have some kind of analysis of the general process, but it inevitably breaks down, human vanity being what it is, into rather pompous and self-defeating claims after titles. The grades of Ipsissimus, Magus, Illuminatus, Adept and so on may have a certain measure of reality if properly understood, but tend to degenerate into a tawdry panoply of pseudo-mysticism and bogus occultism. That such levels of consciousness and relationship exist is true — but they are not measured out with Mr Prufrock's coffee spoons.

There are various states of mystical grace recognised in Sufi mysticism that may be experienced without reference to the stages we have already described. These stages are indeed like steps towards God that can be taken by the effort and application of the individual soul, but such is the illogical and bountiful nature of God, (along with the unknown factors that rule a soul's destiny), that there is also a range of experience that comes solely from God and by the grace of God alone.

In the Sufi mode of analysis these are ten in number. They are not given in any order of ascending or descending importance for there is no way of measuring their 'merit', and they may come and go quite arbitrarily it seems, as the wind that bloweth where it listeth. They are marks of the grace of God, as spontaneous as gifts of a parent to his child.

Inner awareness of God's presence in the soul, or of God's awareness of one's own inner condition. This may occur in various degrees, from an instinctive warding off of unworthy thoughts to a complete obliviousness to the outside world while the condition lasts.

Sense of the Nearness of God, a realisation that God is closer than breathing, nearer than hands and feet, revealed by all created things.

Passionate love of God, that sees God as a supremely beautiful and desirable being who loves the soul with a requiting passion and tenderness. To this we see the metaphysical lineaments of Courtly Love and Dante's vision of Beatrice.

Fear of the Lord, though it may be a feeling of immense awe in some souls, it is more the filial respect and reverence of an obedient and loving child to its parent.

Confident hope in the grace and bounty of God that is based not so much on a hope of obtaining anything from God, but rather a union with God.

An intense longing for God that in some instances may be like the call to a Quest, particularly if the soul, through upbringing or background, does not realise what it is that is longed for with this strange tender desire.

A loving familiarity with God that is almost the opposite of the above. There are some souls who have a kind of 'companionage' with God that may manifest almost as a sort of bantering between two friends.

Trust in God that all that He brings in the way of life experience, pleasant or unpleasant, is of good.

Contemplation of God, or in the nearest possible analogy, the *Vision of God face to face* as described in the Qabalah. The realisation of Him as He is in all His glory.

Certainty, or complete *Union with God*, rooted in contemplation and sure knowledge of His power and glory.

We have followed the way of Sufi mysticism in describing our mystical states, though one does not need to be confined by it, for human souls are human souls throughout the whole of creation, and God is God throughout the length and breadth of it. We have chosen Sufi mysticism for two reasons. Firstly because it is firmly within the tradition of influence that caused a mystical revival in the Christian West immediately after the Dark Ages. Secondly because, having established the central importance of Christianity as an approach to truth, we wish to avoid the parochialism that can see nothing in the mystical insights of other human faiths.

This has already been realised by a number of modern Christian churchmen, some of whom have written books on the subject, for instance. Fr. Dechanet's *Christian Yoga*. Cyprian Rice's *The Persian Sufis*, or Raymond Pannikar's *The Hidden Christ in Hinduism*. Some, such as F. C. Happold or Joseph James have taken the trouble to make mystical anthologies showing the essential unity of mystical experience as indeed must exist in approaches to the One God, from whatever doctrinal direction the soul may be proceeding. And Sidney Spencer has written a highly interesting survey on *Mysticism in World Religion*.

The Christian Church is not necessarily the sole repository of divine knowledge. In our view it is the most accurate, but it is important to realise that others may have equal or even on occasion more perceptive insights into certain aspects of man's relationship to God. The same applies to the mystical experience of other parts of the Christian Church, such as the Eastern Orthodox.

Sidney Spencer points out that the developed mysticism of the Christian Church in both the East and the West reveals a definitely Platonic influence and that medieval Western mysticism was indebted to an incalculable extent to 'Pseudo-Dionysus', sometimes called St. Denis. He was thought in medieval times to have been a contemporary of St. Paul but it has since been discovered that he lived much later, probably in the sixth century, but certainly no earlier than the third. He was a considerable influence on the writer of the great anonymous English work of mysticism that we have already examined, *The Cloud of Unknowing*, a handbook of the *via negativa*, the approach to God without images.

There is a considerable emphasis on the direct experience of God, especially as a Divine Light, in Eastern Christian mysticism. And in the life of Christ considerable emphasis is placed on the Transfiguration. Rather than the imitation of the earthly life of Jesus, which is more the attitude of the Western church, it is the attempt, by prayer and contemplation, to share the divine radiance that illumined him. As Spencer points out:

> At the Transfiguration, it was held, there was no change whatsoever in the earthly form of Jesus, for he lived perpetually in the light of his divinity. The change occurred in the consciousness of his disciples, who then saw him as he truly was. The mystics sought to identify themselves with Christ in his divine glory. There is no parallel among Eastern saints to the stigmatisation of St. Francis, but again and again Eastern saints have felt themselves to be transfigured by the divine Light which shone through Jesus.

There was some controversy over this doctrine in the fourteenth century, but it became recognised as an article of faith in the Orthodox Church at the Synod of Constantinople in 1351.

Another Orthodox Christian practice is of an inner stillness by repeating a prayer over and over again a form of *mantra yoga*. The 'Jesus prayer' — '*O Lord Jesus Christ, Son of God, have mercy on me, a sinner*', is intoned at each breath, which is regularly controlled, again as in *pranayama yoga* practices, for it is held that there is a divine energy in the very name of Jesus itself.

There is also an ascetic tradition, though it is not one of hating the things of the world. One of these ascetics, Isaac the Syrian, who spent most of his life alone in his cell, writes that a loving heart is a heart which is burning with love for the whole of creation — for men, for the birds, for the beasts, for the demons — that cannot bear to see, or to learn from others, of any suffering being inflicted upon a creature; that is moved to pray for all beings, for evil doers and enemies of truth, and for the animals, even for the reptiles; moved by the infinite pity which reigns in the hearts of those who are becoming united to God.

The Platonic influence in the Western church comes particularly through St. Augustine who was a Neo-Platonist before his conversion to Christianity. And as Sidney Spencer points out:

> In teaching and experience of Augustine as indicated in the "Confessions" there are already laid down the main lines of Western mysticism. The Platonism which he accepted became an essential feature of the mystical tradition. Through him the Platonic doctrine of Ideas or archetypes of all that exists in the world, regarded as elements of the eternal Being of God, passed into the current of mystical thought. Yet in the developed system of teaching which Augustine worked out there is marked duality. Many of his ideas, such as human depravity and the fore-ordination which doomed a great part of mankind to everlasting Hell, are altogether inconsistent with his insight as a Platonist and a mystic. He illustrates strikingly the difficulty which has always confronted the orthodox Christian mystic, of combining the illumination which comes to him as a mystic with dogmatic tradition radically divergent from it.

It is not our intention to become involved in the subtleties of mystical theology except to point out that our own inclination is to pay close attention to those mystics who, by their experience, consider man to have an element of his being that is of the same 'substance' or quality as God. This insight, although it has fallen foul of orthodox theological belief from time to time, accords with much traditional occult belief and experience.

St. Teresa pointed out that she felt God to be present everywhere (and note that this is not the same as falling into the monist error of saying that everything is a part of God). And by 'everywhere' she includes the human soul, when she speaks in *The Interior Castle* of the different mansions as his dwelling place — 'the little heaven of the soul, where dwells the Creator of Heaven and earth'.

St. John of the Cross defined this more accurately by pointing out that though God dwells in every soul, 'even that of the greatest sinner', this is something quite distinct from the conscious experience of Union with God, and the transformation of the soul thereby.

The fourteenth-century English mystic Julian of Norwich also speaks of a part of the soul that is eternally united with God, though she rather charmingly and illuminatingly puts it in a way that prevents us from seeing God cut up into little pieces of separate Godhood. The soul of Christ is 'full high in the glorious Godhead, and verily where the blessed soul of Christ is, there is the substance (the eroded being) of all the souls that shall be saved with Christ'. As Julian confidently expected all humanity to be saved, this description is therefore true of all human beings.

This is rather different from the idea commonly held in esoteric circles of a Higher Self and a Lower Self, with the former, (sometimes confused with the Holy Guardian Angel), being regarded as perfect. The terms Evolutionary and Incarnationary Personality were introduced at one time by an influential school, the Society of the Inner Light, defining the former as the sum total of the experience of many lives, (and thus still far from perfect), and the latter its current projection into form life, preferring to confine perfection to the level of the Spirit. In other schools the Spirit may be combined with the idea of the Higher Self in what is sometimes called the Essential Self.

What we speak of here as Spirit is, as Lady Julian implies, a part of the soul that is, in its essence, uncreated. Meister Eckhart had indeed previously taught this explicitly. 'There is something in the soul that is so akin to God that it is one with Him ... It has nothing in common with anything that is created.' And he was charged with heresy as a result of it.

There is, however, no Satanic pride in putting the soul on a level with God, as was feared from the Orthodox Church viewpoint. The idea of an essential core of divinity within the soul does not necessarily diminish the possibility of sin, the falling away of the human soul from its essential divine truth and reality.

This idea stems from Neo-Platonism and was prevalent particularly in the Rhineland mystics, who were also followers of the *via negativa*, the Dionysian school of the 'divine dark', which came to flower in *The Cloud of Unknowing*.

Meister Eckhart, despite being a leading German Dominican and influential preacher, was, as we have said, accused of heresy for ideas of this type. And it is easy to see why, because the ideas easily fall into error. The 'negative' idea of God without qualities can lead to the idea that he is somehow non-existent — or at best something like the void at the centre of Taoism or Buddhism. This has become prevalent in some aspects of modern occultism where God is seen, by misunderstanding of the doctrine of the Qabalistic *Ain* (Nothingness), *Ain Soph* (Limitless) *Ain Soph Aur* (Limitless Light), to be a kind of remote nothingness manifesting himself by some kind of precipitation or crystallisation. There is truth here, and it gives some insights into certain aspects of the Creation, but it can easily lead to error if the mind takes over from the heart or will, and tries to fit God into a mould cast by nineteenth-century ideas of evolution and science.

The essence of the true Neo-Platonic Christian thought is given by Spencer in *Mysticism in World Religion* in that:

> Man, as they conceive him in accordance with their Neo-Platonic outlook, belongs in his essential being to the eternal order, which comprises the ideal archetypes of all things. The ideal archetypes are elements in the eternal Being of God: in their totality they are the Word or Son of God, who is eternally begotten by the Father. As Suso puts it, they have "an existence identical with God's life, God's knowledge and God's essence..." So the Flemish mystic, Ruysbroek, says: "Through the eternal Birth all creatures have come forth in eternity, before they were created in them. So God has seen and known them in Himself." It is man's ideal archetype, the divine image of himself, which is in God eternally, that is the spark or ground of the soul. Man is thus eternally united with God in his deepest being. He "receives without intermission the impress of his eternal archetype", and it is this "union between God and our spirit in the nakedness of our nature" which is "the first cause of all holiness and blessedness".

This is amply demonstrated in *The Divine Comedy* of Dante, though in the full flowering of the *via positiva*, where Beatrice, the divine companion of the soul, is in one respect, the divine aspect of the soul itself. And it is significant that although Dante, in his peregrinations through the inner worlds, can be guided through Hell and Purgatory by Virgil, representing human wisdom and magical knowledge, he can only be taken to the higher reaches of the Terrestrial and Heavenly Paradise by Beatrice. Wisdom has to give way to Love. Or should we say that Earthly Wisdom has to give way to Divine Wisdom — which is synonymous with Love.

EXERCISE FOR CHAPTER V

The tide of light shall rise about you like a Flood,
And with its shining you shall be identified.

The next symbolic exercise that we do is, magically, a technically important one, and marks a major stage in the series of exercises prescribed in this book. It concludes the personal preparation prior to the performance of objective magic.

We have delineated a pure place of working with the Sphere of Light, we have dedicated ourselves with the Spear, we have invoked our latent powers with the Rod, and we have opened our hearts to the Will of God for us in the formulation of the Holy Grail within our hearts. It is now our task, privilege and joy to prepare ourselves for objective work. This is done by realising the presence of God everywhere, though it is not merely an intellectual exercise. We endeavour to realise this with the whole of our lower being, by physical and psychic action, which affects not only the physical body but also the subtler bodies and the psychic centres.

The basis of this exercise is regular and rhythmic breathing, combined with seeing and feeling ourselves being gradually submerged in a Sea of Light. Feel this as a rising tide of golden light that closes over the head. This is best done by breathing steadily, rhythmically and fairly deeply, feeling the waters of light rise with each in-breath. The speed of this may vary according to taste, but four to six in-breaths may generally be found to be a good average rate. After the Sea of Light has been felt to close over the head then continue to breath deeply, identifying with the surrounding light. Feel it swirling through every pore and part of your body, as if you were a submarine creature in this Sea of Light. You are in fact but becoming aware of what is a continuing and ever-present reality.

This is far more than subjective imagination. Subjective imagination it may be in the first instance, but subjective imagination is the magic key that, fitted into the right lock, opens the door to the inner worlds — both psychical and spiritual.

The exercise is similar to the Eastern Yoga technique of *pranayama*, which is concerned with the direction of psychic energies through various channels of the subtle bodies. Psychic energy is very much concerned with the breath, and the analogues are not difficult to find in the religious traditions of 'the Word', the creative 'Fiat', and the Spirit of God moving upon the face of the waters, the Spirit itself being likened to the wind or to breath. By linking the imagery of water to this idea we also call to mind the Waters of Baptism, the traditional form of religious purification and initiation to which even Jesus himself submitted at the hands of John the Baptist in the Jordan, the point heralding the commencement of his divine ministry.

The simple deep breathing that we advocate is probably best done to a count of four—four steady beats to the in-breath and four steady beats to the out-breath. This is advice for the average person and the number of counts can be varied according to taste as long as the principle is maintained of a steady even rhythm. Simple as this exercise is, it is the foundation upon which all further progress and activity stands.

As an aid to concentrating the mental faculties to the task in hand a further device may be used that has its parallel in the East in *mantra yoga*.

A classical *mantram* much used in the Eastern Orthodox Church and latterly recommended by Israel Regardie is the 'Jesus Prayer' of which a shorter version, '*Lord Jesus Christ have mercy on me*', can be broken up into four beats, '*Lord-Je-sus-Christ*' on the in-breath, '*have-mercy-on-me*' on the out-breath. An alternative is the very ancient Greek form of this, '*Kyrie Eleison – Christe Eleison*'.

Or, as a preliminary to the magical and spiritual objective practices that are to come, and as a help at any times of inner stress or danger, there is the ancient invocation known as *St. Patrick's Breastplate*, which can be used with a half-line to each in-breath and out-breath:

> Christ be with me, Christ within me,
>> Christ behind me, Christ before me,
> Christ beside me, Christ to win me,
>> Christ to comfort and restore me.
> Christ beneath me, Christ above me,
>> Christ in quiet, Christ in danger,
> Christ in hearts of all that love me,
>> Christ in mouth of friend and stranger.

Combined with the visualisation of the baptismal Sea of Light this is an identification and betrothal of the human soul and spirit to the Lord himself and is an act of deepest faith.

Complex breathing techniques and visualisation there may be that can be developed from this, as in various yogic and magical systems, but without this simple groundwork performed in faith they remain but psychological techniques and a source of error and delusion. In occult science, unlike physical science, it is impossible to divorce practical result from spiritual dedication and intention.

It is also delusory to divorce them in physical science, as the true alchemists realised, and which some of the results of man's technology are beginning to bring home to a number of people today.

CHAPTER VI

The Table Round

The world is a big place, at any rate from man's limited physical viewpoint, and particularly so when we consider its inner reaches as well as its outer. Just as mankind is a corporate body that intercommunicates with itself as an organism on the physical husk of this terrestrial globe, so is it also a corporate body when viewed beyond such physical limitations.

This has deep implications for the occultist, for by study of the inner side of creation so does communication with the inhabitants of the inner side of creation come about. And from this stems the important question, which is seldom asked, but often taken for granted, who is in a better position to teach what to whom?

It is generally assumed, once the awe of the possibility of such a communication fades away, that whoever is contacted, by virtue of their presence on the 'inner planes' is, by that very fact, a source of wisdom and inspiration.

It can be so, some of the sentimental and platitudinous vapourings notwithstanding. There are indubitably as many wise men off the physical earth as there are on it. But it is a dangerous assumption to think that all who cry 'Lord, Lord' or 'Hear ye, Hear ye!' are necessarily very spiritual or very wise. However, it is an assumption that is often made, with the result that the most trite or unlikely 'messages' or 'teachings' are treated with a reverence that, had they come from a person of flesh and blood, would scarcely warrant a second glance. Their supposedly elevated esoteric origin seems to cause a complete lapse of any critical faculty on the part of many recipients.

If we take examples of material that has been received and promulgated as teaching by various bodies, we find there is a considerable difference of attitude and teaching between various communicators. Some may teach reincarnation, others may deny it, some may be Christian in their phrasing (often in varying degrees of orthodoxy), others base their views on oriental religions, yet others claim to be denizens of other planets or on orbiting flying saucers from various parts of space.

Dion Fortune has perhaps done as much as anyone in the West to try to achieve a balanced attitude to the existence of inner plane communicators of worth —usually known in esoteric circles as 'Masters' or 'Inner Plane

Adepti'. And in an article in the *Inner Light Magazine* in September 1931, she foreshadowed the very problem with which we are now attempting to deal. So we will quote her at length:

> Theosophical literature has made us familiar with the idea of the Masters — beings once human, now superhuman, who accept the cooperation of incarnate disciples and train them for the work they are required to do. In the accounts of the early days of the Theosophical Society and in the letters of Madame Blavatsky and other pioneer Theosophists, we read of the visits of these Masters, of their manifestation to psychic vision and the messages that they gave both clairaudiently and by automatic and inspirational writing. We may think, after studying them, that these messages vary in value, but it nevertheless remains that a great work was done by their instrumentality.

> Their first knowledge of Initiation and the Ancient Wisdom has come to a very great many through the work and publications of the Theosophical Society; and many, myself among them, have been inspired to follow the Path and seek a Master by its propaganda. But when setting out to find a Master and taking their directions from the Theosophical literature, many people are confronted by a difficulty. The Masters with whom the T.S. gives contact are Eastern Masters, Koot Hoomi, Morya, and others. That it gives contact with these Masters, and that they are of the Right Hand Path, I am prepared, from my own experience, to agree. But when it comes to contacting the Western Masters, as many, possibly most Westerners would normally desire to do, it is a different matter. I have so far come across no convincing evidence that such contacts are made; and in such statements of Bishop Leadbeater, that the Master Jesus is at present incarnated in a Syrian body and living in Asia Minor, I find evidence which convinces me that the contact, in that instance at any rate, has not been made. The two greatest Western Seers of recent times, Eliphas Levi and Rudolf Steiner held quite other views. Be that as it may, however, for when all is done, "by their fruits ye shall know them", Theosophists of the orthodox school, that is to say, of that point of view which is in sympathy with the present leaders of the Society, for the most part make little attempt to pick up the Western contacts, finding their spiritual needs met by the Masters Koot Hoomi, Morya, or the Lord Maitreya.

> In the days when I was a member of the T.S. no attempt was made to develop the contacts of the Master Jesus. In fact He was never referred to as the Master Jesus, so far as my acquaintance with Theosophical literature goes, until I introduced the name. He was declared to be a virtuous Jewish youth, of mediumistic powers, who lent his body for the manifestation of the Lord Maitreya in the same way that Mr. Krishnamurti is believed to do for the

present incarnation of the same entity. The Liberal Catholic Church, though using Christian ceremonial aimed at contacting, not the Master Jesus, but the Lord Maitreya, in fact, in Theosophical circles the Master Jesus was very much the poor relation. This no doubt was due to the fact that a great many Theosophists turned to the Eastern Masters and their systems in a reaction against an overdose of dogmatic Christianity. Mme. Blavatsky herself was essentially a rebel against all the traditions of her day and hated organised religion with a furious hatred, and not without grounds. All the same, the influence of her antipathies has been unfortunate from the point of view of religious toleration. When the announcement was made that the World Teacher had come, it was obviously felt in the Society that the day of the Master Jesus was over, and that any attempt to develop his contacts was diverting support from the Lord Maitreya. Feeling ran high in consequence, and revealed the fact that the spirit of religious persecution is not the special failing of any particular faith, but springs eternal in the human breast.

This spirit naturally revealed itself, implicitly if not explicitly, in the publications and propaganda of the Society, and as no other occult organisation carried on a publicity campaign of anything approaching the dimensions of that conducted by the T.S., the general public naturally came to the conclusion that the Society spoke for occultism in general, and the occult schools were one and all anti-Christian.

There is much that could he read between the lines here as regards Dion Fortune's personal difficulties with the personalities responsible for running the Theosophical Society at the time, though there is little point in pursuing such speculations here. Nor need we dwell on the unfortunate fate of the Star in the West movement, which attracted a huge following which was eventually shattered by Krishnamurti repudiating the role as Avatar for the New Age that had been wished upon him by his guardians. It can still serve a purpose however in a dreadful warning that those who call for action in the name of 'the Masters' are as prone to error as any other members of the human race. And that either the Masters have feet of clay or else their mode of communication is so inaccurate as to be hazardous to say the least.

We need to look a little closer perhaps at Dion Fortune's coining of the title 'the Master Jesus' which would seem to imply that she is still regarding him as a human being of a particular esoteric 'rank'. That she meant more than this is revealed in other writings of hers but we shall not find much reliable guidance there, for intelligent and dedicated woman though she was, she lacked the training or guidance that would have prevented her from falling into some very elementary theological errors. She was pointing generally in the right direction, however, and in a following article refers to Jesus as 'the Master of Masters' to whom the Lesser Masters are 'as glow-worms to a star'.

There is, in fact, a noticeable tendency in occult literature to confuse the function of the 'Masters' and to consider them as gods. We see something of this even in Dion Fortune's remarks above in referring to them as *'beings once human, now superhuman'*. In the writings of others we find a capital letter used, in a pronoun referring to a Master, such as is generally reserved only for the Deity. This is a practice particularly current in the orient, being applied even to spiritual teachers or *gurus* in the flesh.

So we tend to have a two way confusion the 'Masters' being raised up as gods, and the Christ regarded as a human 'Master' who happened to do a particularly important esoteric task in the bearing of 'the Christ-force' during the period of his earthly ministry. Attractively simple as this seeming trend towards synthesis may appear, it is superficial and just will not wash.

For one thing we must be suspicious of the term 'superhumanity', which is part and parcel of a Theosophical evolutionary theory whereby stone goes through super-stone to become vegetable, vegetable through super-vegetable to become animal, animal through super-animal to become human, and human through super-human to become god. The same trend of thought then goes on to see gods becoming super-gods and so on *ad super infinitum*. We would submit that an animal in its fulness is very close to the God who made it, as is a flower, or any other artefact of creation, and that humanity in itself is no mean thing to be, without introducing speculative conceptions of superhumanity.

The Christian Athanasian Creed teaches the taking up of manhood into Godhead in a mystical translation, whereby humanity remains what it is, but *in* God rather than divorced from Him. Thus we must ask are the 'Masters' *in* God, like the saints, or outside Him?

The traditional test of spirits laid down in John 4 v. 1–3 is 'By this you know the Spirit of God: every spirit which confesses that Jesus Christ has come in the flesh is of God, and every spirit which does not confess Jesus is not of God. This is the spirit of antichrist.'

Then, as now, there were some who held the view that Jesus was a man temporarily possessed by a certain divine force, and this test was a help and warning to them — that Jesus is wholly God and wholly man. The early Fathers saw quite clearly that the descent of a 'Christ-force' on to a man is not a genuine incarnation of God into the world but simply an intensification of what the prophets had experienced, with Jesus as a kind of super-prophet.

Again the passage in I John 5-6, 'This is He who came by water and blood, Jesus Christ, not with water only but with the water and the blood', means that it was not simply at the baptism in Jordan that the Messiahship descended upon Jesus, but that it was a full incarnation by physical birth. The meaning of *'blood'* in this context is in the same sense of *'physical birth'* as it is used in John 1 v. 13 in describing Christians as being born of God, 'not of blood, nor of the will of the flesh, nor of the will of man'.

Canon J. Stafford Wright, in his book *Christianity and the Occult*, claims that in every case he knows where an instructed Christian put the test of John, 'the spirit has refused to admit the Deity of Jesus Christ and His true incarnation, and has made an end of the séance'. He goes on to say:

These tests are rare, since instructed Christians do not usually attend these séances. If they do, their presence often inhibits any communication at all. In the only private séance that I attended, with a view to the writing that I was doing on spiritualism, we sat for some 45 minutes without any communications, and the medium commented that the spirits were slow in coming through. The communications that eventually came bore all the marks of being faked.

Then he cites further instances where he considers séances were broken up or rendered abortive by a convinced Christian praying silently in the Name of Christ. Canon Stafford Wright, we should say, is a committed evangelical Christian, with a firm conviction that the Bible condemns all attempts at spirit communication. In our opinion his view is oversimplified, but it is particularly interesting in that it indicates some of the grave difficulties of communication.

As to the moral aspect of communication with beings on the 'inner side' of creation, we make no comment. We do not share the Canon's view that it is defiance of God's Law and that it leads inevitably to disaster. Arguments of the type that polarise 'Christianity' versus 'the occult' are really as outmoded, and confused as to the real issues, as the old nineteenth century arguments of 'Christianity' versus 'Science' — for as we have said, occultism basically is a science of the inner side of creation. It can be used for good or ill, as can physical science. The points we wish to pursue are more on the subject of the technicalities and psychology involved.

With regard to prayer breaking up a séance, this may well have been true, but one would like to know a little more about the nature of the prayer. We certainly know from practical experience that emotionally felt intellectual disagreement is also quite capable of breaking up communications of this nature. Thus it is not necessarily the direct action of the Christ we have in this instance, but may simply be the magical thought power of the individual, horrified though he might be to realise that he was himself working 'magic'.

We know of a case of a Methodist lady who disapproved of her son going out with girls and who used to meet in 'prayer meeting' with other members of her Christian congregation and pray that he be kept from such activities. The prayer was extremely effective, and almost drove the lad neurotic, but we submit it was more of the nature of Black Magic than the manifestation of the grace of the Christ.

We see therefore that we have two points at issue here. One is that it is possible by the power of emotionally powered thought to affect communication between inner and outer sides of creation; the other is that it is possible to be misguided as to one's application of the practical issues involved to the point even of making a false 'God image' into a magical tool for the influencing of another's will.

Grotesque though our example of the possessive mother might be, it shows that an incorrect attitude to God is as possible inside the Church as out of it, and there are scientific technicalities involved that the institutional Church ignores at its peril. Just as it would be foolish to ignore the natural laws of structures and stress in erecting its buildings.

This has been realised by some discerning members of the clergy. For instance, in an article in the highly respected theological journal *New Fire* for Summer 1973, we find A. D. Duncan writing:

> There appears to be, in the rising generation, a considerable increase in what we may describe as "psychical awareness". In addition, there is a very real and growing desire for God. There is, however, a massive impatience with institutionalism and a real questioning as to the relevance of the institutional Church to things of the spirit at all. Our public preoccupation with "relevance" and self-preservation has not helped us, *but far worse has been the long tradition of ignorance in matters of an interior nature, our mistrust of mysticism and our rejection without very much attempt at comprehension of the "psychic".*   [Our italics. G. K.]

This 'long tradition of ignorance' has, we might add, had unfortunate consequences outside as well as inside the Church. As Duncan goes on to say:

> The great Christian heritage of mysticism and contemplation is going by default through sheer ignorance of it, and through the widespread gap in communication between those seeking God in meditation and those able to help them within the institutional Church, the clergy in particular.

The effects of this communications failure are dolorous. The terminologies are in hopeless confusion and the distinction between meditation as a *technique* and "meditation", when what is meant is "contemplation", is quite blurred. Meditators seek "Samadhi" and there is nobody to tell them that this is the same as "the Prayer of Union", and that the techniques employed, although potent, can only lead to the threshold of contemplation, and that technique is not the same thing as prayer. Furthermore, the techniques because they are techniques only, can be used for many purposes. They can be used prayerfully, they can be used to simply induce an inner peace or silence without conscious desire to pray; and they can also be used to explore the unconscious mind, and this is not the same thing at all as prayer, although many practitioners of the occult think that it is.

We have now quoted two instances of clerical views of the occult. The one taking a stand against it on grounds of Old Testament injunctions which he considers have not been rescinded by the New Testament; and the other aware of the great relevance of the Western mystical tradition and seeing it as the pearl of great price that occult students are ignoring because of its being covered with the long ingrained muck of centuries of ecclesiastical institutionalism. May we say that we agree with the second opinion and also find it regrettable that more occultists do not show a little more discernment. Anti-institutional Church prejudice has grown to a blinding degree, and in view of the short-sightedness of many Christian organisations, not without reason. But this is really no excuse for the corresponding myopia of those on the occult side.

One area of confusion is in the use of the word 'meditation' in two wholly different meanings. **Occult** meditation, as taught in many occult schools, is a centering of the mind upon a certain symbol or complex of ideas. The aim is to bore through the shell of concrete ideation and to tap a pool of intuitional realisations. **Mystical** meditation on the other hand, as taught and practised by the contemplative orders of the Church, is a bringing of the soul into an approach to God prior to a period of colloquy or inner communion with God.

It is usually forgotten, for instance, by occult students who cite the very 'occult' Spiritual Exercises of St. Ignatius of Loyola, that these exercises were not ends in themselves but a preliminary to mystical prayer.

The difficulties that this confusion brings in its train is that occult students are not quite sure whether they are approaching God, their own 'inner selves', or an objective 'inner plane master' or other entity. The results are that they can, if they are not very careful, either come to regard God as a cog in an intellectual cosmogony of their own making (if they are of an intellectual turn of mind), or else (if they are of an emotional bias) to set up other beings or archetypes of the unconscious as objects of reverence or even worship.

An exaggerated devotion to the 'Masters' leads to many disappointments and abuses. On the part of the Master (and let us state here that from personal experience we affirm their existence) it can only be a distraction and an embarrassment, clouding any proper communication. And in the case of the more numerous lesser types of communicating entity there is an unhealthy temptation to thrive upon it. This can happen with occult teachers on the physical level also. Such are only too willing to make and maintain contact with a group of students eager to give limitlessly of their credulity and adulation. This can result in a kind of devotional vampirism. And it can happen at all levels of communication, from the naïve tumbler turners who sit in the back parlour to receive advice from some *soi-disant* 'guide' to the organised fraternity where there is an inner circle of devotees devoting hours of voluntary service to the production and distribution of duplicated sheets of the Masters' views for an outer circle of lesser students.

At the centre of it all may well be a demonic entity, though more often it will be a relatively harmless opinionated cosmic windbag. However, all communication, whether good or indifferent, is subject to tenuous and subtle forms of interference, for all types of subjective communication — be they trance or psychic, unconscious or intuitional are easily disturbed and distorted. Thus what may purport to be a communication from one source may well have interpolations in it from various other minds, effected deliberately or accidentally. All communications must therefore be submitted to the cold analysis of common sense and spiritual integrity.

The subject of communication with 'higher' beings on the inner side of creation has been fraught with much difficulty so let us examine the matter at some length.

A principle text about their existence is, C. W. Leadbeater's *The Masters and the Path*, first published in 1925. It assumes an Eastern religious standpoint and Theosophical worldview and is written in an easy style. It is an interesting book, for although we might accept much of its contents as true if stripped down to their bare essentials the author's personal embellishments often make it painful reading.

The exaggerated devotion to, and almost religious worship of the inner-plane communicator is seen, for example, in this passage, from the section entitled *Messages from Adepts*:

Many of us have been long meditating daily upon our great Masters — some of us for years; we have drawn ourselves near to Them by the intensity of our reverence and devotion, and it often happens to the more fortunate among us to come into personal touch with Them and sometimes to be charged by Them with messages for less fortunate brethren.

Sincere, if naive, though C. W. Leadbeater may have been, one sees all the signs here, capital letters and all, of confusion between mystical religion and occult communication. Note the difference between the communicating 'sheep' and the less fortunate 'goats', and also the statement that the way to join the charmed circle is by applied reverence and devotion to the alleged communicator. The potential spiritual dangers are enormous. In what human organisation on the physical level would such demands of reverence to an unseen eminence be tolerated outside of a police state?

Let us say that we do not impute improper motives to C. W. Leadbeater or his colleagues. The evidence is that they acted in the best of faith. We simply point out the dangers. There is no doubt, for any who have had their own experience in these matters, that there was sincere communication with some 'Masters' in this case, from the descriptions that are given. In describing such communication Leadbeater states:

The thought of an Adept showers upon His pupil a kind of hailstorm of lovely little spheres, each of which is an idea with a relation to other ideas quite clearly worked out: but if the pupil is fortunate enough to remember and clever enough to translate such a hailstorm, he is likely to find that it may need twenty pages of foolscap to express that one moment's deluge, and even then of course the expression is necessarily imperfect. Furthermore, it has to be recognised that no words have been given to him — only ideas; and therefore he must of necessity express those ideas in his own language. The ideas are the Master's, if he is fortunate enough to have caught and interpreted them accurately; but the form of expression entirely his own. Therefore his idiosyncrasies will certainly appear, and people reading the message will say: "But surely that is so-and-so's style" — referring to the intermediary to whom the message was confided. In saying so they are of course quite right, but they must not allow that obvious fact to blind them to the importance of the message.

There is much good sense here, although the visual imagery of 'hailstorms' of ideas can be misleading and cause many students to go seeking for truth in the form of astral pyrotechnics. What is important is the content of the message, not the colour of the form it comes in, or the alleged infallibility of its mediator or source.

And here again we would question C. W. Leadbeater's later assertion that 'when a person of the development and extensive experience of our great President (for example) conveys a message, we may be quite certain that its sense is accurate and that the form of its expression is the best that can be attained on this plane'. With all due respect to the President, we would doubt that. No one is infallible, and it is a little incongruous to find many who claim that they have escaped from the 'trammels of religion' going seeking for infallible Masters in place of an infallible Bible or an infallible Pope.

Let us, however, turn from the words of a proselytising occultist to those of an influential psychologist. This may show how important is the personal equation of the subject's attitude to the inner communicator. In the following passage we see it acting in another way — with a scientific rather than a devotional bias. We refer to C. G. Jung's autobiography *Memories, Dreams, Reflections* and what he calls a vision figure.

Philemon was a pagan and brought with him an Egypto-Hellenistic atmosphere with a Gnostic colouration. His figure first appeared to me in the following dream.

There was a blue sky, like the sea, covered not by clouds but by flat brown clods of earth. It looked as if the clouds were breaking apart and the blue water of the sea were becoming visible between them. But the water was the blue sky. Suddenly there appeared from the right a winged being sailing across the sky. I saw that it was an old man with the horns of a bull. He held a bunch of four keys, one of which he clutched as if he were about to open a lock. He had the wings of the kingfisher with its characteristic colours.

Since I did not understand this dream-image, I painted it in order to impress it upon my memory. During the days when I was occupied with the painting, I found in my garden, by the lake shore, a dead kingfisher: I was thunderstruck, for kingfishers are quite rare in the vicinity of Zurich and I have never since found a dead one. The body was recently dead — at the most, two or three days and showed no external injuries.

Philemon and other figures of my fantasies brought home to me the crucial insight that there are things in the psyche which I do not produce, but which produce themselves and have their own life. Philemon represented a force which was not myself. In my fantasies I hold conversations with him, and he said things which I had not consciously thought. For I observed clearly that it was he who spoke, not I. He said I treated thoughts as if I generated them myself, but in his view thoughts were like animals in the forest, or people in a room, or birds in the air, and added, "If you should see people in a room you would not think that you had made these people, or that you were responsible for them." It was he who taught me psychic objectivity, the reality of the psyche. Through him the distinction was clarified between myself and the object of my thought. He confronted me in an objective manner, and I understood that there is something in me which can say things that I do not know and do not intend, things which may even be directed against me.

Psychologically, Philemon represented superior insight. He was a mysterious figure to me. At times he seemed to me quite real, as if he were a living personality. I went walking up and down the garden with him, and to me he was what the Indians call a guru ... In my darkness ... I could have wished for nothing better than a real live guru, someone possessing superior knowledge and ability, who would have disentangled for me the involuntary creations of my imagination. This task was undertaken by the figure of Philemon, whom in this respect I had willy-nilly to recognise as my psychogogue. And the fact was that he conveyed to me many an illuminating idea.

More than fifteen years later a highly cultivated elderly Indian visited me, a friend of Ghandi's, and we talked about Indian education — in particular, about the relationship between guru and chela. I hesitatingly asked him whether he could tell me anything about the person and character of his own guru, whereupon he replied in a matter of fact tone, "Oh, yes, he was Shankaracharya."

"You don't mean, the commentator on the Vedas who died centuries ago?" I asked.

"I mean him," he said to my amazement.

"Then you are referring to a spirit?" I asked.

"Of course it was his spirit," he agreed. At that moment I thought of Philemon. "There are ghostly gurus too," he added. "Most people have living gurus. But there are always some who have a spirit for teacher."

This information was both illuminating and reassuring to me. Evidently, then, I had not plummeted right out of the human world, but had only experienced the sort of thing that could happen to others who made similar efforts.

Most of this and of other figures who came to Jung's mind as independent creatures (called Elijah, Salome, Ka and a feminine figure who took on the attributes of a female patient of his) caused Jung, as scientist, no little disquiet. His struggle to come to terms with it is recorded in *Memories, Dreams, Reflections* and from this he formulated his ideas of the 'archetypes' of the unconscious.

This is where he differs from the occultists, who would feel there was sufficient evidence to take such beings, bizarre though they might be in name or appearance, at their face value rather than demote them to figments of consciousness. Actually in Jung himself this is probably not a question of 'demotion' though it easily becomes so afterwards in the limited conceptions of followers, just as the pioneer occultists' ideas became distorted into superstitious reverence.

For many years Jung turned to these beings, particularly the woman, when he felt in need of guidance, and he inevitably got it. On another occasion when pressure was building up for him to write down an important piece of work at their behest the whole house became heavy with inner presences and even paranormal phenomena began to happen.

> It began with restlessness, but I did not know what it meant and what "they" wanted of me. There was an ominous atmosphere all around me. I had the strange feeling that the air was filled with ghostly entities. Then it was as if my house began to be haunted. My eldest daughter saw a white figure passing through the room. My second daughter, independently of her elder sister, related that twice in the night her blanket had been snatched away; and that same night my nine-year-old son had an anxiety dream … Around five o'clock in the afternoon on Sunday the front-door bell began ringing frantically … The atmosphere was thick, believe me!

The upshot was that he wrote the *Septem Sermones* (privately printed and pseudonymously, subtitled *The Seven Sermons to the Dead written by Basilides in Alexandria, the City where the East toucheth the West*) … 'it began to flow out of me, and in the course of three evenings the thing was written. As soon as I took up the pen, the whole ghostly assemblage evaporated. The room quieted and the atmosphere cleared. The haunting was over.'

Again, such an experience gave him as scientist pause for much thought and without intellectualising it down to insignificance, he felt that it must be thought of as a particular constellation of the unconscious.

We may perhaps feel, at this point, that we are drifting towards a central field which may be the same thing under different terminology and from a different viewpoint. The depth psychologist sees it as 'the collective unconscious', the occultist sees it as 'the inner planes'. In our view, both these concepts are wrong. They are certainly limiting if we take them at their face value — such is the deflating effect that verbal labels have.

What we are trying to deal with, the 'inner side of Creation', is neither *only* a subjective part of consciousness, nor *only* a somewhat idealised and tenuous replica of the physical world. It is, and can be, both of these, but is a great deal more besides — just as the physical creation is something very different from what might be described, in turn, by the specialist eyes of a landscape painter or a civil engineer.

It is certainly a powerful place. Jung thinks that without his work and his family to 'earth' him to physical reality he might well have lost his reason during this critical early period when all this was first formulating.

He cites Friedrich Nietzsche as one who failed to maintain the contact with earthly reality in similar circumstances with disastrous consequences to his work and his sanity.

And though we suspect that some devout evangelicals might well feel that this is only to be expected, and that we are dealing with the emissaries of Hell, we have the testimony of Jung that:

> Today I can say that I have never lost touch with my initial experiences. All my works, all my creative activity, has come from those initial fantasies and dreams which began in 1912, almost fifty years ago. Everything that I accomplished in later life was already contained in them, although at first only in the form of emotions and images.

We can see, however, that a certain danger may exist to those who pursue these matters in the occult spirit and form quasi-religious groups to promulgate the teachings they receive. This can be a very effective way of cutting off the reality that the basic problems of existence and relationships in the world give; and a group of people going into an 'agreement' over various basic matters can start to feed on each others illusions. A lack of practical reality and common sense may soon appear in their work and demeanour, all of which does nothing for the public repute of occultism as it develops another outcrop of adherents on the 'lunatic fringe'.

We have mentioned the difficulties of accurate communication. When communications become invested with a reverent or even infallible aura in an occult group, then the minor personal idiosyncrasies of the individuals at the centre receiving such messages become a distorting influence that permeates the entire group.

In one instance, for example, the marriage problems of the leader of such a group led to a body of teaching that held celibacy to be a *sine qua non* of spiritual development. And one of the problems of modern occultism as a whole has been a lack of any informed spiritual directors, as occur in contemplative orders of the Church. This leads to a tendency not only for the group leadership to take itself at its own valuation but for it also to regard the communicating being on the inner planes to be the fount of all knowledge and wisdom.

The occult is the study of a particular branch of nature, such as chemistry or physics might be, and it does itself great disservice by trying to pose as omniscient. An occult adept, however long his training may be or wide his experience, is really no more qualified to pronounce upon the problems of humanity at large than a doctor of physics or chemistry. An occult adept is not a superior human being. He is a human being specialising in and trained to a particular function. And this applies to those who occupy bodies in the physical world and those who do not. Being discarnate is not in itself an occult diploma.

A science gains nothing but harm from trying to become a *quasi-religion*. Although we must immediately qualify this by saying that physical science has lost much by cutting out the 'wholeness' of the devotional attitude of its workers, or 'adepts', that characterised say alchemy or astrology.

Let us now turn to another source of witness in the works of Alice A. Bailey, most of which are stated to be the direct teachings of a Tibetan Master. The general tenor of the teachings is an expansion upon those first formulated by Helena Petrovna Blavatsky and the Theosophical Society. As such we would not necessarily agree with all of them but a close reading of the text inculcates a respect and even affection for the communicator responsible for them — highhanded though he may be in tone at times. The Tibetan states in a much quoted foreword:

> The books that I have written are sent out with no claim for their acceptance. They may or may not be correct, true and useful. It is for you to ascertain their truth by right practice and by the exercise of the intuition. Neither I nor A.A.B. is the least interested in having them acclaimed as inspired writings, or in having anyone speak of them (with bated breath) as being the work of one of the Masters.

One can read between the lines, with some sympathy, the frustrations that an inner communicator must sometimes feel. In one of his works, *Telepathy and the Etheric Vehicle*, he gives an estimation of the validity of occult teaching from an occult inner plane Master. In percentage terms he considers that 93 per cent of such communications are of subjective origin. 85 per cent come from the nicer areas of the sub-conscious mind of the individual, and 8 per cent from his or her own genuine higher consciousness. And of the remaining 7 per cent, only 2 per cent actually emanates from the Master, the remaining 5 per cent coming from inner-plane disciples under training. We might also do well to remember that these figures do not even bother to take into account the vast amount of sentimental and fatuous material that is got about by various less discerning enthusiasts, to say nothing of deliberate charlatans.

The Tibetan gives in his books a vast amount of technical detail on the process of raising consciousness to the point of being able to contact the Master at will — as for instance in *A Treatise on White Magic*. Stimulating and informative though this may be, its dependence upon purity of consciousness and motive may make it appear to be a kind of religious quest, but the way of attunement to an inner-plane entity's consciousness is not necessarily the way of attainment to heaven. It is *not* the way that all must go in order to be at one with God. It is rather a specialist discipline for the dedicated occult scientist with a genuine vocation for such work.

From what has been said it may be apparent that much of the task confronting the frontiers of present-day occultism is not so much the receiving of a body of teaching. This has been done in large quantity in the past hundred years. It is more a question of a proper evaluation of that which has been so received.

We have spent much time on the Masters. They are important to the occult student who is going to go any distance in the work, though they are in truth but a small part of the Creation as a whole. They form an Order or Brotherhood called sometimes the Great White Lodge, and though some teachers have, in our opinion, erred in making organisation charts of how they are supposed to run the universe, we do best to take such teachings as an example of how an inner teaching can be distorted by reflection into a physically limited consciousness (although of course an inner plane consciousness may well be equally limited, if in a rather different way).

A more correct way of looking at such a conception might be to imagine any other religiously oriented benevolent fraternity on the physical plane with a keen interest in the affairs of the world. It might have sections and officers devoted to study and work in various departments of human affairs but would not, by this token, be running the universe. Whatever they may be, the Masters are not an inner-plane branch of the Civil Service.

Generally, one may expect a similar kind of organisational 'free for all' on the inner side of creation as on the outer — with correspondences of churches, friendly societies, business enterprises, police forces, armies, criminal gangs, pressure groups, educational institutions, hospitals, learned societies, occult fraternities and so on.

One of the points that occult students tend to forget is that there is this great mass of human activity of which occult teachings take little account. The first task of occult training is the raising and refining of consciousness of the student so that he may be attuned to the teacher. But raising or refining of the consciousness is not, as we have said, necessarily the goal and destiny of all humanity. This is the first hard lesson that many a proselytising occult aspirant has to learn. In the first flush of learning of the occult worlds it can be very tempting to rush round to friends and relations to tell them the good news — only to meet with disinterest or rebuff.

This painful lesson is an early indicator that the way of occult training is very much one of shattering of illusions, and may appear very often as a matter of continued 'dis-illusionment'. A serious error can arise from this however. If the student thinks that the way he is on is the way that *all* must tread eventually, it is a short step to the presumption that he must be 'better' or 'more evolved' than his 'ordinary' friends and relations.

Now it may be true that he has received a high calling, but this does not make him 'better' than anyone else, any more than a concert violinist is necessarily a 'better' person than his less talented contemporaries. Unfortunately a fair proportion of popular occult teachings goes to perpetuate this error. Perhaps this is why it is popular! But it brings the subject into disrepute with the intelligent outsider, and makes the eventual awaking to reality a more painful process for the aspirant.

We have spoken much of human Masters but we must also take into account those beings who are not humans, but who also serve the cause of the Great White Lodge. There are two principal categories of these, the Elemental and the Angelic. It would be foolish to be dogmatic about the nature, constitution and cosmic destiny of these other orders of being when we are hard pressed to account for our own. There is, of course, much speculation and 'teaching' of various kinds. Some of it written more as pap for the credulous than as serious contributions to human knowledge.

It may be of help if we take a fairly broad traditional rule of thumb and consider the Angelic kingdoms as the 'thoughts' or 'ideas' of God. Or, in other words, created for specific functions or purposes of a relatively specialised nature. Similarly, the Elemental Kingdoms could be considered as the ensouled and conscious mechanisms laid down to maintain what we would call the 'laws of nature'.

Having said this, we need immediately to qualify it in the light of experience, for when we define something intellectually we tend to degrade it to the level of an inanimate object. But any who have experienced even the 'touch of an angel's wing' will know that they have been in the presence of beings mighty and glorious (and which are, incidentally, a far cry from the magician's formulation of angelic telesmatic images).

Similarly the experience of Elemental beings can be of a presence as mighty as a rushing wind, a roaring furnace, a tide at flood, or the deep stillness of a cave —compared to which the being of man seems like a dry leaf. This again is a far cry from 'fairies at the bottom of the garden' — not that we would dismiss even these out of hand.

We do well to remember that just as there is a vast range of beings in the human kingdom in infinite individual diversity, and in groups of races, nations and times, so there is in the parallel living kingdoms of God's creation — from the conventional cherub to the great Archangel, or from elves and pixies to the great Pan or the Elemental Kings.

Similarly there are many beings of the other evolutions who are indifferent to humanity (as many humans are indifferent to them) or who may even be hostile — and perhaps with very good reason. We should realise that all is not sweetness and light on the inner side of creation. It is as much subject to the consequences of the Fall as the physical outer creation — though this may not apply, by definition, to most of the Angelic kingdoms.

Gustav Davidson, in his encyclopaedic *A Dictionary of Angels* has admirably summarised the doctrine of the Church on angels:

> ... that angels, like human beings, were created with free will, but that they surrendered their free will the moment they were formed. At that moment, we are told, they were given (and had to make) the choice between turning towards or away from God, and that it was an irrevocable choice. Those angels that turned towards God gained the beatific vision, and so became fixed eternally in good: those that turned away from God became fixed eternally in evil. These latter are the demons, they are *not* the fallen angels (an entirely different breed of recusants which hatched out subsequently, on Satan's defection). Man, however, continues to enjoy free will. He can still choose between good and evil. This may or may not be to his advantage; more often than not it has proved his undoing. The best that man can hope for, apparently, so that when he is weighed in the balance (by the 'angels of final reckoning') he is not found wanting.

Mr Davidson also notes that according to Abbot Anscar Vonier in *The Teaching of the Catholic Church* (1964), angels still enjoy free will and that this would seem to be another or new interpretation of Catholic doctrine on the subject. So let us simply note that the subject is a vast one, on which there is little conclusive evidence, in the scientific sense, available, but that all who have experienced the contact with angels have not been left in much doubt as to their existence.

Let us quote from Anthony Duncan's *The Sword in the Sun*, that records a contact with such a being, to a most surprised Christian.

> The following day, the angel came again; but it would be more truthful to say that I became aware of his presence, for as I well know, he is always present with me. Once more, he spoke:
>
> **Angel:** I am glad you have written that I am always with you, for as you know, I am your Guardian Angel.
>
> **Me:** I very well remember the occasion when you first showed yourself to me. I was making my thanksgivings after offering the Eucharist, when suddenly,

you were there! I saw you with an inner vision; a man-like shape, apparently made of a bright, copper-coloured flame. The overwhelming impression I received was of a quite unfathomable love, and directed, of all persons, to me! I fear my description is a poor one and unflattering!

Angel: You saw me as I am! The previous day your consciousness was raised in prayer until you found yourself in the presence of many angels and of discarnate human souls. Do you remember both the sense of copper-coloured flame and of beings robed in white? The images of heaven in Holy Scripture have become debased in the minds of mortal men, but their reality is unaffected, as all mortal men shall shortly discover.

Me: I have asked this question before, but because we are to be overheard, I will ask it again. Has every human being in this world his own personal Guardian Angel?

Angel: No. But all have guardians of a sort. Most are human guardians; human souls with whom they are eternally associated. Some have guardians from among the angels. It all depends upon the needs of each and every individual soul. There is no idea of rank or merit; every guardian partakes of the Mind of Christ, and loves his charge with the Love of Christ.

Me: The term 'guardian angel' may mean, for us, either a human or an angelic being. Either may fulfil that office. Tell me, does this office ever fail?

Angel: Never! But your free will is forever inviolate. You can make yourself impossible to guard. Your integrity is the key to all things.

Me: Tell me, if you will, the difference between angels and men. I read somewhere that the great theologian Origen thought they were the same beings. Other theologians think 'angels' in the Scriptures are mere literary devices, or names for divinely given intuitions.

Angel: You and your theologians! It is as well for us all that our Lord cares nothing for theology! Origen was mistaken. Angels and men belong to wholly different orders of creation. First the angels were created, and then man. And we are happy to serve our little Brothers. Notice; I am your guardian: you are not mine.

Me: 'I am among you as he that serveth'. In a topsy-turvy world, normality itself seems upside down, and the idea of the greater serving the lesser is one which we find hard to grasp. And yet the best of human leaders spend themselves in service to their subordinates. I am about to talk nonsense; guard me, my Brother!

Angel: Men have not always had angel guardians. This is a fruit of the Incarnation. Before our Lord's Resurrection, men had no guardians at all, either human or angelic. This guardianship is a temporary thing: at the end of the age it will cease; after then it will no longer be needed.

Me: Then we are in an age of transition? Guardianship, angelic or human, belongs to the period between our Lord's Incarnation and his Coming Again? What happens then? What happens to this world? Will it be destroyed? Does the whole of Creation undergo a catastrophic change?

Angel: You ask too many questions at once! Why are you so concerned about the world at the Second Coming? You are doing your very best to destroy it yourselves, and yourselves with it. Why this sudden concern? Does God love the world even less than you do?

Me: I think we love ourselves, and love the world only because we identify it with ourselves. We will exploit it, but we fear to lose it. I think we are remarkably stupid; a moment's thought is enough to show us how we should conduct ourselves—but we cannot behave even if we have thought about it. I blame the Fall! But I am, in part at least responsible for the Fall, and it is no good blaming the past all the time. We talk too much about the Fall, and yet — its effects are manifest. I think we are in a bad way.

Angel: What do you know about the Fall? Your mythology gives expression to what your folk-memory remembers; but the memories are vague. You only know the effects; you can only guess the cause. The whole truth of the Fall is altogether beyond your knowing. You are right; you talk too much of the Fall. St. Paul never intended Adam and Eve to be so obsessively rediscovered! You are redeemed; your frailty is made a means of Grace. Forget the Fall! You are to live the Risen Life, and in this age of transition, your guardians are there to help you. This very age, terrible though it is, is itself a means of Grace as you shall discover.

Here, our conversation came to an end. I had asked a lost of questions, and had both questions and answers in reply. You who read this: ask your own questions and take nothing as proven until it is true for you. The age of dogmatism is past!

Amen to that. As with all communications with the inner worlds there is little point, and indeed positive harm, in taking any communicator or communication at face value. We have in the last analysis to make up our own minds, based on the apparent worth and integrity of the communication, judged according to our lights.

We have also mentioned Elemental creatures. Of these, in his useful little book *How to Develop Clairvoyance* W. E. Butler writes:

The Devas or "Shining Ones", the "Lordly Ones" of Celtic tradition, the Naiads, the Dryads and the Oreads of Grecian belief, and the fairy folk, the Spirits of the Elements; all these live and have their being in the etheric and astral realms. Some of these entities you may see as your clairvoyance begins to unfold, and their activities form a fascinating field of study for the clairvoyant investigator. It is in this field of clairvoyant work that you will need to exercise the greatest care, for you will be making conscious contact with living beings of many different kinds, and not all of them will be friendly. You will also have to cultivate the power to resist the "glamour" which some of these beings can exert over you unless you have so trained yourself to resist this.

At this point let us return to our former script, which also records a contact with an Elemental hierarch:

Angel: It is time we introduced a third party. Here is Pan!

Me: Pan? Does he really exist? Who is he? What am I to make of him?

Angel: Pan is the hierarch of the Elemental creatures on earth. If you like, you may call him the King of the Fairies. Like me, he is your brother in Christ.

Me: You said that men would call me mad! I believe you, as you know: but what of all those who may overhear our conversation?

Angel: Does any of this matter? Men must make up their own minds. Are we to do their thinking for them?

Pan: I am standing by your right shoulder; I have come in from the garden.

Me: Do you live in the garden? Where? What do you do?

Pan: I live everywhere on earth; my children live in your garden, the garden is full of them.

Me: Why can't I see them? I can feel their presence sometimes; I have been taught to sense them, and to sense the life in trees and flowers, and in rocks and hills too. Why can't I see you or your children?

Pan: We don't live in this world in the same way that you do. We live in this world as it really is. You live in it in a strange way we cannot understand.

Me: Is this house real to you? Are our roads and railways and factories and cities real to you? Are we driving you out and making life difficult for you? What can we do to become more aware of you? We must do you terrible mischief! I am sorry!

Pan: You cannot understand. Your house is here, and then again, it is not here. It is not in our world, but we are in both worlds. This must seem very difficult for you.

Me: Yes, very difficult! But in some strange way I can understand. It is as if we live on two different wavelengths in the same world; different, but close to one another. If my house is not in your world, what is here in its place? And what about me? Where am I if I am not here in your world?

Pan: You ask too many questions; I do not know all the answers! As to your house; in your world it is here, in my world we are in the middle of a lake. My world is nicer. And you? You are in both, and yet, not in both. I cannot explain. Let us leave you in your house, it is easier that way.

Angel: You are right about the wavelengths. Pan does not know these things because they are not his concern. And you shall not know how it is that you are in both worlds at once until the end.

Me: But what of our misuse of this world, our spoiling of it, our pollution of its atmosphere the sea and everything else? Do we harm the Elementals or their world? We play havoc with the plants. What of the animals? How much damage can we do?

Angel: You cannot do as much damage as you think, and you are paying for that which you have done. I will not elaborate, but meditate upon the sorrows of your world of men. Are you happy in your cities? Do you enjoy your riches? And is war a truly entertaining pastime? You harm the Devas of your world; you harm the animals that belong to your world and the harm rebounds upon your own heads. But no harm is permanent, and all is passing and shall soon be past.

Me: Who are the Devas? You have told me, but I would hear it again.

Angel: Hear their King! He will tell you.

Pan: They are the spirits of wood and water, field and tree, and plant and stone.

Me: Are they the same as the Fairies, or are they of another order? And are you their King too?

Pan: They are of another order, but they are my children. This world of nature is my Kingdom under Christ.

Me: Then what am I doing here? What is our relationship? And what, please tell me, of the animals?

Angel: Pan does not know the answers to these questions. He lives ever in the present moment for this is the nature of Eternity. You men came here by the Fall, and your world evolved to catch you as you fell. Pan is your Brother in Christ, and you are King of the animals in your world. The plants belong to Pan.

Me: What a horror for the animals! And what an outrage on a royal Brother! What restitution can I make?

Angel: Your restitution is your own unhappiness. All judgements in Eternity are self-inflicted. You exact revenge upon your own self. There is no escape; but have no fear, you are redeemed.

Me: What can I do, if not to make amends, yet to befriend a Brother? How do I conduct myself to Pan?

Angel: Acknowledge that he is. And you will find the whole world come alive before your eyes. You will have begun within yourself a cure for your own blindness, and when next you pluck a flower, it will be, 'by your leave!' Courtesy is the hallmark of Heaven!

Me: Then Pan, my Brother, I acknowledge you and all your children. And I ask your pardon for my trespass. And I trust that we may come to glorify God in partnership and rid the world of man-made sorrows.

Pan: I am well pleased! And now I go about my world. Call me, Brother, when you will, for I am everywhere to be found.

Angel: And that will do for one day's work! All you who overhear, take note! But do not take too much at once; just think it possible that the conversation was real!

In the light of this recorded 'conversation', let us return to W. E. Butler, who continues: .

The non-human intelligences of this astral level do not possess any form similar to that of man, but they do have their own forms, though these cannot be described in earth terms. If the human clairvoyant does come into contact with such non-human beings, his subconsciousness gives to them "a local habitation and a name". This usually is embodied in a traditional image. Thus, the elemental lives of the four modes of matter, the four elements, so-called, were visualised in medieval times as Gnomes, Sylphs, Undines and Salamanders. In other nations and at other times, they were given different forms by man, and Shakespeare in the Midsummer Night's Dream has caused innumerable 'fairy-forms' built up by the visualising imaginations of countless theatre goers. Such forms are quickly seized and made use of by the elemental spirits, and in such guise they are often seen by clairvoyants. So in many ways, this great world of the astral is well-named the World of Illusion. At the same time, the illusions are in the artificially created appearance of that world; in itself it is as real as any other realm of Nature.

We have now drawn from several witnesses the existence of inner worlds and of the denizens of them. We are mainly concerned, from a practical point of view, with the aspects of companionage between such beings and ourselves, which companionage in a common cause is embodied in the symbol of the Table Round. And it is with this principle in mind that we have deliberately quoted from various other sources throughout our discussion of it. The time now comes for us to discuss our practical exercises based upon this principle.

EXERCISE FOR CHAPTER VI
A table round, and there, a place for you
To come and go at will in Contemplation.

The Table is a symbol rich with power and significance, particularly when related to a meal or banquet. When the Holy Grail appeared it was generally when all were seated at table, and the appearance of the Grail roused everyone there to have before him that which he liked best. Charles Williams has suggested that what is here intended is that under the Grail influence all men saw with transformed eyes of the spirit, so that they saw the best in and accepted fully whatever was before them.

In Grail Legend there were three tables, the Round Table at which the companionage of Arthur's knights sat, the Table of Joseph of Arimathea, who was first guardian of the Grail, and ultimately the Table of the Last Supper where God Incarnate initiated the symbolism and institution of the Mass, whereby he is mystically present to his faithful at any time and place unto the end of the world. There are other tables also — the disciples of Jesus were all sitting at table when the Holy Spirit descended upon than at Pentecost.

We do well to keep in mind these high antecedents of the 'table' which we seek to build and whose companionage we seek to join. As Francis Rolt-Wheeler has suggested in *Mystic Gleams from the Holy Grail* there are several levels at which one may view the love in fellowship and mutual service that is symbolised by the Table Round:

i)   as a mutual interest group — often materially selfish, the type of organisations seen in business or politics;

ii) a chivalrous and altruistic friendship — as in a club or charitable organisation;

iii) a romantic cult — of which the equivalent would be the modern religious or occult group of various degrees of ethical behaviour and effectiveness;

iv) a mystic devotion — which is really what we are after, for it is as at-one-ing under and in God to do his works within his Creation. The Round Table becomes almost, as it were (and we speak with all due reverence), a 'central nervous system' in the Body of Christ.

Be aware then, first, of the origins of the Table and the wonder and power of He whose table it is at which you aspire to sit. Then be aware of your companions, visible and invisible, human and nonhuman, who also serve.

The Table is a symbol of the corporate nature of anyone's service and in one way it could be said that the Grail does not manifest until all are sitting at the Table Round. It behoves us then to welcome in our minds all our unseen brethren at this point, imagining ourselves, with them, sitting at the circumference of a great Round Table at which Christ Incarnate sits as King at the Eastern Quarter.

Your initial awareness of them may be dim, but at times upon the way, certain steps have to be taken in faith, and the faith in the presence of one's unseen brethren, and in the strong links that are forged by mutual dedication and service, will one day, as the result of gradual process of sustained faith burst forth into the reality of 'never being alone' in the service of the Great Work.

For the time being it is sufficient, first to orientate the origins and patronage of the Table to God (and no other), and then to extend one's love and greeting to the others also there.

CHAPTER VII

The Upper Room

We are about to embark upon a study of magic, and this differs in many respects from mysticism. We have examined all this in earlier chapters so we will not repeat ourselves, but it may help to refer back to those points, for it is important that the difference is clearly understood.

Briefly, we are about to examine techniques of inner orientation. These are not necessary for the pure mystic, who is automatically oriented by his pure love of God. The magician, however, devotes his attention and energies to the 'many mansions' of God's inner creation and as such needs to have some kind of map-reference system. So what we are about to undertake is a study of technique but technique that is concerned with *states of consciousness*.

During the first years of our physical lives on earth we spend much time and effort simply trying to orientate. Seeing, hearing, are very much activities that have to be learned, as is the interpretation into meaningful concepts of the confused mass of sensations impinging upon our bodies from the external physical environment.

We have exactly the same problems to confront when we are entering upon the inner levels of creation — which is why magic is hardly a matter that can be learned from a book or without long practical training.

The principal vehicle of consciousness by which we come to terms with the inner side of creation is the visual imagination, and early magical training consists in the development and disciplining of this faculty.

Once the ability to hold the mind, the emotions, and the imagination steady has been achieved (with the delicate balance that allows the perception of changes in those aspects of consciousness to be affected by objective sources, without upsetting the whole orientation), then communication is possible between inner and outer creation.

Communication is, in general, all that is required, for it gives the ability to direct energies from one level to another. It is possible to operate entirely on the inner side of creation, in forms of trance, or what is known as etheric or astral projection, but this is a fairly rare condition, as rare as its corollary, the physical manifestation of a being of the inner-creation to physical perception. The amount of energy required is so great that generally speaking it does not appear in the battery of techniques of the average magician. It is true that there are some with a particular kind of nervous and psychic constitution that gives them the facility to do this. The experiences have been described at length in that occult classic on the subject *The Projection of the Astral Body*, by Sylvan Muldoon, assisted by psychical researcher Hereward Carrington. More recently, an American businessman, Robert A. Monroe, has published a book describing similar experiences in *Journeys out of the Body*.

These are worth study, for they show how sensitive the inner world conditions are to their states of consciousness. A mere wandering of attention will deflect the course and purpose of the travelling 'phantom' to a marked degree. And the harbouring of resentful feelings can result in most unpleasant attacks.

The actual ability to project is not a hallmark of high occult adepthood though its spectacular aspects, particularly as embroidered by occult fiction writers, have led it to hold a high degree of wonder in the eyes of the general public and the student first coming to these affairs. Whether one has the facility or not, it is important that the groundwork of control of the mind, imagination and emotions be achieved — at any rate in the context of magical operations. Upon this, further specialisation may follow, according to our natural gifts and the destiny to which we are called.

We must first, then, build compass points on the 'inner' so that we can orientate ourselves if and when we find ourselves there. There are many ways in which this structuring can be done and all occult symbol systems, be they the Tree of Life of the Qabalists, the Tarot, the Chinese I Ching, the magician's circle or Mandala, the prick symbols of Geomancy, the image of the heavenly sphere of Astrology, are all methods towards this end. Properly speaking they are models of the Universe (inner and outer) and by learning to find our way about the model so do we the better equip ourselves to orientate in respect of the larger actuality.

Naturally, these principles are often misunderstood, and one finds the rather sad spectacle of occult students quarrelling over symbol systems, and where such and such an image should or should not be attributed. The occult symbol systems fortunately have an element within them that prevents them from being locked into a rigid system by the human intellect. The slight fluidity that they have (symbolised by the Fool in the Tarot, about which much fruitless argument has occurred) enables them to be adapted to the needs of each particular soul or group of occult workers.

Let it be said that the symbol system that is valid is one that, though based on tradition, has been formulated in its precise details by an individual or a group. It then becomes that individual's or group's unique means of coping with the inner-creation realities.

Much controversy having raged over the 'correct' attributions of the Tree of Life, let us for the purposes of this chapter go back to an earlier tradition in the literature and examine the Cube of Space, as described in a very early Qabalistic text, the *Sepher Yetzirah.*

The Cube of Space is a kind of three-dimensional Mandala that can help us, in our three-dimensionally conditioned consciousness, to formulate, contact and cope with further dimensions.

A Mandala is a regular figure, usually four fold. It has been fairly widely written about since the psychologist C. G. Jung drew attention to its importance as an aid to structuring the psyche. Literally the word means 'magic circle'. In recent years such basic magical ritual devices as the Pentagram Ritual have also been much publicised. This is a basic pattern for much ritual work, and here again one sees the building of four stations at the Cardinal Points, with specific Archangelic and Elemental figures, colours and so on.

We also have, in a rather less rigidly formalised structure, the Breastplate of St. Patrick, that we have already quoted, with its '*Christ behind me, Christ before me, Christ beside me, Christ beneath me, Christ above me*' and in a number of abstract situations also.

Any and all of these are perfectly valid systems. But the real value of these devices is in the work that we ourselves put into them.

There are variations in the text of the *Sepher Yetzirah* (or Book of Formation) as translated by various hands since its written origin, in possibly the third century A.D., but the translation we shall take is that of Dr Wynn Westcott — for no better reason than that we personally happen to like it, and in practical magic there can be no better criterion. Let others find what suits their own psychic structure and build from there. What we intend to do here is to exemplify a method. If students wish to use it as it stands they are welcome to do so. If they wish to introduce their own private variations they are also at liberty to try.

In so far that we are dealing with the symbolism of the Hebrew letters we also hope it will serve to redirect attention to these ideographs, which are the oldest and purest parts of the Qabalistic system, yet which have become somewhat overlaid and neglected with the modern preoccupation with Tarot cards, astrological symbols, 'flashing colours' and so on.

The Hebrew alphabet consists of 22 letters basically (ignoring the expanded and final forms, and also the vowel pointings which are a later addition) and can be split into three sections. These sections are the three Mother Letters, the seven Double Letters, and the twelve Single Letters.

It may help us if we tabulate them in this fashion, giving their traditional shape, their Hebrew name, and what the name means. It will be obvious that we have a numerical structuring of 3, 7 and 12 that is found in a number of other occult symbol systems. We will not concern ourselves with cross-references to these, however, at this point. That can come later as the student wishes. Let us simply build up this system upon its own interior devices and see what we have at the end of it.

Mother letters			Double Letters			Single Letters		
א	Aleph	Ox	ב	Beth	House	ה	Heh	Window
מ	Mem	Water	ג	Gimel	Camel	ו	Vau	Nail
ש	Shin	Tooth	ד	Daleth	Door	ז	Zain	Sword
			כ	Kaph	Palm of hand	ח	Cheth	Fence
			פ	Peh	Mouth	ט	Teth	Serpent
			ר	Resh	Head	י	Yod	Hand
			ת	Tau	Cross or mark	ל	Lamed	Ox-goad
						נ	Nun	Fish
						ס	Samekh	Prop
						ע	Oyin	Eye
						צ	Tzaddi	Fish-hook
						ק	Qoph	Back of head

The three Mother Letters, to begin with, we may use to formulate the foundations of our magical universe.

The tooth (Shin) is a very hard object in the human body, that which is likely to survive as an entity long after the rest of us has mouldered away. It is also the means of preparing nutrition into assimilable form for the interior organs of the body — that which cuts and grinds — almost like 'the mills of God'. We take this letter therefore to represent the Eternal, the Spirit, God Himself; and indeed the shape of the letter suggests the Trinity, the three-in-one, with the fourth element, the potential part of the Creation that will become at-one-ed with God, as the horizontal bar.

Water (Mem) is directly related to the basis of creation — the waters over which the Spirit passed in the Genesis account of the creation. One could in fact visualise, if one wishes, the Spirit, as Shin, passing over the waters, Mem. The reflection of the one within the other would give the word, or Holy Name, ShMSh, which in the Qabalistic system is the name given to the Sun, particularly relevant to invocations concerning the central, balancing Sephirah Tiphareth. We mention this magical Qabalistic technicality in passing as a simple guide to how words and 'names of power' may be built up. Here again their importance and potency depends very much upon the student who formulates and uses them. Parroting ill-understood names from a book is worse than useless.

The letter Mem, in our system, then, stands for the basic stuff of the Creation. It could be called the Anima Mundi, the Soul of the World, and it is the *prima materia* of the alchemists (not quite the same thing as the Collective Unconscious, though this modern concept goes some way towards it). It is evocatively described in *The Chemical Marriage of Christian Rosenkreutz* as a sleeping naked virgin, the Lady Venus, secluded in a deep and most secret dungeon of the castle.

The third Mother letter is the one with which we shall be most concerned. This is the letter Aleph, which to our anglicised ears seems like a vowel, but which, in common with all the Hebrew letters is a consonant, though it is simply a light aspirate — rather like the pause that comes with the hyphen in the word 're-echo'. Its meaning, an Ox, may seem somewhat incongruous until we cast our minds back from our modern times to the technology of the early peoples who gave us the symbolism of the Hebrew alphabet. Then we see the Ox as the driving power upon which civilisation is based. It is the motive power that drives the plough and grinds the grain, that pulls the harvest wagon home. Its modern equivalent might be the internal combustion engine, or more basically, fuel oil, or electricity, or ultimately the power within the atom that gives atomic and nuclear power, the very power that rages forth within the sun and all the other stars, and is latent in every piece of matter throughout the physical universe.

We have, then, our three Mother letters, so called because traditionally all the other letters sprang from them, representing a three-fold basic universe. Shin — the Spirit, the eternal matrix; Aleph — the driving power within; Mem — the reflective substance within which the whole edifice of forms is built.

We may see ourselves building our Cube of Space 'within' the letter Aleph, looking beyond it to Shin for our authority and inspirations, and expecting the result of our actions to be reflected ultimately in the substance of Mem.

According to the *Sepher Yetzirah* the seven Double letters point out seven localities, or cardinal directions — Above, Below, East, West, North, South and 'the place of Holiness in the midst of them sustaining all things' — the Central Point.

Thus each of them represents a plane, or face, of the Cube of Space, with the exception of Tau, the last letter of the alphabet, which marks the central point between them all. The Double letters are so called because each has two methods of pronunciation, hard or soft, according to whether a doghesh is placed inside them, thus:

Beth   ב (b)   בּ (v)
Gimel   ג (g)   גּ (gh)

Daleth ‏ד‎ (d)   ‏ד‎ (dh)
Kaph   ‏כ‎ (k)   ‏כ‎ (kh)
Peh   ‏פ‎ (p)   ‏פ‎ (f)
Resh   ‏ר‎ (r)   ‏ר‎ (rh)
Tau   ‏ת‎ (t)   ‏ת‎ (th)

Some of these variations in pronunciation are difficult for Westerners to appreciate, owing to different structure of language, but this is not a point that need concern us in practical magic, at any rate at this stage.

We may now construct our Cube of Space diagrammatically (Figure 14) assigning Beth to the Above; Gimel to the Below; Daleth to the East; Kaph to the West; Peh to the North; Resh to the South; and Tau to the Centre.

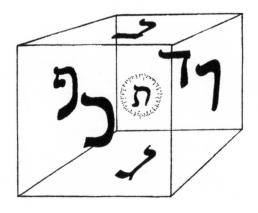

Figure 14

We have now a system of seven 'gates' or functions in and about us as we visualise ourselves standing in the centre, as in a cube shaped room.

The central **Tau** (Cross or Mark) is the point coinciding with our own heart, and represents a most important 'inner' gate, upon which all the others are centralised. Meditate upon this —all valid magical work must spring from the heart.

Above us shines the letter **Beth**, meaning a House, an indication that it dwells over a complete, unified system, of roof, walls, floor and foundations. Though we may remember that the original signification would have been a tent, which is also transportable — and more readily thrown up as a protection about ourselves from the elements. It can be quite an illuminating experience to actually put up a tent and lie in it, listening to the sounds of nature without, feeling the walls swaying in the wind, hearing the rain pattering on the walls and roof, and reflecting upon it as one's own structure and shelter in the midst of the universe.

The movable aspect is reinforced by the letter below us — **Gimel**, the Camel, which as every schoolboy knows is 'the ship of the desert'. That which can take us, and all our belongings on far treks into distant lands, across dry and forbidding territory. In our modern days of comparatively easy travel we tend to miss out on the profound significance and effect upon the soul of a pilgrimage, with its physical trials and tests for the sake of an inner goal or inspiration of the soul.

In the East, traditionally the most holy place and place of dawning light, we have the letter **Daleth**, a door. The way by which we can go forth into the inner worlds — this is the gateway to experience and adventure, and its facing East, the most holy place, is so that it will be a doorway at which our Maker and Lover stands, 'Behold I stand at the door and knock; if any man hear my voice, and open the door, I will come in to him, and will sup with him and he with me.'

Taking the 'gates' in the order as given in the *Sepher Yetzirah* we turn to the North, traditionally the place of greatest symbolic darkness, yet also the place of wisdom — the starry wisdom of the night sky. Here the letter is **Peh**, a Mouth, and it is the mouth that is a means of communication of the word, and a means of ingesting food, which ensures our survival upon the physical level. It can also imply the consuming of spiritual food, and it is not without significance that the Sacrament of the New Covenant instituted by Christ is a sacrament in terms of food. The seemingly crudely cannibalistic 'eating the flesh and drinking the blood' of the Saviour which has caused so much theological misunderstandings over the centuries is the nearest equivalent in words to expressing a great Mystery. And this should remind us of the inadequacy of words in expressing Mysteries, which, by definition are beyond the reach of the mind. However, another way of expression of wisdom, the oracle of words, is by the seal of love, a kiss. All these meanings and more besides are involved in the concept of the Northern Gate.

To the West is the Hebrew letter **Kaph**, the Palm of the Hand, and as the West is traditionally the place of reception of that light which comes through the door of the East so the palm of the hand is that most basic of cups. One may think of the nomad coming to an oasis after many parching days of march through the desert and throwing himself down by the still waters. The palm of the hand is the first and natural means of carrying water to the lips. At the same time the hand is, of course, in its clasping activity, a receiving agent for any tool — or weapon — or the clasp of a friend. It is also traditionally the map of destiny in that the lines of the palm designate the impress of fate upon the soul. And its receptive aspect may also give weight to the Indian practice of holding a pool of ink in the palm of the hand, as an alternative to the costly clairvoyant's crystal ball.

Turning to the South, the source of heat and fire and activity by tradition (and these directional traditions are based on the very elemental and age-old movements of the sun in the Northern hemisphere, particularly in those latitudes that formed the cradle of our civilisation) we have the letter **Resh**, meaning Head, in all its senses of physical head and leader of a family or people. And so we have the tradition corroborated of leadership and activity being the province of this quarter, which is that of the Sun, the primal symbol of life and light, during the day period, when all activity takes place.

This completes the attributions of the Double letters to the Cardinal directions of the space of our inner universe, and we may now go on to add the twelve Single letters, which add to and modify the major significations of the Double letters. These are:

North East	Heh	West Above	Samekh
South East	Vau	West Below	Oyin
East Above	Zain	North Above	Teth
East Below	Cheth	North Below	Yod
South West	Lamed	South Above	Tzaddi
North West	Nun	South Below	Qoph

and we will lay these out in diagrammatic form where we may see that the Cardinal Directions will share some of the Single or Simple letters, which in this respect act as linking agencies (Figure 15).

The four Single letters towards the Eastern Gate share the principle of dealing with division — between one plane or state and another. **Cheth** (the Fence) is a boundary separating two states; **Zain** (the Sword) is that which defends and maintains such boundaries. To left and right we have **Heh** (the Window) which allows one to see through solid boundaries, and **Vau** (the Nail) is that device which keeps two separate things together. All these are amplifications of the fact that Daleth is a door in the East to other worlds and it is through this that we shall go on our magical ventures.

To the North the Gate is crowned by **Teth** (the Serpent), the creature of wisdom. **Heh** (the Window or Tent-flap) is also relevant to this oracular Gate of Wisdom because it gives insight into other conditions of existence. To the left is an indication of the hidden depths of wisdom in **Nun** (the Fish) which lives and moves and has its being in another element from

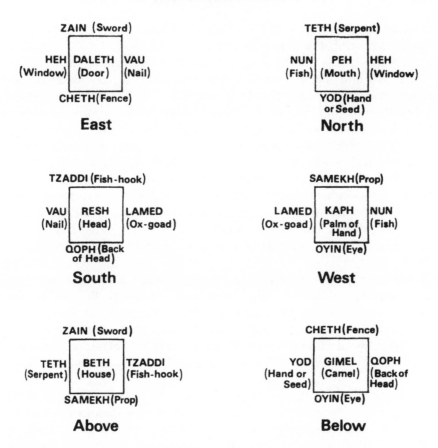

Figure 15

ourselves; and below, **Yod** (the Seed), which unless it be buried in the ground and die, does not bring forth fruit. The usual symbolic attribution of Yod is the Hand, but as Crowley points out, this is really a euphemism for the spermatozoon — the creative or initiatory seed. The hand can be allied to this as the basic element which gave rise to the possibility of human craft and civilisation and the embodied wisdom of technology, by its unique ability to meet forefinger and thumb to grasp and control tools. In his novel *The Greater Trumps* Charles Williams equates the hand with Tarot archetypes.

To the West, the Gate of Reception, **Samekh** (the Prop or Support) is appropriate as the passive support and receptor of the active principles with which the magician deals. **Oyin** (the Eye) as the principal form of perception is appropriate to this perceptive quarter; whilst the sides are **Nun** (the Fish) indicating more this time the depth of experience of material, magical or spiritual principles, and **Lamed** (the Ox-goad), that indicates control of power.

Turning to the South we find elements of control at each side of this active and forceful quarter. **Vau** (the Nail) again, which makes connections, and **Lamed** (the Ox-goad) which directs and keeps power going. **Tzaddi** (the Fish-hook) catches by attraction, controls and then lands into another dimension; whilst **Qoph** (the Back of the Head) the area of autonomic and automatic reactions, the base of consciousness from which all else builds, and signifies the deep motor automatic drives. As Robert Fludd points out, man and woman are but the agents of a new birth, it is God who makes the increase, who laid down the forms of bone, muscle and sinew, and brings it through growth and to the birth. It is something of this natural process upon which we are so dependent, and of which all mankind's technology is but an imitation, that is signified by Qoph.

We have now covered all the Simple Letters but we have still two directions to consider — the Above and the Below. Beneath us we have a basic outline of the human condition, the basic psycho-physical framework represented by Qoph in which we are enclosed by the fence of Cheth, endowed with the means of perception (Oyin) of our conditioning environment and with the ability for creative initiatory action (Yod) upon it.

Above us we have the helps and guards available to us in this condition. The Serpent of Wisdom (Teth); the Prop (Samekh) which in this context can be taken as the Cross of Calvary or the Staff of Moses on which a brazen serpent was impaled as a means of saving and inspiring the people in the wilderness seeking for the Promised Land; the Sword (Zain) of the Cherub who stands guard outside the Garden of Eden, the Earthly Paradise; and the Fish-hook (Tzaddi), that dreadful yet merciful implement of the Big Fisherman — and only one who has experienced it knows how a soul may be, like a fish, attracted, played and caught up into a new life.

All these symbols, it will be seen, have extensions and ramifications for the pursuit of meditation and contemplation; and we are now in a position to lay out our full construction diagrammatically (Figure 16).

This gives us the basis of a magical 'universe' on which we can build our own superstructure as a means of orientation on the inner side of creation.

This is where so many would-be students of magic go astray, if in fact they go anywhere at all. The principal injunction of magic is the fourfold 'To Know, To Will, To Dare, To Keep Silent'. We have now laid out the bare bones of knowledge, it is up to the student to have the will to use it,

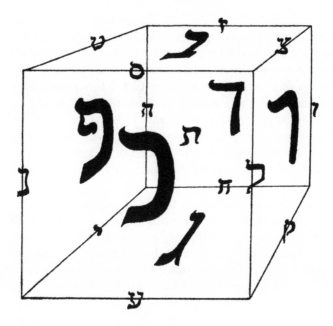

Figure 16

the courage to use it, the wisdom to keep silent for a due period afterward until the psychic stresses come to rest in a new equilibrium.

So many, however, will expend their time and energies in 'playing' with symbols and symbol systems instead of using them.

As an example, it would be possible to extend astrological symbolism on to the framework of letters that we have made. In this way one could extend one's reach into various aspects of the inner worlds. But the tendency for a number of students of the armchair variety will be to quibble about which attributions should go where. But comparing other people's ideas, ancient or modern, or awaiting some new revelation from another source, is a waste of time and effort, when the only source of revelation is within ourselves if we will only *use* what we already have.

The reason for extending the symbolism into other systems is to enrich the basic conceptual framework from which we started. If it only causes confusion, argument and muddle it is better to leave things simple.

For instance, build the Cube of Space in the imagination with yourself standing in the centre. Concentrate on the six main directions initially and reflect on their general function and meaning. Then it becomes a matter of following your nose. The details of the minor directions may be filled in. It may then well occur that certain figures may appear more or less spontaneously in any particular direction. These might be astrological figures, or Tarot pictures, or William Blake's four Zoas, or images quite independent of any known system. Simply take them for what they are worth and use them in the immediate context in which they arise.

What seems to be little realised is that all those symbolic figures can be used as means of communication between the inner and outer creation. It is rather like the flag signal code traditionally used on ships. Our aim, when one crops up (say the Tarot Trump I, the Magician, in the East), is to consider what it may mean — not to rush away and start to rack our brains on yet another mental construction of images on how to allocate all the rest of the Trumps around the Cube. This is to substitute reason for intuition.

We have our basic structure in the Cube of Space on which we have affixed the Hebrew letters and their immediately associated symbols. That is the fixed central part of our magical generator. We need to let the other parts revolve around the fixed part if the generator is going to work. The principle is just like an electrical machine, a rotating coil and a fixed one, which can be used to convert motion to power or power to motion — it is a two-way energy converter in consciousness.

It can be a help to externalise some of the symbolism with which we are dealing. This takes us into the realm of ritual or ceremonial magic, if in an elementary way. Full scale ceremonial consists of several operators in a carefully prepared place, preferably used for no other purpose, dressed in special regalia performing in a trained way an elaborate pre-arranged ritual drama. It calls for facilities that few possess, but the principles are just as readily used in less elaborate circumstances.

A shrine cupboard is an excellent device if a whole room cannot be devoted to the purpose, and the ideal is one of wardrobe size from which the upper shelves have been removed. The size of this causes it to cover most of the angles of vision when the doors are open, and so helps to give more focused concentration. The magician stands between the open doors, which can be painted in symbolic colours on the inside. The waist-high shelf serves as an altar and any reserve equipment or symbols can be kept in the lower shelves, which are covered by a cloth hanging from the topmost shelf. This is in accordance with the old Lodge tradition that all the magical implements are kept within the altar. When closed and locked the cupboard looks just like any other ordinary cupboard (see Figure 17).

The practical use to which the shrine cupboard is put is to furnish it symbolically — which is in itself a training in magical consciousness — and a valuable magical tool when it is complete. The way this is done is best left to the imagination of the operator, for there is little educative value in simply laying out symbols to a ready-made blueprint. But as a rough guide, one such shrine cupboard that we have come across has the space divided into four areas for each of the Cardinal directions, in which are placed the appropriate suits of a deck of Tarot cards, corresponding Platonic solids made from appropriately coloured cardboard, corresponding semi-precious stones, and representative symbols relating to the Elements — Cup, Candle, Incense Burner, Dish. There is a fifth area containing The Tarot Trumps and a home-made set of cards of Hebrew letters, also with stone and Platonic solid, and at a focal point a box or casket in which special intentions or talismans may be placed, surmounted by a figure of the Risen Christ and a large diagram of the Tree of Life. There are also planetary and polarity symbols and in fact the ramifications are endless.

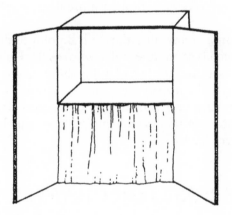

Figure 17

A dynamically operated cupboard such as this will develop a kind of cyclic life of its own, the symbols changing, being rearranged, simplified, made more complex, according to changes in the operators' consciousness. Temporarily discarded symbols, or those kept in reserve, are housed in the bottom of the cupboard in which may also be kept ritual robes, if used, and a battery of incenses — though these items are optional and are perhaps best excluded if one has unsympathetic neighbours. Incense, although a sovereign concentrator of consciousness, tends to make its presence felt for quite a distance.

The shrine is really working when appropriate symbols seem to come the way of the student in ordinary life, seemingly of their own accord.

We will not go into more detailed and specific uses just yet. Our first aim is the building of a direction finding apparatus, a device for 'orienteering' on the inner creation. It is important not to become preoccupied with techniques only. They have their validity and use at their own level but we must remember that we are building a *model* universe, not an actual one.

We are operating in the mental sphere only, as exemplified by the letter Aleph. There is the whole world of physical objectivity and its etheric matrix, represented by Mem, and also the whole of spiritual reality, represented by Shin. To neglect either of these is to court delusion — if not disaster. The neglect of Mem leads to unreality on the physical levels, to the crank, the eccentric, cut off from his roots. The neglect of Shin is perhaps worse — the prideful assumption of the individual will as being the centre of the universe — cut off from spiritual roots.

One can even have both conditions with the aspiring magician capering around in public in robes and symbols considering himself a superior being to all others — though more likely a spiritual and social cripple.

Above all we must remember the central point of the Cube of Space we have built, which is sometimes referred to as the Holiest Point. It is in fact the human heart. And the fact of doing things from the heart, instead of through intellectual curiosity, or social convention, or whatever, adds another whole dimension to our magical operations. The thought of the human heart as the central crystallising point of Aleph is a meditation that may prove very fruitful.

EXERCISE FOR CHAPTER VII

An upper room, symbolic of the world redeemed
In which you shall abide in your redemption.

We have already described a number of exercises that can be performed with advantage in the body of our chapter. The field of magical technique is a vast and fascinating one, though based on a few simple basic principles.

The above quotation gives us an overall view of the purpose behind our magical orienteering, and is a corrective to our getting too closely concerned with the mechanics of magic, the psychic nuts and bolts, and losing sight of the greater reality.

We should think of ourselves as preparing an Upper Room. We shall not be doing this in the same way that the ordinary religious or the contemplative mystic would do so but that is because we are not ordinary religious or contemplative mystics. This instruction is not for the world at large, nor even to the religious world, but to those few who have a genuine spiritual vocation to be white magicians. Fortunately this no longer needs the heavy footed secrecy of the past, which led to many abuses and misunderstandings.

It may help us to recall the circumstances as described in the New Testament of the selection of the Upper Room — the place set apart for the enactment of a great Mystery — the institution of the New Covenant. '… his disciples said to him, "Where would you like us to go and prepare for your Passover supper?" So he sent out two of his disciples with these instructions, "Go into the city, and a man will meet you carrying a jar of water. Follow him, and when he enters a house give this message to the householder: The Master says, "Where is the room reserved for me to eat the Passover with my disciples?" He will show you a large room upstairs, set out in readiness. Make the preparations for us there."' (Mark 14 v.12-15.)

We have, in effect, been preparing an Upper Room. But we must remember that its real use is yet to come — by the indwelling of the Christ and his disciples for the institution of the New Covenant. And that magical preparations are but peripheral and preparatory to this central purpose.

Put in more abstract symbolic terms, we have prepared our place in Aleph, so that Shin may indwell the Tau, and profoundly affect Mem to achieve a new synthesis.

In practical terms it is important, when building our magical cube, to spend time seeing it also in more human terms of the Upper Room at the Passover Supper, seeing all the disciples present, and ourselves among them. And it may well occur that one may come, in a very profound and moving way, bearing bread and wine, that will truly put our magic into proper perspective.

CHAPTER VIII

The Light of Christ

The matter that we now concern ourselves with is the keystone of the structure of the last two chapters. For communication with beings of the inner side of creation, and the building of a magical system are fraught with the risk of delusion and deception if they are not undertaken in the Light of Christ — without which we are literally working in the dark.

We will base our thoughts upon the Qabalistic Tree of Life for it is this pattern of relationships that has formed the basis of a whole philosophical school of Western occultism. Its roots can be traced, furthermore, prior to its modern occult form, back to its mystical roots in Judaism. Also as I myself have written a fairly large work on the subject (*A Practical Guide to Qabalistic Symbolism*), taking for granted the accuracy of the modern occult analysis, what we say here may be used as a corrective and aid in the study of that and similar works. Dion Fortune's *Mystical Qabalah*, for instance, however good it may be as a descriptive text based on occult meditations, is very far from being 'mystical' in the true sense of the word.

The Tree of Life is a system of relationships that pertains to the structure of the psyche and, by extension, to the universe itself (inner and outer), and also to God. In the traditional occult presentation that is based on Hindu monist religious philosophy, the universe and God are often seen to be synonymous. But this is not so in earlier Qabalistic texts. The Tree of Life *may* be applied to God, but similarity to an archetypal pattern of activity or structure does not mean identity with it. In fact there need be no confusion if the traditional Qabalistic doctrine of the Four Worlds is taken into account, but this is a doctrine that has been consistently misunderstood, not to say fudged, by many Qabalistic writers of modern times. It is an area that gives most difficulty of understanding to Qabalistic students, and the reason why this is so is because it has not been properly comprehended by their teachers — and indeed cannot be properly comprehended as long as they encumber themselves with the irrelevant and alien presuppositions of a monist theology.

The Four Worlds are those of **Atziluth, Briah, Yetzirah** and **Assiah,** usually translated as Archetypal, Creative, Formative and Material. We can place these in diagrammatic form as in Figure 18.

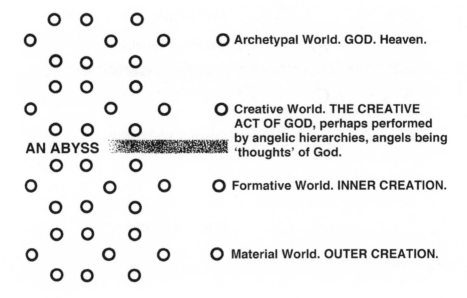

Figure 18

But the Tree of Life, being a most adaptable diagram, can also be put in another form, using just one Tree pattern in a vertical position, as in Figure 19.

Here we see the importance of the Abyss in the scheme of things. It is that which differentiates between Creator and Created. If this is ignored or misunderstood then we are in a monist system where God and Creation are one.

It may be thought that we make heavy weather of this monism issue but it does have profound practical applications. If God and his creation are one, then we are parts of God and by various exercises we are able to make ourselves more important parts. It simply requires knowledge and application. The techniques of this are to be found in the various forms of yoga. But these lead not to God, but to the basic ground base of universal consciousness — and universal consciousness is not God. At best they provide a clearing of the ground prior to a real mystical relationship. And a real mystical relationship recognises the Creator as a separate being and conceives a great reciprocal love for the Creator. A prodigal son has returned to the Father.

In this way the Abyss may be bridged; and attempts to formulate a Sephirah there (Daath) are really stumbling intellectual attempts to find some rationale for the great power of love. And it is love that will cross

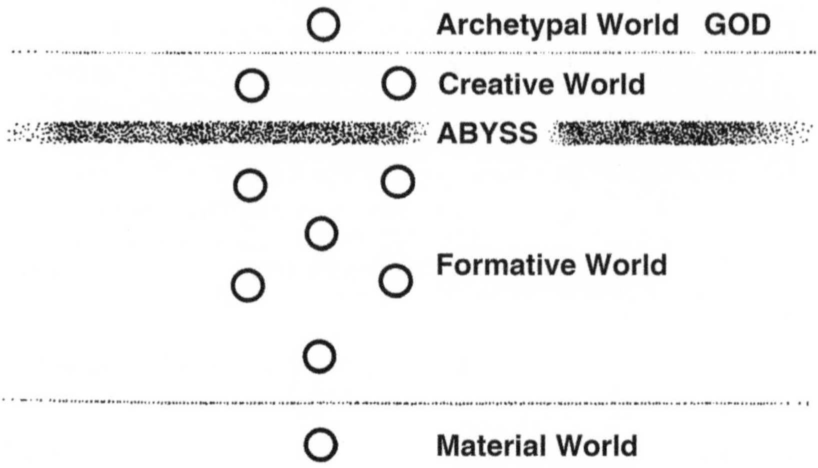

O   Archetypal World   GOD

O   O   Creative World

ABYSS

O   O

O

O   O   Formative World

O

O   Material World

Figure 19

the Abyss, not knowledge, or non-attachment. (This notwithstanding the fact that Daath means Knowledge. We take 'knowledge' in the Biblical sense of the greatest possible loving intimacy of sexual union. In another way Daath can be seen to be a redeemed Malkuth, which, if taken from its fallen position to the place of Daath creates a more balanced Tree diagram.)

This is by no means a new issue, and has been dealt with at some length for instance by the Flemish mystic, von Ruysbroek, who writes in his *Spiritual Espousals*, that:

> ... whenever man is empty and undistracted in his senses by images, and free and unoccupied in his highest powers, he attains rest by purely natural means. And all men can find and possess this rest in themselves by their mere nature, without the grace of God, if they are able to empty themselves of sensual images and of all action.

He goes on to say:

> These men, are, as it seems to them, occupied in the contemplation of God, and they believe themselves to be the holiest men alive. Yet they live in opposition and dissimilarity to God and all saints and all good men...

Professor R. C. Zaehner, who deals with this theme in his book, *Mysticism, Sacred and Profane*, points out:

It will be remembered that Christ said, "No man cometh to the Father but by me." It is, of course, possible to take this saying in an absolutely literal sense and thereby to dismiss all non-Christian religions as being merely false. It is, however, legitimate and certainly more charitable to interpret this saying, so far as it applies to mysticism, to mean that unless one approaches the Father through the Son and as a son with the trust and helplessness of a child, there is very little chance of finding Him — none at all it would appear, if you insist either that you are identical with the Father or that the Father is an illusion.

Hence a sharp distinction must be drawn between those forms of religion in which love or charity plays a predominant part and those in which it does not. In Christian mysticism love is all-important, and it must be so, since God Himself is defined as Love. In Islam too, because the Muslims inherited more than they knew from the Christians, it assumes ever-increasing importance despite the predominantly terrifying picture of God we find in the Qur'an.

In Hinduism this religion of love breaks through in the Gita and in the cults of both Visnu and Siva, and, of course, in the worship of Rama and Krishna as incarnations of Visnu. "I am the origin of all," says Krishna in the Bhagavad-Gita, "from me all things evolve. Thinking thus do wise men, immersed in love (bhava), worship Me. Thinking of Me, devoting their lives to Me, enlightening each other, and speaking of Me always, they are contented and rejoice. To these worshippers of Mine, always controlled, I give a steady mind by which they may approach Me, for I loved them first."

This and very much else that is similar will be found in Hindu literature, yet always the shadow of self-satisfied monism stalks behind it. And in monism there can be no love — there is ecstasy and trance and deep peace, what Ruysbroek calls "rest", but there cannot be the ecstasy of union nor the loss of self in God which is the goal of Christian, Muslim, and all theistic mysticism.

And all of this equally applies to the occult field, today, whether it be Qabalistic or structured according to any other fashion. And we need to take care, for a device such as the Qabalistic Tree of Life, or any similar occult philosophical 'construct', by its universality, can be regarded in either fashion.

The Tree of Life has been construed as a monist system by most modern occult writers, though to the original Jewish Qabalists and the original translators and interpreters of the Qabalah to Christian Europe, such as Pico della Mirandola, it was a theistic vision and an aid by which to love and see God as well as to understand his creation.

Returning to Ruysbroek to emphasise this point, for it can hardly be overstressed:

> And therefore all those men are deceived whose intention it is to sink themselves in natural rest, and who do not seek God with desire nor find Him in delectable love. For the rest which they possess consists in an emptying of themselves to which they are inclined by nature and by habit. And in this natural rest men cannot find God. But it brings man indeed into an emptiness which heathens and Jews are able to find, and all men, however evil they may be, if they live in their sins with untroubled conscience, and are able to empty themselves of all images and all action. In this emptiness rest is sufficient and great, and it is in itself no sin, for it is in all men by nature, if they know how to make themselves empty.

And the issue is summed up by Professor Zaehner:

> ... there are two distinct and mutually opposed types of mysticism — the monist and the theistic. This is not a question of Christianity and Islam versus Hinduism and Buddhism; it is an unbridgeable gulf between all those who see God as incomparably greater than oneself, though He is, at the same time, the root and ground of one's being, and those who maintain that soul and God are one and the same and that all else is pure illusion. For them Christian mysticism is simply bhakti or devotion to a personal God carried to ludicrous extremes, whereas for the theist, the monist's idea of "liberation" is simply the realisation of his immortal soul in separation from God, and is only, as Junayd pointed out, a stage in the path of the beginner. He is still in the bondage of original sin.

> Hinduism has its theists as well as its monists. This is a quarrel that cuts clean across the conventional distinctions of creeds. In each of the great religions there have been upholders of both doctrines. Even Christianity has not completely avoided the monistic extreme even though it makes nonsense of its basic doctrine that God is Love.

Let us place this on the Tree of Life then, remembering that the Tree of Life is but a card index system that can be applied to discuss (with reverence) the attributes of God, or to codify the structure of God's Creation, whether inner or outer.

The original Jewish Qabalah speaks of the highest level of the Tree (Atziluth) as being infallible — almost too holy for contemplation. This is reflected in the Gentile Qabalistic occult tradition not to use the King Scale of Colours as being too dangerous for ordinary meditation work —

the Queen Scale (of Briah), attributed to the Archangelic level, being the colour scale made most familiar in the literature. Let us try to express this diagrammatically, by the Four Worlds drawn laterally, from left to right, with a ground plan underneath of how the plan might be applied to a single Tree conceived in another dimension (Figure 20).

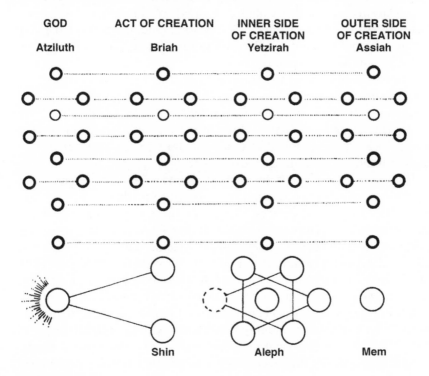

Figure 20

When considering the Tree in Atziluth we may regard the traditional Sephirothic qualities as our stumbling attempts to make some description of God — as One God (Kether), All-Wise (Chokmah), All-Understanding (Binah), Benevolent (Chesed), Just (Geburah), Beautiful (Tiphareth), Powerful (Netzach), Glorious (Hod), Strong and Pure (Yesod) and Stable and Orderly (Malkuth).

It may help the Christian to anthropomorphise this in the figure of Jesus, God made Man. The Jewish Qabalist (not being Christian) also anthropomorphised it into the figure of a Great Countenance. It is not one that may appeal to the modern Christian but it is valid as an expression of love and reverence for a personal *God*. This is what we want to emphasise. The Tree in Atziluth is not simply a set of abstract concepts as is sometimes implied, but the lineaments of the living God, as discerned by certain of his human creatures.

The next level — the Act of Creation, which some may see as a level of Archangelic powers that may ensoul the archetypal patterns of our Cube of Space, may be regarded essentially as the creation and stabilisation in inter-relationship (the Chokmah and Binah of the horizontal Tree) of the qualities of Unity or Coherence, Wisdom, Understanding, Rulership, Justice or Fairness, Beauty or Harmonisation, Power, Glory, Strength and Purity, and stable Foundation.

From this emanation of patterned qualities the psychic stresses of these qualities are formed in Prime Matter (the Virgin of the World) which concrete finally into the outer world of the physical creation.

On the Qabalistic Tree of Life framework we see a method of theosophical classification that is able to take in the concept of both Creator and the Creation.

This is not so evident in Eastern forms of occult diagrammatic speculation, which often depend on a structure made up of projections of the human psychic centres. From this there is posited a planetary head, heart, sacral centre and so on, a similar set of solar centres, a more comprehensive one based on seven solar systems, and so on into infinity until an ultimate (as far as human understanding goes) One About Whom Naught May Be Said. To our mind, a OAWNMBS is a poor substitute for the Living God who became man and took up manhood into Godhead.

It is however quite possible to bring the Eastern system into line with the Qabalistic insight by aligning the chakras with the central Sephiroth of the Tree of Life. But what has tended to happen in modern Gentile Qabalistic exegesis is the reverse: the Tree of Life has been aligned with the chakras and then projected into space, as it were, like the psychic centres of the Hindu based system. This is an error that betrays and runs counter to the whole religious and mystical tradition of the Jewish Qabalah.

An interesting half-way house position is seen in an inspirational work by Dion Fortune called *The Cosmic Doctrine*. Here the evolution of God is claimed to be represented and it all starts off in a vast cosmic analogy of 'inner space' moving and forming itself into an opposition with itself and thus building into more and more complex forms until a spherical figure subdivided into twelve 'rays' and seven 'planes' is formed, within which are 'atomic' consciousnesses, or 'Great Entities', one of which becomes the God of our Solar System.

So far it is identical with much Hindu theological speculation. But there is then a radical difference. Each God 'projects' or 'creates' its own universe, using as its helpers in this act of creation the lesser 'entities' grouped around it, some of whom include you and me, the human race, in our essential essences.

If it were a universe so created, and not just a solar system, this could well be in line with Western Christian theological tradition, but each God being allocated to a solar system shows a polytheistic Hindu influence. The book claims to unify the polytheistic and monotheistic in that while there are many gods spread throughout the Galaxies, each God is omnipotent and omniscient to its own Universe.

There is however, a difficulty here, for if God is all that there is, God-wise, to his created Universe, then by definition it is impossible for any of his creatures to be conscious of what lies beyond him. It can only be conjecture passed off as revelation — and this is largely what *The Cosmic Doctrine* (in common with other such cosmologies) seems to be. And the fact that the conjecture may be on the part of an 'inner plane' communicator really adds nothing to its claims to accuracy.

The inner psychic structure of every heavenly body reflects the archetypal pattern of the universe. From the point of view of a subjective consciousness within such a planetary etheric sphere, with no consciousness of the presence of God, God may well be identified with the totality of that which is perceived, with the additional supposition that beyond the limits of apparent awareness all is formless chaos or 'unmanifest'.

But in reality all is held within God. And the true state of affairs is the converse of what so appears to such a soul, whose 'fallen' viewpoint has robbed the whole dynamic of love and life, so that the forms seem mechanical and bound by inexorable laws.

It is to such souls that reincarnation may be a necessity, for in a discarnate state they are less able to re-identify with the spiritual archetype of humanity and of nature which is in the Mind of God.

God is utterly unimaginable to man — just as a thought in a mind cannot imagine the person in whose mind it resides. We do best, if we must use analogies to try to describe God, to go to the warmth of human relationships rather than to the cold abstraction of geometric shapes, illuminating though the latter can be if properly approached — as for instance through contemplation of the Platonic solids or the insights of Projective Geometry.

If we start from the axiom that man is made in the image of God this must mean that he has the autonomous freedom of will to act towards the rest of the Creation, and even to God, as he sees fit. His actions, however, will affect the quality of life, and if they are out of harmony with reality then he will bring suffering upon himself and the lives of all about him.

But there is also the response of God to man. And any abuse of man's free will and creativity is met by the redeeming love of God. This may work through the integrity of other men (on inner or outer planes) or indeed through other kingdoms, such as the angelic. Every grave error is compensated for in some way, thus adding to fallen life a quality of redeeming love that was not there before.

The Fall of Man was not a once for all thing in some historical past but is repeated over and over again by every individual who fails to live according to his or her own creative spiritual integrity. This causes more unbalance and suffering but at the same time gives the opportunity for further intercession of God's redeeming love.

The Redemption of Sin brought by Christ at the Incarnation is often too narrowly understood. It was, and is, a mark of the forgiveness and redemption of *all* human error, past, present and yet to come. By our sin we make the universe a prison house for ourselves. But this is transformed by God's redeeming love into a school for godhead, with the earth as a classroom and the angels and saints of God as the teachers. The curriculum of the school is the realisation and acceptance of the reality of our own sinfulness, and the seeking with all our heart, mind and strength for the love of the God whom we have rejected. This is not a matter of learning 'obedience' in its usual submissive or authoritarian sense, but the learning of love, from which obedience, or common purpose, naturally follows.

The pattern laid before us in the Incarnation is that of the Risen Christ. And we must learn to live the life of the Risen Christ, even if in the current fallen state of our physical existence it may have to be by faith. This applies to the individual life of every one of us and it applies to the human race as a whole. Our whole 'progress' is more a matter of lurching from one fallen state to another — although in another sense it is a continual demonstration of our God-given creativeness and the continuing love of God.

The technological progress, for instance, of the last two or three centuries is but an intellectual rediscovery of much that was intuitively known to man in ancient times. Great ancient works of civil engineering still remain, a testimony to what could be achieved without benefit of modern reason-based technology.

It is human reason that seems to have got out of hand, and although valuable in its own right and just proportion, to have usurped the role of intuition.

The intuitive faculty gives an appreciation of the archetypal structure of the created universe, and our rightful place within it, in relation to God and our fellow creatures. And the principal method of training and regaining the intuitive faculty is by the practice of occult meditation.

Such meditation has its dangers, but if we have integrity of purpose then we have little to fear in terms of temptation to the abuse of inner power. And meditation is best done, and indeed is more effective, if performed as an act of worship. It may then lead on to the state of contemplation.

However, meditation without worship is better than no meditation at all, and it has been found that such meditation, when it opens up the intuitive faculty, naturally leads on to a realisation of the need for worship, because of the awakened intuitional awareness of the relationship of the soul to God.

Meditation leading to contemplation is indeed the highest form of worship for it involves the whole being; and a realisation of the archetypal configurations of the inner as well as the outer creation, subjective and objective, and of their relation to God, the Creator of them all.

It is one of the results of the Fall that the practice of meditation and action has been so scandalously neglected by the institutional Christian churches. This has reached the point where they themselves are as overbalanced with a rational theology as science is with a rational methodology. On the other hand, and to a large extent because of this, a number of intuitionally aware people have turned to oriental systems of meditational technique. But because of the lack of sound theological basis by which to test their intuitive insights, much irrelevant and dubious speculation has been allowed to run wild under the guise of 'ancient wisdom'.

This results in the monist bias of which we have spoken; and in confusing the Creator with the creation in an abstract form of pantheism, or putting God in the position of a remote grey eminence in inner cosmic space. What in fact has happened is that a fallen, telescope's eye view of the outer universe has been used as an inverted archetypal image for the inner universe.

It is true that life revolves in cycles, and that there are cycles within cycles, but we lose a whole dimension of reality if we see it all as a cosmic machine of inexorable Law. Rather is it a great and joyful dance, created by the Cosmic Christ (the Word that was in the beginning) and actively participated in by the Risen Christ (the Word made flesh) as Lord of the Dance.

The dance is created upon archetypal patterns, acting upon all levels and in many different ways. There are, for instance, archetypes of race and nation, and the concept of a rootless international man is a dangerous, even demonic, one. Man needs to have a home, and roots, and though we do not suggest that all should be serfs bound to their native village, there is certainly much truth in the idea that man is, in an archetypal way, the conscious rational mind of the countryside he inhabits. Jung, the psychologist, has pointed out that the soil has this effect upon races, and that this occurs even with physical characteristics — the modern American, of very mixed origin, beginning to take on some of the characteristics of the Red Indian, his predecessor in walking the American lands.

Other archetypes are revealed in number — the three, four, six, seven, twelve and thirteen, for example. The roots of these are revealed in mathematics. The four sided figure is the simplest Platonic solid, and consists of four three-sided planes. Six circles of equal diameter will exactly encircle a seventh, and twelve spheres exactly enclose a thirteenth. In man the five is of importance, the spiritual factor in the Cross of the Elements, expressed magically in the Rose Cross or the Pentagram. All these show the archetypal patterning of the universe — which does not mean we should worship them — but rather regard them as pointers to their Creator.

And we must also avoid the danger of building them into a philosophical system — for an archetypal construct, useful though it may be as a tool of magical operation upon the inner side of creation is not necessarily the secret pattern of the entire cosmos — still less an anatomical diagram or electro-encephalograph of the mind of God.

A great deal of the cosmology which has been mediumistically conveyed to occult investigators by denizens of the Inner Creation emanates not from a vantage point on a par with, or even beyond the limits of God, but from the psychic structure of the inner Earth. There is, as we have said, sufficient archetypal correspondence between the psychic structure of the planetary spheres (as indeed in the auric sphere of man, and the stellar sphere of the inner solar system), for such cosmologies to contain great glimpses of truth, but their whole contextual terms of reference may be in error. In a way it can be rather like describing a molecule and thinking it a universe. Parallels exist but there are considerable differences of size and function!

Just as one atom has similarities with a solar system, because built on the same 'star and satellite' archetypal pattern, or the sea shell in the ocean resembles in its shape the whirl of intergalactic nebulae, so revelations of the psychic structure of the Earth, described by the Earthbound, may give the appearance of an entire universe. In *The Cosmic Doctrine* for example, spiritual beings are described in terms of 'atoms'. It has a certain validity. One could equally talk of human beings in terms of cells in an organism, or bees in a hive. Yet whatever unusual perspective this might give to archetypal interrelationships, when the fabric of human life is kept in mind such a conception is basically dehumanising — just as when applied to God it is basically, if unintentionally, blasphemous.

Unfortunately our scientific method tends to deceive us into regarding such microscopic-eyepiece world-views as somehow 'objective' and so the more true. One is reminded of the type of modern man who bares his soul at the slightest opportunity, thinking it demonstrates intellectual integrity, honesty and courage, whereas what it more often indicates is a lack of moral integrity, social values or shame. The objective becomes the inhuman — and ultimately the demonic. Such a person can become badly cut off from forming any worthwhile human relationship. The relationships of family will seem to be petty, parochial, tame, platitudinous, limiting as compared to what is considered to be a wider vision. Yet this 'wider vision' is in reality a constricting shell. And until the shell breaks no real life or love can get in.

So for many 'teachers' on the 'inner planes' the universe they see may be but the psychic structure of 'sheol' or 'Hades', the shadow world of the astro-etheric counterpart of the physical globe. Because they have no conscious love awareness of God they think they understand God in the analogies of the archetypal nuts and bolts of the inside of Creation. Earthbound as they may be, they may regard themselves perhaps as 'advanced souls' who could have gone off to higher spheres but have elected to stay behind to teach their 'lesser evolved' brethren. The definitions are their own, though shared by those, their disciples, who are prepared to accept them at their own valuation. And such disciples are encouraged in their belief by the teaching that they themselves are 'advanced' and 'elect' because they have been selected to receive such teachings! It is something of a vicious circle — a spiritual trap — even black hole!

To such souls, God and the Creation are one. But man was saved from the limitations of this earthbound discarnate state by the Incarnate Christ and specifically by his 'preaching to the spirits in prison', in his descent into hell (i.e. *sheol*, or Hades, the underworld of the dead, not the punitive Hell of medieval speculation).

It should hardly be necessary to say that those spirits who elected to remain in prison will not be piteous squalling creatures conscious of their own ineffable loss, but proud spirits very content with their own views of the entire universe and ever ready to impress their views on others. They may even appear very reasonable and even spiritual, if in a muted kind of way.

By their fruits shall we know them. And this must remain an individual assessment. But there seems to be a lamentable lack of stature amongst the esoterics of this type, despite the high claims (often given in terms of modesty) as compared to the stature of the mystics of the Church, however handicapped some of these may have been by physical, psychological or social disadvantages. St. John of the Cross is, for instance, sometimes cited as being a manic depressive — but for a manic depressive to achieve what he achieved betokens an inner stature somewhat out of the ordinary.

The Word, the Son of God, the creative principle of the Godhead (reflected in man by the primary imagination in Coleridge's sense) abides at the centre of Creation and is also at every heart of every lesser part of the creation, just as he is at the heart of every human being — unless denied or rejected.

The same might be said for any human institution. Institutionalisation reflects a human need, and is based on an archetypal hierarchical structure, but if the loving heart of God is not beating at its centre then it can become a dire charade — even if masquerading under a guise of piety.

It is for this reason that Jesus referred to himself as the Way, the Truth and the Life, for without that active principle of divine love in human form the way is crooked, the truth obscured and the life diseased.

Christ is like the Fool in the Morris dancers. The Morris dancers consist of a side of twelve men dancing in a set of patterns and thus representing human conformity to archetypal laws. The Fool, on the other hand, skips around at will with a blown-up pig's bladder, not destroying or disrupting the dance, but in an expression of free will in unfettered relation to the dance.

The same could be said of the Tarot pack wherein much midnight oil has been expended on disquisitions as to where the Fool should be positioned in the array of Tarot Trumps. The very fact that the Fool defies the most strenuous efforts of men to codify and categorise him into a fixed place in the system demonstrates his validity and the redeeming wisdom behind the Tarot that defies the categorising efforts of modern intellectualising savants.

The Fool is the Christ. And it is interesting to note the divinatory definitions given to the card by various commentators — which range from 'great wisdom' to 'madness and folly'. And no doubt in terms of Mr Worldly Wiseman, the life of Christ, and indeed of those who follow him, is an exemplification of madness and folly — an idealistic Jewish youth, with delusions of grandeur based on theological speculation, and some natural healing gift, who met his deserts as an alleged political criminal.

So the Christ (as Fool) prevents the man-operated archetypal system from clogging up. And he can be hard put to do this — and not least of all within his own Church, in whatever of its denominations. It can also happen at the individual level — producing that walking bureaucracy, the ecclesiastical bigot. An indication of this state is when 'Christianity' becomes more important than Christ. As Coleridge put it: 'He who begins by loving Christianity better than truth will proceed by loving his own sect or church better than Christianity, and end in loving himself better than all.'

The emphasis on truth is an important one. If Jesus is the Way, the Truth and the Life, any genuine searching after the truth, even though it may appear to move away from him, can only end in coming closer to him. Thus the importance of free will and spiritual integrity.

This has been exemplified by a very typical modern 'saint', who although having a tremendous influence on modem theological thought, never became a formal member of the church. This was Simone Weil.

It may help us if we take and examine the vision of this very modern follower of Christ in conjunction with the great medieval vision exemplified in Dante. They provide two poles, between which we may best chart our course in the work that is to come.

In the vision of Dante as described in *The Divine Comedy* the poet finds himself wandering in a dark wood striving to make his way to a fair green hill, as in a nightmare world, he finds himself unable to get to this land of desire. The wood grows ever more dark and entangled, and he finally finds, to his horror, that he is also being stalked, and cut off from the green hill irrevocably by three ravening beasts — a leopard, a lion and a wolf.

The wood is indicative of the Physical World in which he finds himself, and the green hill the state of Earthly Paradise towards which he fruitlessly strives. Not only is his striving in vain because he does not know the way, but he is also stalked by his own sinfulness, which can be categorised into three types of sin. Those of the leopard include the sins of youth — perversity of appetite, lust, gluttony, squandering, hoarding, wrath. Those of the lion are principally of violence, either to oneself or to others, or indeed against nature, art or God. Whilst those of the wolf are the more devious and deceitful sins of pandering, seduction, flattery, hypocrisy, theft, fraud and treason.

Beginning to despair, in his terror Dante is almost relieved to see a ghostly figure standing before him, who reveals himself to be the great poet and philosopher of pagan antiquity, Virgil. Virgil may be taken to represent the higher reason in man, the highest reaches of wisdom that man can get by his own efforts. He undertakes to guide Dante to the Earthly Paradise, and has indeed been assigned to do this from Heaven, but it is needful that the way they go is through the kingdom of Hell.

Dante agrees and they make their way to a great cave leading down into the earth which forms the mouth of Hell. Here the first thing they meet before actually getting to Hell, the spiritual condition of the wicked, is a great mob aimlessly running backward and forward after a banner

— the army of the futile, those who are neither very good nor very bad but simply aimless when it comes to the direction of their Spiritual Will. Those who have really hardly attained humanity, nor made any real use of the gifts that distinguish them from the animal kingdom.

Dante and Virgil cross the River Acheron that divides the futile from Hell and find first a kind of sealed off area, that appears to be a reasonably pleasant place to live in. This is Limbo, wherein reside the great virtuous pagans. Those who, like Virgil, and this is where he comes from, have lived good lives according to their lights and so, although free from the pains that afflict the sinful in Hell or Purgatory, are not yet capable of the great beatitude that Heaven offers.

We should, in this and all that follows, bear in mind that what is being portrayed so vividly, and often in so ghastly a fashion, is not a crude method of punishing the wicked. It is the condition that souls inflict upon themselves through their own volition. And although Dante describes actual people in various parts of hell, either contemporaries of his or well known historical or literary personages, what we are really being shown are archetypal images for each particular type of sin.

So the Inferno is not a geographical description of an actual metaphysical place, but a review of the state of soul that may be associated with various human weaknesses and errors. Those in Limbo, for instance, are not there by historical accident because they happened to be born before Christ. They are those who prefer their own wisdom to that of the revelation of God. Whilst deeper in the bowels of Hell the various predicaments and torments we meet exemplify the self destructive, self-tormenting condition of soul, actual or potential, in every man.

Generally speaking the sins get worse and worse as Virgil and Dante proceed into Hell, which is structured like a dark terraced funnel going down to the very centre of the Earth.

At the commencement of Hell great storm clouds of lust are seen blowing figures through the sky, two of whom come to speak to Virgil and Dante. These are Paolo and Francesca, who tell of how they softly dallied over a book about Lancelot and Guinevere and their illicit love, and then, lingering upon that thought, drifted into an adulterous relationship themselves. Here is exemplified, in a very tender fashion, the first dangerous, seemingly innocent, flirting with the idea of sin, and then sliding down the gentle slope of declining standards into sin proper.

From this not altogether horrific condition of being blown about in constant tempests Virgil and Dante pass on to the more disgusting results of the sins of the appetite, from the gluttonous wallowing in mire like pigs, to the continual bickering and mutual condemnation of the misers and the spendthrifts and the frightening circle of the wrathful.

Here they come to a city — the great dark towering walls of the City of Dis — the perverted reflection of the Heavenly City. Here even Virgil blanches as they are taunted from the walls by demons and furies. But by revealing his Heavenly mandate Virgil is able to compel the horrors to let them in.

Upon entering the city we move from the sins of appetite (those of the leopard) to those of violence (those of the lion), passing the circle of the heretics. We should here perhaps strike a note of caution. We must not over-react to medieval Christian terms. To get the most from Dante we need to forget the abuses of ecclesiastical organisation and to concentrate upon the actual root meaning of his terms. Thus heresy, as understood in this approach to Dante, is not a disagreement with the ideas of ruling church dignitaries, but wilful disregard of *truth*. And in this sense heresy is a condition developing from that of those souls in Limbo — it is a condition of wilful ignorance as opposed to contentment with natural ignorance. (Dante later reveals that there are pagans in Heaven — those who remain in Hell or Limbo do so only by their own choice.)

We proceed from here to the hellish circles of those who have done violence to their neighbours (and are appropriately immersed in a river of boiling blood); those who have done violence to themselves (the wood of suicides, who are transformed into the vegetable life of withered trees); and the violent against nature (in a burning lifeless desert — perhaps indicative of what we are preparing for ourselves ecologically with our technological violence against the planet!)

We mention the torments allocated by Dante merely to warn against reading this part of *The Divine Comedy* in the wrong manner. It can be read like a grand guignol horror film script, but whilst the punishments described by Dante have a certain appropriateness and validity, we should try to get to the psychological reality behind the horrors described. Dante intended his writings to be understood on four levels of meaning and there is not a single image he uses which has not been carefully selected and which does not contain many ramifications and depths accessible to thought and meditation.

There then comes a great barrier before the steep descent of terraces confine those who are marked by the sins of the wolf, consisting for the most part of malicious frauds, until at the very deepest and darkest part of the funnel of Hell come the traitors, with the arch traitor, Judas Iscariot, at the base, crunched in the teeth of the Devil.

The Devil is a huge figure, encased in ice, at the centre of the Earth. The beating of his great dark wings forms a desert of ice all about him. Here is the ultimate degradation. Death in life and life in death. Utter isolation.

But Virgil guides Dante past this great figure of perverted will along a narrow passage that comes out eventually at the other side of the world, to the isle of Purgatory, which is represented as a high steep mountain up which the sinful but repentant can climb. It is important for us to realise that the horrors of Hell are only for the unrepentant — those who deliberately choose and wallow in their evil. And again we must realise that many of us *do* prefer the enjoyment of evil to the enjoyment of good.

There is, as with Hell, a kind of antechamber condition, and on the low terraces about Mount Purgatory are those who opted out of Hell almost by technicalities at the last possible moment. Dante sees these as the excommunicate who repented their defiance of truth only at the last moment, with no time for formal reconciliation or satisfaction.

There are three other types of late-repentant. The first and lowest of these are the indolent, those who — though in the fold of the saved — were too idle to care very much or to make much effort. The second degree are those who died by violence or unexpectedly and so were deprived to some extent by circumstance from putting themselves right with God. And the third degree are those who failed in their religious duty because preoccupied with other affairs.

After these we enter the seven cornices of Purgatory proper, and this can only be done by going through Peter's Gate, which has three steps to it, indicative of Confession, Contrition and Satisfaction. Again we should not be put off by these terms but read them in a universal rather than ecclesiastical context.

If we have turned our love and will away from the Love and Will of God then the first requisite is that we recognise the fact. This is what is meant by Confession. It is a confession of unpalatable truth to oneself. The ceasing to kid oneself any more.

Following from this must come Contrition. Some sorrow for the evil done — although perhaps unfashionable in our objective and psychoanalytic times — is a *sine qua non* for the health of the soul, for it shows an ability to appreciate the relative values of good and evil.

And finally, if the Confession and Contrition are sincere, will come the desire to give Satisfaction — to make amends in some way for all the evil that is past.

This opens the way to the purification of the soul that is symbolised by Purgatory. Those of us brought up in a Protestant tradition tend to look askance at the doctrine of Purgatory and Hell. But properly understood they give very revealing insights to the condition and purification of the soul. Hell is self-chosen — no one is in that condition unless they want to be. Purgatory is not a vindictive torture any more than Hell is. It is a cleansing process. And many who would wrongly object to the concept of Purgation as commonly understood (or misunderstood) may quite happily accept the thought expressed it terms of evolution, or alchemical purification and transmutation.

In Purgatory the root difference from Hell is that love is an under-lying factor of all. However, in the lower reaches of Purgatory that love may be misdirected, into proud, envious or wrathful channels. In mid-Purgatory is defective love, where the principle difficulty to be overcome is sloth. Whilst in the higher reaches of Purgatory are the levels of excessive love for a secondary object, manifesting as covetousness, gluttony or lust.

It may be discerned that the levels of Purgatory correspond to the traditional Seven Deadly Sins — Pride, Envy, Wrath, Sloth, Covetousness, Gluttony, Lust. These sins also appeared in Hell, but in Hell they were revelled in for their own sake. In Purgatory they are recognised as sin and efforts are made to recognise this fact and to try to grow out of them.

At the summit of this Christian initiatory way is the Earthly Paradise, a fair green place that is recognised as the Hill towards which Dante was striving when we first met him in the enchanted wood, when, hounded by the spectres of sin, the leopard, the lion and wolf, he was saved by Virgil — representative of the higher reason, the highest level to which man, unaided by the grace and revelation of God, can aspire.

Whilst Virgil was able to guide Dante (though not without risk) through the depths of human folly in Hell, it is notable that through Purgatory, the ascent of which requires a love of God assisted by Divine Grace, he is less able to guide, and needs to be assisted by various souls already resident there. At the environs of the Earthly Paradise however, Virgil can come no further and has to give way to the heavenly figure of Beatrice.

Beatrice was the Florentine girl for whom Dante conceived a great romantic love. This is described in his earlier little book *La Vite Nuova* — *The New Life*, which is also a manual of romantic poetry. In the sense of *The Divine Comedy* she represents the vision of perfection of the love of God, projected onto a human person.

Having reached the Earthly Paradise, the condition in which the Earth should be if we had not fallen into sin and degradation, Dante is conducted into the Heavens.

It will be of interest to Qabalists that these correspond to the Sephiroth of the Tree of Life. Dante is of course using the Ptolemaic astronomical system whereby the planets are seen as being attached to concentric spheres revolving about the Earth. That this has been discarded by modern physical science need not deter us, the inner validity remains.

The first three Heavens, those of the Moon, Mercury and Venus are within the shadow of Earth and they are marred by a certain dichotomy.

They are inhabited respectively by those who, though participators in the bliss of heaven, are in a relatively lowly state of it because of the counter-attraction of various Earthly pleasures.

The 1st Heaven (the Moon) is inhabited by those who have been inconstant in their vows.
The 2nd Heaven (Mercury) by those with ambitions in the outer, or active, life of the world.
The 3rd Heaven (Venus) by those who love others, besides God, with a consuming passion.

Once beyond the shadow of Earth the Heavens are inhabited by those appropriate to their type.

The 4th Heaven (the Sun) by teachers, historians and theologians.
The 5th Heaven (Mars) by warriors.
The 6th Heaven (Jupiter) by the just.
The 7th Heaven (Saturn) by contemplatives and martyrs.

From here there is a Celestial Ladder to the 8th Heaven (the Fixed Stars) wherein Dante meets Christ, the Blessed Virgin Mary, Saints Peter, James and John and also Adam.

There is much very deep symbolism and teaching in all of this. Adam is the prototype of fallen man, a forerunner of Dante himself as Everyman. The Blessed Virgin Mary is the prototype of unfallen humanity, the redeemed Eve, the forerunner of Beatrice. The three saints are those particularly close to Christ, who witnessed the Transfiguration, when Christ demonstrated the unfallen or redeemed state of Resurrection on Earth before his Passion.

We will not go into all these ramifications here. It is really a matter for individual meditation and contemplation, but we wish simply to point out that there are deep symbolic Mysteries in the orthodox Christian tradition far outweighing in depth and richness any attenuated or orientalised 'esoteric' Christianity.

In the 9th Heaven, the Crystalline Sphere of the Primum Mobile (Kether on the Tree of Life) are the angelic hierarchies beyond which, in the Qabalistic Ain Soph, or Limitless Light, is found the 10th and ultimate Heaven, corresponding astronomically to the Empyrean, where is seen a great white Mystic Rose.

This image of the Rose represents the ultimate Heavenly reality, for all the company of Heaven are gathered here, like petals about the golden centre of God. All the apparent denizens of the lower heavens were no more than projections of the spiritual beings who make up this Heavenly Rose, the *rosa mystica*.

It is this Rose which, in the Rosicrucian tradition, is blood red and fixed to the Elemental Cross of Matter.

Beatrice is transformed in radiance at this point, her function (amongst many) of personification of Divine Truth, or True Theology, giving way to the Revealed Presence of Truth Itself. Her place as guide is taken by St. Bernard of Clairvaux who undertakes the final instruction of Dante before he comes face to face with God himself, the Three in One, symbolically expressed as three spheres.

We can only quote directly from Dorothy L. Sayers' gloss of her translation of *The Divine Comedy* to give some indication of how it concludes (or perhaps the credit should go to Barbara Reynolds, who completed the work after Miss Sayers' death):

> The final vision, the crown and climax of the whole work, consists of two revelations. First, Dante perceives in the Divine Light the form, or exemplar, of all creation. All things that exist in themselves ('substance'), all aspects or properties of being ('accident'), all mutual relations ('mode') are seen bound together in one single concept. The Universe is *in* God. Next, having glimpsed the whole of creation, Dante beholds the Creator. He sees three circles, of three colours, yet of one dimension. One seems to be reflected from the other, and the third, like flame, proceeds equally from both (the Father, Son and Holy Ghost). Then as he gazes, the reflected circle shows within itself the human form, coloured with the circle's own hue. As Dante strives to comprehend how human nature is united with the Word, a ray of divine light so floods his mind that his desire is at rest. At this point the vision ceases, and the story ends with the poet's will and desire moving in perfect co-ordination with the love of God.

Or, as it is contained in the closing stanza of the poem:

> High phantasy lost power and here broke off;
> Yet, as a wheel moves smoothly, free from jars,
> My will and my desire were turned by love,
>
> The love that moves the sun and the other stars.

The Divine Comedy is not an entirely easy work to read, containing many local allusions to Florentine politics of the thirteenth century, and replete with medieval horrors and much piety and scholastic metaphysic that do not make things easy for the modern reader. However, it is certainly no more difficult than the esoteric texts or early oriental religious scriptures that many students of the occult spend much time and trouble on.

It is also much, much, more rewarding, and is rooted in the European Christian heritage and tradition. It is well worth purchasing a copy and making your own diagrammatic representation of Dante's vision. This will enable you to avoid some of the difficulties of the text and to get more value from the general conception and structure. This exercise will in turn make the text more readily understandable.

But by way of counterbalance from this great high medieval vision we can turn briefly to a modern Christian, hailed by some as a saint, but who was so devoted to Christ she refused to have anything to do with the institutional church. This was Simone Weil (1909-42), who demonstrates another, perhaps polar opposite (yet in another sense identical) identification with the Heart of the Universe.

Concerned always with the ideal of rigorous honesty in her search for truth she made herself intimately acquainted with the afflictions of the human condition, working for extended periods in the Renault car factory and as an agricultural labourer. She also spent time with the Republican Army in Spain on the Catalonian front. Always in poor health, her last illness was aggravated by the fact that she refused to eat anything more than her compatriots in German occupied France. She was a qualified teacher of philosophy and a particularly deep student of Greek and Hindu philosophy — which she read in the original Greek and Sanskrit. Of her experience of the worst that modern society can do to the unprivileged she wrote: 'What I went through then marked me in so lasting a manner that still today when any human being, whoever he may be and in whatever circumstances, speaks to me without brutality, I cannot help having the impression that there must be a mistake...'

Her experience of the power and reality of the Christ came just before the War. She had acquired an acquaintance with the English metaphysical poets and had learned by heart George Herbert's *Love*, which she used to recite to herself as a distraction to help her through the violent headaches she used to suffer. It goes:

> Love bade me welcome: yet my soul drew back.
>   Guiltie of dust and sinne.
> But quick-ey'd Love, observing me grow slack
>   From my first entrance in.
> Drew nearer to me, sweetly questioning
>   If I lack'd any thing.
> 'A guest,' I answer'd, 'worthy to be here:'
>   Love said, 'You shall be he.'

'I the unkinde, ungrateful? Ah my deare,
    I cannot look on thee.'
Love took my hand, and smiling did reply,
    'Who made the eyes but I? '
'Truth Lord, but I have marr'd them: let my shame
    Go where it doth deserve.'
'And know you not, sayes Love, who bore the blame? '
    'My deare, then I will serve.'
'You must sit down.' says Love, 'and taste my meat:'
    So I did sit and eat.

It was during one of these recitations, she recounts in her spiritual autobiography, that:

> Christ himself came down and took possession of me. In my arguments about the insolubility of the problem of God I had never foreseen the possibility of that, or a real contact, person to person, here below, between a human being and God. I had vaguely heard tell of things of this kind, but I had never believed in them. In the Fioretti the accounts of apparitions rather put me off if anything, like the miracles in the Gospel. Moreover, in this sudden possession of me by Christ, neither my senses nor my imagination had any part; I only felt in the midst of my suffering the presence of a love, like that which one can read in the smile on a beloved face.

> I had never read any mystical works because I had never felt any call to read them ... God in his mercy had prevented me from reading the mystics, so that it should be evident to me that I had not invented this absolutely unexpected contact.

> Yet I still half refused, not my love but my intelligence. For it seemed to me certain and I still think so today, that one can never wrestle enough with God if one does so out of pure regard for the truth. Christ likes us to prefer truth to him because, before being Christ, he is truth. If one turns aside from him to go towards truth, one will not go far before falling into his arms.

> After this I came to feel that Plato was a mystic, that all the Iliad is bathed in Christian light, and that Dionysus and Osiris are in a certain sense Christ himself; and my love was thereby redoubled.

> I never wondered whether Jesus was or was not the incarnation of God; but in fact I was incapable of thinking of him without thinking of him as God.

She then goes on to discuss her reading of the Bhagavad Gita and her later difficulties and realisations about prayer, which really resolved themselves by simply repeating the Lord's Prayer, as indeed C.S. Lewis records, he found quite adequate for himself for years after his own unexpected conversion.

One of Simone Weil's great contributions has been her inclusiveness that prevented her from formally joining the Church because this would make her part of an exclusive organisation. She writes:

> Christianity should contain all vocations without exception since it is catholic. In consequence the Church should also. But in my eyes Christianity is catholic by right but not in fact. So many things are outside it, so many things that I love and do not want to give up, so many things that God loves, otherwise they would not be in existence. All the immense stretches of past centuries, except the last twenty are among them; all countries inhabited by coloured races; all secular life in the white people's countries; in the history of those countries, all the traditions banned as heretical, those of the Manicheans, and Albigensian for instance; all those things resulting from the Renaissance, too often degraded but not quite without value.

This and much more can be examined in the paperback volume which contains her spiritual biography and letters, entitled *Waiting on God*.

It is with some of these "things resulting from the Renaissance, too often degraded but not quite without value" that we have been mainly concerned about in this book. But now having cleared the ground and formulated the foundations, we can go on to examine its practical applications in the final part of this work.

EXERCISE FOR CHAPTER VIII

A lamp is there for you to light your way,
I am your way, your Light, your Destination.

Having performed all the preceding exercises described at the ends of the Chapters so far, be aware of standing in the Upper Room, at your place at the Round Table, with the presence of the Christ before you, holding before him bread and wine and also a brilliant lantern.

Imagine him giving you of the bread to eat, at the same time that he says, 'Take, eat: This is my Body that is given you for you. Do this in remembrance of me.'

Then feel him giving you of the Cup to drink saying, 'Drink ye all of this: for this is my Blood of the New Covenant which is shed for you and for many for the remission of sins. Do this, as oft as ye shall drink it, in remembrance of me.'

Then hear him say, 'My peace I leave you, my peace I give unto you' and take the lamp from him and hold it aloft.

You should then recite the Lord's Prayer slowly, reflecting upon each phrase.

CHAPTER IX

The Winding Stair

One of the most important influences that Dante had was on a fellow Florentine, over a century later, Marsilio Ficino, from whom stems the greater part of Renaissance magic.

Ficino was another of those important figures we find from time to time in our study, standing at the crossroads of two cultures in an esoteric or religious sense. He was employed by Cosimo de Medici as a translator of the ancient Greek texts that were just being rediscovered and which brought in the second phase of the Renaissance, that was concerned with Greek as opposed to the slightly earlier recovery of Roman culture and learning.

He was assigned to translate the works of Plato but in 1460 a monk returned from Macedonia with a manuscript of the *Corpus Hermeticum* and so important was this thought to be that he was ordered to translate it in preference to Plato. It was considered so important because its authorship was accredited to Hermes Trismagistus, believed to be an ancient Egyptian theologian contemporary with Moses.

In fact, the Hermes Trismagistus literature was written by many hands and dated from the first or second centuries A.D. It was a direct result of the impact of Christianity on paganism, but did not run to some of the dualist and earth denying excesses that caused Gnosticism to be condemned by the early Church.

The Hermetic literature is thus important for us today because it represents the best of the two spiritual cultures. We would put it forward that this was an example of the old pagan law, the natural religious impulses of man, being redeemed by the Christian revelation of God, which came 'not to destroy but to fulfil'.

It was thought highly important in Ficino's day because, being credited, if mistakenly, with a very early pre-Christian date, it seemed to foreshadow the decline of Egyptian religion and the coming of Christ.

Renaissance culture held to the theory that there was an early Golden Age from which our modern ages fell away. Thus ancient manuscripts were highly prized for their possible wisdom. Of these, the Old Testament was obviously the principal text, but the Hermes Trismagistus literature was placed almost on a par with it.

It is true the *Corpus Hermeticum* did reflect the teachings of earlier times. The world of the second century A.D. was weary of contemporary philosophy of the Graeco-Roman type that never seemed to get anywhere, and the easy communications of the Roman Empire allowed for intermingling of religious ideas. Thus there was an intense interest in the early Greek Pythagoreanism, based an esoteric geometry and numerology, and in Indian, Persian and Chaldean religious philosophy. Above all, there was an interest in the Egyptians and it was still possible to make a pilgrimage to a functioning Egyptian temple. A number of contemporary 'seekers' did so — there to pass the night in its environs hoping for some vision or divine dream. It was believed that ancient Egypt was the repository of profound religious wisdom under the custodianship of a priesthood who performed high magic in subterranean chambers. All this is in the Hermes Trismagistus literature, and as it obviously contains contemporary Greek and Christian references, it was, by this token, thought to have been written by an all-wise ancient prophet who, though pagan, lived in an unfallen Golden Age, and who had foreknowledge of Greek and Christian times.

This belief in an ancient Hermes Trismagistus as a real person was accepted by early fathers of the Christian Church, particularly Lanctantius and Augustine. Lanctantius, writing in the third century A.D. saw the Hermes writings as an ally in his campaign of using pagan wisdom in support of the truth of Christianity. Lanctantius never has a critical word to say about the Hermes literature and thus became an important source of defence for the Renaissance magus defending himself from accusations of heresy. Augustine however does attack the use of magic, as described in the *Corpus Hermeticum*, for attracting divine forces into god-forms. He considers this to be the imprisoning of demons into idols. Others were later to speculate if this modus operandi could, or should, be applied to the Catholic images of saints.

This magical element weighed heavily on Augustine, who, whilst admitting Hermes to have been a great pagan figure, considered him to have obtained his prophecies by illicit and dubious means And he cites Isaiah as the case of a true prophet inspired by God.

Augustine was making this attack on magic, however, after experiencing the pagan reaction to Christianity (after Lanctantius' time) under the Emperor Julian the Apostate — and also in the context of the views held by Apuleius of Madaura, who was (mistakenly) held to have translated the *Corpus Hermeticum* into Latin, and this was the text that Augustine was using. Apuleius did in fact write that popular novel of the Isiac Mysteries, *The Golden Ass*, which is very much in sympathy with the tone of the Hermetic writings and indeed contemporary with them.

The Golden Ass is worth reading, not only as a classic novel but as an example not only of the philosophical heights of which the Pagan Mysteries were capable, but also of the depths of evil witchcraft and sorcery. On the one hand are the great myths of the condition of the soul, in Psyche's love for Cupid, which like the Song of Solomon, is almost capable of direct Christian mystical interpretation; and on the other hand of corpses having to be guarded lest they be mutilated for magical purposes. And running through all this is the most bizarre level of credulity and superstition.

The medieval church had driven magic into a hole and corner existence, where its worst elements flourished. The Renaissance, with the revival of classical learning, revived magic as an elevating means of therapy for the soul. And the first Renaissance magician of note was Marsilio Ficino, translator of the Hermes literature, though there were others of the same period, and the mosaics of Siena Cathedral show Hermes as a legitimate part of the Christian heritage. These were laid in the 1480s.

The Hermes literature is not the work of one man but is a collection of manuscripts which indeed contradict one another in parts. Some of the scripts are philosophically pessimistic and dualist — that is, they believe there to be equal powers of good and evil and that we must free ourselves from evil matter in order to attain to the good of the higher spheres. Other scripts demonstrate an optimistic gnosis and see all matter as being impregnated with the divine, and the earth, the planets and stars and all the parts of Nature, as living beings. Such a belief has no fear in trying to draw down the good powers of the universe by sympathetic magic, invocations and talismans.

Both forms of belief assume an astrological framework to the world and, mixed up together, could, by their superficial similarity, be regarded as aspects of a whole uniform teaching. As the Hermes account of the Creation has marked similarities to the Genesis account; and as a Second God, or demi-urge, is described as 'the Word', created by the First, and creating the world, this could easily be interpreted as reference to Jesus as Second Person of the Trinity, and also as the Word described in the Gospel of St. John.

This was the philosophical side to the Hermes literature, though the name Hermes had long been associated with the magical arts throughout the middle ages. One of the most important of the practical magical texts is the *Picatrix*, which although not ascribed to the pen of Hermes Trismagistus, mentions him frequently as an authority. This was originally in Arabic, written probably in the twelfth century, and links up with our previous remarks about the influx of esoteric ideas from the Arab world as a result of the Crusades. The *Picatrix* was never printed but it is known to have had an enormous manuscript circulation.

The *Picatrix* sees a three tier Universe created by God (who is also inscribed as *prima materia*). These three sections are

i)   *Intellectus* or *Mens*
ii) *Spiritus*
iii) *Materia*

The whole art of magic according to this scheme consists of attracting and guiding *spiritus* into *materia*, which is largely done by talismans made of the right materials and inscribed with the right signs and sigils made potent by the right planetary invocations. The objectives are completely practical — curing disease, acquiring business success, overcoming enemies, escaping from bondage, attracting love, achieving long life and so on.

The *Picatrix* is virtually a magical recipe book, though we would not regard it as necessary reading for the modern magus by any means, because it is the principles of the art that are important, and the mere repetition of ancient formulae from such sources, of dubious origin and with many copyists' errors, is useless if not dangerous.

The above division of the Universe into three tiers, plus the formless God, is obviously similar to the principles of the Tree of Life we have already described.

There is also a passage in the *Picatrix* giving an orienteering device in the guise of the plans for a magical city constructed 'in the east of Egypt' twelve miles (miliaria) long within which is a castle with four gates.

> On the Eastern gate he placed the form of an Eagle; on the Western gate, the form of a Bull; on the Southern gate the form of a Lion; and on the Northern gate he constructed the form of a Dog. Into these images he introduced spirits who spoke with voices, nor could anyone enter the gates of the City except by their permission. There he planted trees in the midst of which was a great tree which bore the fruit of all generations. On the summit of the castle he caused to be raised a lighthouse (rotunda) the colour of which changed every day until the seventh day after which it returned to the first colour, and so the City was illuminated with these colours. Near the City there was abundance of waters in which dwelt many kinds of fish. Around the circumference of the City he placed engraved images and ordered them in such manner that by their virtue the inhabitants were made virtuous and withdrawn from all wickedness and harm. The name of the City was Adocentyn.

Here again, the student magician's own construct is to be preferred to any incompletely understood ancient formularies. But it can readily be seen that the principles are valid and similar.

In so far that astrology was closely intertwined with the science of the times, Ficino's work, *Libri de Vita*, could be regarded as an ordinary medical textbook. He was a physician as well as a priest and translator and in this book he introduces a form of Christian talismanic magic in a medical context.

The elementary principles of it are laid down in his advice to those whose profession calls them to intense study, which if overdone, can lead to depression or melancholia. As these matters are traditionally under the influence of Saturn, Ficino recommends a life in which the attributes of counteracting planets are brought to the fore, that is, the Sun, Jupiter and Venus. He includes recommendations for a non-Saturnian diet, and for walking in the fields contemplating the flowers particularly associated with these planets, such as the crocus or the rose. All this is little removed from basic psychology such as any medical practitioner might give, although nowadays tranquillisers might be more readily prescribed than astrology.

Ficino then goes on to introduce more specialised techniques for the attraction of Jovian, Venusian and Solarian qualities, and bases this theory upon a three tier system of:

i)   an intellect of the world — in which are archetypal ideas
ii) a soul of the world — in which are a corresponding number of 'seminal reasons'
iii) a body of the world — in which are the forms of matter depending in turn from the 'seminal reasons'

If there are any malformations in any aspect of the body of the world then it should, theoretically, be capable of being put right by intelligent manipulation of the 'seminal reasons' of the soul of the world.

This is done, according to Ficino, by working upon the *spiritus mundi*, which is a plastic medium between the soul of the world and the body of the world. Note that 'spirit of the world' to which it might be translated, does not apply to the word 'spirit' a high abstract sense as is common in many modern occult writings, but to a level that would probably nowadays be called 'the etheric'. The word 'spirit' is used in a sense similar to its meaning in such terms as 'natural spirits' or a 'horse of spirit', meaning, broadly speaking, 'vitality'. And one of the principle ways of working upon the *spiritus*, or 'etheric', is by use of talismans.

A talisman is a material object in which the essence or *spiritus* of a particular planet or stellar constellation is concentrated. This is the rationale behind all the psychological attributions to the planets and zodiacal signs. The 'decans' were much used in magical texts of the time (the 36 ten-degree divisions of the Zodiac), though Ficino used only planetary figures. Of course the principles could be applied to any body of esoteric symbolism which can be used to form a construct of the Universe as a whole, be it Tarot, I Ching, Hebrew alphabet, or whatever.

The talisman is made by constructing it of a material traditionally attributed to the planet — say copper in the case of Venus — and inscribing thereon, at the proper planetary hour, the relevant signs and sigils, whilst surrounded by appropriate planetary colours and objects and burning the appropriate planetary incense.

It is for this reason that magical operators set such great store by traditional tables or 'correspondences' but, as we have said, this can cause much futile argument if we fail to see the wood for the trees. Whilst we should avoid a completely arbitrary or idiosyncratic use of symbols, the important thing is what they mean to us. And to approach them in the same attitude as one might go to a cookery book is not, generally speaking, to be encouraged.

Ficino developed other aspects of magic from this. One of these was the preparation of a 'model universe' in which all the astrological influences could be represented by various coloured lamps. Then, if one were afflicted by particular astrological configurations in the sky one could counteract such influences by setting up one's personal model universe in a fashion which provided a counterbalance. Here again we have a similarity to our Cube of Space, which could be used in a similar manner by concentrating upon particular aspects of it.

Whilst physical representation should not be abandoned it would be generally agreed that the force or power from such an operation comes very much from the faith, intention and will of the operator and that a cursory moving of objects around would be likely to have little effect — though in a well 'run in' magical cabinet such as we have already described, even this, reflecting as it does the consciousness of the operator, could have a marked and by no means negligible talismanic effect, 'earthing' a particular intention.

Ficino thus covered the two related fields of talismanic magic and sympathetic magic. He also developed a form of incantatory magic by performance of the *Hymns of Orpheus*. These date once more probably from the second or third century A.D. though in Renaissance times they also were credited with great antiquity. Orpheus, like Hermes, was considered a great pre-Christian prophet who had foreseen the Holy Trinity.

The Orphic Hymns have been translated into English by the eighteenth-century Platonist Thomas Taylor. We may take the opportunity to digress here by quoting from Kathleen Raine's essay *Thomas Taylor in England* (from *Thomas Taylor the Platonist – Selected Writings* edited by Kathleen Raine and George Mills Harper) to show how Ficino and Taylor parallel one another in Renaissance and modern times.

> It was Thomas Taylor who took upon himself, at the close of the eighteenth century, the task of placing before his contemporaries the canonical Platonic writings, in which are embodied the essential learning of the imaginative tradition. The texts Taylor placed in the hands of the Romantic poets were the same that Ficino had made accessible to Botticelli, Raphael and Michelangelo; Coleridge and Shelley alone among the Romantic poets habitually read their Greek authors in the original; Taylor's translations were the texts, his interpretations the guide. Flaxman and probably Blake were close friends of Taylor during the formative years of all three; Shelley's friend Thomas Love Peacock knew him in later life. Keats, though not a scholar, may at a remove have caught the enthusiasm of the Greek polytheism from Taylor; and the gleam from Plotinus that illuminates Wordsworth's most famous Ode (and other of his poems) certainly comes through Taylor. Samuel Palmer, F. O. Finch, George Richmond and Edward Calvert affirmed, in the name by which they called themselves, "the Shoreham Ancients", an intention to revive, in their art, a traditional vision, restored to their generation by the rediscovery not only of the arts, but the philosophy of ancient Greece... Volumes of Taylor crossed the Atlantic, there to fertilise a flowering of American culture. Emerson, Bronson, Alcott and their friends dreaming of an America that should approach to Plato's never-to-be-realised Republic, read the same books that a generation earlier had inspired Blake's prophecies of an England whose national life should reflect, like Plato's city, the order of eternal perfection, and in this century, when 'the sceptre of intelligence passed to Dublin' we find that the same works were fertilizing the thought of AE and the poetry of Yeats.

It is interesting how the image of a perfect model city recurs in our studies. One finds reflections in the New Jerusalem of *Revelations*, the Jerusalem of the Crusaders, the Florence of Dante, the Adocentyn of the *Picatrix*, and it features also in the teaching of later Renaissance Magi such as Campanella. Very often great tragedy is brought about when such visions are brought into a political context, and there may, as Frances Yates has described in *The Rosicrucian Enlightenment*, have been such an episode in relation to Bohemia and the Rosicrucians in the seventeenth century.

We quote one of the shorter Orphic Hymns from the translation of Thomas Taylor to show the type of lyric that Ficino was setting to music.

TO JUPITER
(*The Fumigation from Storax*)

O Jove much-honor'd, Jove supremely great
To thee our holy rites we consecrate,
Our pray'rs and expiations, King divine,
For all things round thy head exalted shine.
The earth is thin; and mountains swelling high,
The sea profound, and all within the sky,
Saturnian king, descending from above.
Magnanimous, commanding, sceptred Jove;
All-parent, principle and end of all.
Whose pow'r almighty, shakes this earthly ball;
Ev'n Nature trembles at thy mighty nod,
Loud-sounding, arm'd with light'ning, thund'ring God.
Source of abundance, purifying king,
O various-form'd from whom all natures spring;
Propitious hear my pray'r, give blameless health,
With peace divine, and necessary wealth.

Ficino had his own system of musical composition, based on symbolic principles, and accompanied himself on a *lira da braccio*. What little is known of the details are described in Professor D. P. Walker's book *Spiritual and Demonic Magic from Ficino to Campanella*, though we should once more advise caution in the use of terms, for as we have mentioned before, 'Spiritual' in this context refers more to 'animal spirits', vitality, or the 'etheric'; and 'demonic' is perhaps better rendered as 'daimonic', as it refers not to the hellish assistance of the devil but to all types of spirits, including angels, and such as Socrates' *daimon* which some would equate with a kind of 'higher self'.

Ficino was much concerned with keeping within the bounds of Christian orthodoxy, and besides quoting favourable parts of Thomas Aquinas in support of himself, and emphasising the influence of the Plotinus rather than the magical *Picatrix*, he was at great pains to point out that he was performing *Natural* Magic. That is, he was not invoking spirits but working with the forces of nature, in an aspect of scientific endeavour, though of course in those days science did not have the prestige it had today — and even scientific enquiry could fall foul of hunters of heresy.

The magic of Ficino is certainly a much higher thing than the magic of the Middle Ages, as Frances Yates points out in her scholarly work *Giordano Bruno and the Hermetic tradition* to which we are much indebted in this chapter. She points out that 'just as a pagan Renaissance work of art is not purely pagan but retains Christian overtones or undertones (the classical example of this being Botticelli's Venus who looks like a Virgin) so it is also with Ficino's magic'.

The magic of nature, the psychological manipulation of natural forces, of Ficino, took a major step further however in the work of Ficino's younger contemporary, the brilliant Pico della Mirandola, who introduced the Jewish Qabalah to Western Christendom.

The Qabalah, with its ten Sephiroth, which are powers or attributes of God Himself, with corresponding hierarchies of angels and archangels, introduces another dimension to the natural magic of Ficino. No longer can one say one is dealing with science, or nature, only. The introduction of spiritual beings bring the whole study into the sphere of religion.

For Pico, the Qabalah, like the Hermes literature and the Orphic Hymns, was of great antiquity, although of the two principal texts, the *Zohar* was written down from existing oral tradition as late as the fourteenth century, and the *Sepher Yetzirah* at earliest in the second or third century A.D.

Perhaps more significant historically than Ficino, Pico also stands at the gateway of the junction of two traditions or cultures. He unites the Hermetic and Qabalistic types of magic, a union that was to have profound consequences.

Pico was above all a great synthesiser, and in 1486 at the tender age of 24 went to Rome offering to prove in open debate, on the basis of 900 theses he had drawn up from them, that all existing philosophies were reconcilable with one another. He had also prepared an opening oration extolling the Dignity of Man.

He fell foul of the more conservative ecclesiastical authorities however, who took exception to some of his theses, and the debate never took place. He published instead an Apology or defence in 1487 which was based upon them. Twenty six of his nine hundred theses related to magic. In common with almost all magicians, Pico starts by differentiating between good magic and bad magic. The subject has always suffered from a low principled and superstitious element in so far that to the ignorant it has mysterious trappings and appears to offer secret powers and something for nothing.

He emphasises that Natural Magic is a conscious and deliberate linking of aspects of nature, and that it is the characters or images used which are the more important part, rather than the actual material substances used. This puts the study very much in terms of psychology if we care to look at it in modern terms. It also emphasises the gap between the higher Renaissance magic and the debased magic, or sorcery, prevalent in medieval times, where superstitious use of strange substances (bat's blood, nail clippings, parts of corpses, and things of that ilk), for circumventing natural law.

So far this is very similar to Ficino's magic, particularly as Pico also advocates use of the Orphic Hymns. But Pico does come out more into the open and states explicitly that he is talking about Hermetic magic; whereas the more cautious Ficino had introduced it under cover of philosophical — and slightly misleading — passages from Plotinus and Thomas Aquinas.

Having said this, however, Pico goes on to state that Natural Magic is a relatively weak thing if it is not allied to Qabalistic Magic, which introduces a higher realm of forces.

Whereas Natural Magic deals only with the sympathies between the stellar magical images (via the 'spiritus' or 'etheric') and the physical world, Qabalistic Magic links the stellar magical images through angelic correspondences with God Himself. As Pico explains, there are two types of Qabalah, one the philosophical side and the other concerned with practical magic.

On the philosophical side God is conceived in terms of ten holy Sephiroth or 'emanations' as we have, indeed, already described. There is a relationship between the Ten Emanations or Holy Attributes of the Creator and their archetypal reflections in the Creation.

In the stellar or celestial world this consists of a direct correspondence to the ten crystalline spheres conceived to be about the Earth, which we also described when we talked about Dante — those of the Moon, Mercury, Venus, the Sun, Mars, Jupiter, Saturn, the Zodiac and Fixed Stars, and the Primum Mobile or clear outer sphere which gives the primal movement to the others, beyond which is the Empyrean corresponding to Ain Soph in the Qabalah.

It must be remembered that Ain Soph is the hidden side of God whereas the Empyrean is the hidden backdrop of the created universe or, to use another analogy, the saturated solution from which Creation crystallised, the ultimate *prima materia*. If we contact it we may have an expansive experience of *nirvana* or *samadhi* or *satori,* but it is not an at-one-ment with God. To those who cannot conceive of, or accept a personal God, the self-indited cosmic orphans, the Empyrean may take on the attributes of a substitute God, but it will be like a baby mistaking the walls of the maternity ward for its mother.

An important feature of the Qabalah is the hierarchies of spirits, usually called archangelic, which act on behalf of God throughout the Creation. All this is linked to the Old Testament, particularly the Pentateuch and the Book of Genesis, by the importance given to the Hebrew language.

This in turn leads to the other branch of Qabalah, the path of the names, which is also featured in the *Zohar* , but which was principally developed independently by the school of Abraham Abulafia.

The *Zohar* makes disconcerting reading to modern eyes because of the way it treats the Scriptures as if they were a person — in fact God himself. His word is his manifestation or self-revelation in terms of language. Therefore not a line nor a letter may be altered.

This is quite normal rabbinical treatment of it and we find exactly the same approach taken by St. Paul, who, like the rabbis of the *Zohar* finds nothing incongruous in taking any text, or even a disconnected phrase, from the Old Testament and screwing it into any interpretation he likes as justification for a point he is trying to make.

In the *Zohar* indeed this goes to even further lengths by analysing individual words, and a large part of the beginning of the *Zohar* is taken up with the first word of Genesis — *Berashith* (in the beginning) — and even the first letter of this word. Whilst it makes strange logic there is, within all this, the mechanics of a devotional mysticism of profound depth and consequence.

This is rendered more complex by the introduction of certain conventions or codes to obtain further ramifications of meaning, such as Notariqon which allows words to be abbreviations of sentences. One sees this in alchemical form in VITRIOL, which also stands for *Visita Interiora Terrae Rectificando Invenies Occultum Lapidem*. Another method is Temurah, allowing transpositions of letters or anagrams of words. And Gematria, in taking into consideration the numbers indicated by words (in Hebrew orthography, letters are also figures) opens up the vast field of numerology, where words or sentences or names of similar numerical value can be transposed or interpreted in terms of number symbolism.

There opens up a maze of such complexity that the student without the Ariadne's thread of right intention and grasp of principles could spend years of obscure erudition getting nowhere.

We do well to remember that what we are given here is a very flexible means of building our own meanings and intentions into symbolic words or names or talismanic figures. And most of the angelic beings dealt with in magical Qabalism go under names synthesised from occult meanings of letters or syllables, with the suffix '-el' (meaning 'lord') added. For instance, Uriel stems in fact from Aur-iel—Lord (El) of Light (Aur).

However, we begin to tread on dangerous ground if our intention and reverence are not right. It is one thing to provide a higher and more powerful dimension to Natural Magic by a reverent approach to God and the angelic hierarchies, an attitude which makes our magic a form of prayer. It is another thing to attempt to 'push around' or dominate angelic hierarchies, or even God Himself, by manipulating bits of his Creation in a magical manner.

One can see the reason for Ficino's caution, apart from the theological intolerance of the times. And Pico also solemnly recommends a spirit of piety towards God in the performance of all magical operations, at risk of coming into contact with an evil spirit rather than a good one. And indeed to approach the subject in the detached scientific spirit could be but a very short step from doing the work of the devil attempting to set oneself up as a creative agency divorced from the Creator.

Pico goes on to develop the differences between Natural and Qabalistic Magic. Having stipulated that none but Hebrew names are magically powerful, and that the Qabalah is an essential addition to Natural Magic, he states that the reason for this is the power of number that is behind the Hebrew names, but not behind the characters of Natural Magic. Natural Magic is in fact using only intermediary causes whereas Qabalistic Magic goes right back to the First Cause — God Himself.

We are thus now dealing with a form of magic that is very close to mysticism, in the sense that we defined these terms at the beginning of this book. And the link between Natural Magic (close to what we now call science) and Qabalistic Magic (close to mysticism) is to be found in the Qabalistic Tree of Life, where the powers of God in ten-fold majesty are correlated with the celestial spheres and the spiritual beings associated with them.

Pico also found much Christian relevance in the theoretical side of the Qabalah, where by the use of the methods of Notariqon, Gematria and so on, he felt that he could prove the divinity of Christ. It is, of course, possible to prove almost whatever one likes by use of such flexible methods of number and letter counterchange; it is a kind of metaphysical Rorschach Test.

It was this that raised the greatest controversy and protest of the time for it was allied to the proposition as to whether magic should be introduced as a means of reform to the Church. This has to be seen in the light of much controversy of the time as to the alleged wonder-working images and relics in the traditional Church and the possible abuse of such matters. It also led to the shattering question as to whether Jesus Christ performed his miracles by use of practical Qabalistic Magic. To this Pico answered a definite negative. But we can see in all this the possibility of impassioned controversy from many points of view and the cause of the very cautious view of the Church towards magic.

The Church's suspicion of magic was not lessened by the medieval type of magic, which at root used similar sources to the high philosophical magic of Ficino and Pico. The Medieval grimoires are full of fragments of garbled Hermeticism and Qabalah along with their barbarous and filthy recipes. And there was, too, a kind of half-way house where the very religious and pious motives and attitudes of Ficino and Pico give way to a cruder technological spirit, with magicians such as Cornelius Agrippa or Trithemius of Sponheim, whom we have already mentioned as using angelic magic in an attempt to make a communications network, such as science has today in modern telecommunication.

As it was, Pico della Mirandola became the centre of a great controversy. Several of his magical theses were condemned by a commission appointed by the Pope. Nothing daunted, he published his Apology, defending his ideas, but this led to an inquisition being formed and he found it advisable to retract. The Pope then published a Bull condemning all his work, and Pico, in spite of fleeing to France, was pursued by papal nuncios and imprisoned for some time. Later, through intercession of friends in high places, he was allowed to return to Florence where he lived an ascetic and pious life to his early death.

One of the commission who examined Pico, the Spanish bishop Pedro Garcia, wrote a work attacking Pico's Apology. In this he states the Church's view that *any* kind of magic is evil and diabolical. He admits the technical fact of occult sympathies in nature and the celestial spheres but insists that these cannot be used by man without diabolical assistance. He condemns magical images based on the astrological signs or decans, and also talismans. He particularly insists that the Church practice of issuing wax lambs blessed by the Pope, and so on, is not ecclesiastical use of magic, and that such pious observances are efficacious not through the media of stellar sympathies but through the direct power of God.

Pico's side of the case was however favoured by the new Pope, Alexander Borgia, a colourful character who was much interested in magic and astrology and who published Bulls for Pico's absolution. He also wrote a letter, which was published with all editions of Pico's works, calling him a faithful son of the Church, of unimpeachable orthodoxy, and stating that magic and the Qabalah are valuable aids to Christian practice. When Popes fall out, where does the lay-man stand?

Once again we see how much of a knife edge we are placed upon in the study of magic, where one party can see it as diabolical heresy and another as an aid to practice and belief. And also where, divorced from the divine orientation, it becomes a kind of technology — but a technology involving other conscious beings. And there is another body of moral questions attached to this, as might be in any other form of technology dependent for power on sentient creatures — whether such be animals, humans, elementals, angels or demons.

Certainly the influence of Pico in the sphere of magic had its parallels in other spheres of human endeavour. It was the beginnings of the scientific age, and whereas pious belief to that time had seen man as a part of the Creation, albeit a relatively high part, he was still regarded as but a spectator of a Divinely ordained environment.

The ideas of Pico put man on to a higher status, seeing him not simply as a spectator, but also as an operator upon nature, and as such having a profound influence upon the Creation. Thus with the scientific method and the resultant sophisticated technology of our own times, we are posed again with fundamental moral questions as we find we gain power over life and death. Medicine and the life sciences are indeed imminently faced with some appallingly difficult moral questions.

The theological background to Ficino and Pico was provided by Dionysius the Areopagite, whom we have discussed before as having a profound influence on the writer of *The Cloud of Unknowing*. He was in fact a Christian of the first or second century A.D. writing under Neo-Platonic influence, but to the medieval and Renaissance world he was still taken at face value as a contemporary and companion of St. Paul. Whatever his historical pedigree the fact that his ideas could be accepted as part of Christian orthodoxy for centuries, is, in our opinion, a good enough reason for retaining them.

Apart from the *via negativa* that we have already examined, pseudo-Dionysius, or St. Denis, was responsible for a Christian angelology which posited nine orders of angels, grouped in three triads, corresponding to the Holy Trinity. These angelic hierarchies have their being in the Empyrean beyond the Crystalline Sphere of the Primum Mobile.

These ideas were developed by Ficino via no less a Christian authority than Thomas Aquinas and of course Dante, of whom Ficino was a keen student, and who had himself been much influenced by Aquinas. Whereas Pseudo-Dionysius had not specifically defined the activities of each hierarchy, this was done by Thomas Aquinas, and Dante linked these hierarchies with the Celestial Spheres in a system of universal hierarchy as in the diagram overleaf (Figure 21). Dionysius saw the nine orders of angels as:

Seraphim, Cherubim, Thrones pertaining to the Father;
Dominions, Virtues, Powers pertaining to the Son;
Principalities, Archangels, Angels pertaining to the Holy Spirit;
and as with the order of precedence of the Holy Trinity,
the Son begotten of the Father,
and the Spirit proceeding from the Father and the Son,
so do these hierarchies depend and react similarly one upon the other.

In his work *De Christione Religione* Ficino gives further details (deriving from Aquinas and Dante), as follows:

The Angelic Hierarchies
Seraphim, who speculate on the order and providence of God;
Cherubim, who speculate on the essence and form of God;
Thrones, who also speculate, though some descend to do works;
Dominions, who like architects, design what the rest execute;
Virtues, who execute, and move the heavens, and concur for the working of miracles as God's instruments;
Powers, who watch that the order of divine governance is not interrupted, and some of whom descend to human beings;
Principalities, who care for public affairs, nations, princes and magistrates;
Archangels, who direct the divine cult and look after sacred things;
Angels, who look after smaller affairs and take charge of individuals as their guardian angels.

The Universal Order
The Empyrean, where all is stable and the *lumen* of which is a quality of light superior to *candor*;
The Outer Crystalline Sphere, which has simple motion and the qualities of *candor*;
The Eighth Sphere, whose movement is opposite to that of the planetary Spheres and which has qualities of *candor* and *splendor*.
The seven Planetary Spheres, which are not mutable in substance, but are so in quality and disposition;
The Sphere of the Four Elements, which are mutable in substance and quality.

As we saw in Dante, these link up in the fashion of: God, the Holy Trinity, in the Empyrean;

The Angelic Hierarchies in the Outer
   Crystalline Sphere.
The Apostles and Church Triumphant
   in the Eighth Sphere.
The souls of the blessed throughout
   the Planetary Spheres.

   though in
   their essence
   in the
   Empyrean as
   part of the
   rosa mystica

The Physical World including Limbo, Hell and Purgatory; or the Sub-Lunar World.

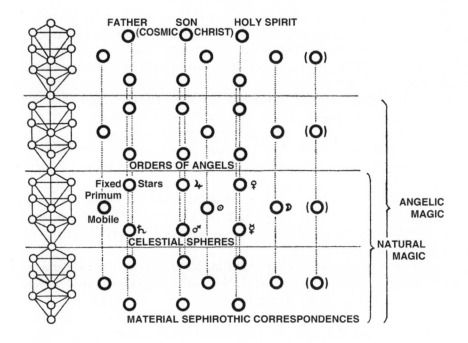

Figure 21

Ficino was thus aware of a succession of angelic hierarchies stretching beyond the scope of Natural Magic, but whether he used them apart from normal Christian prayers and supplications is not known. He was very cautious in his statements certainly. But these hierarchies were brought very much to the fore when Pico introduced the Qabalah to Natural Magic. In his commentary on Genesis, *Heptaplus*, Pico emphasises the 'three Worlds' of the Qabalists;

The super-celestial world (called by theologians the angelic, by philosophers the intelligible);
The celestial world or world of stars;
and **the terrestrial**, elemental or sub-lunar world.

He uses the analogy of Moses' division of the tabernacle into three parts — and here again we see the idea of building a 'model universe'. He also draws attention to the account of the Creation in Genesis where the waters are divided by a firmament. The firmament he sees as the celestial sphere, with the waters above as the super-celestial sphere and those below as the mundane sphere.

We should note that the modern tendency to talk of Four Worlds of the Qabalists is due to regarding God as a 'World'. This is permissible as long as we do not fall into the monist trap of regarding God as abstract matter, matter as concrete God, with the other worlds as levels of attenuation between.

Pico also draws correspondences with the Dionysian triadic choirs of angels who, although situate in their essence in the super-celestial world, have duties commensurate with all three worlds as listed above.

Thus the Seraphim, Cherubim and Thrones are given over to contemplation, ever praising God; the Dominions, Virtues and Powers have celestial functions; whilst the Principalities, Archangels and Angels are concerned with works in the mundane world — the Principalities concerned with the affairs of princes and nations, the Archangels with mysteries and sacred rites, and the Angels with the private affairs of individual men and women.

We have, then, in the work of Marsilio Ficino and Pico della Mirandola a synthesising genius at work that is able to affect a bond of unity between God and the Creation — and the Creation is seen as a hierarchical order, from the angelic hierarchies to physical matter. In the Renaissance magi we see how, with the recovery of the best of classical learning, the higher magical philosophy is also recovered and united with the esoteric elements of the Hebrew mystical tradition and the Christian religion, building upon the foundations laid by Thomas Aquinas and Dante Alighieri. Their chronology may have been wrong in the dating of their sources but their religious instincts were, in our view, none the less accurate for that.

Having reached a high point in Ficino and Pico we do well to trace what has happened to magical philosophy and practice since that date. The ideas caught on rapidly and a whole class of Renaissance magi came into being, who were as high above the barbarous sorcerers of the middle ages as the great Renaissance artists were above the earlier artisan painters. (Incidentally, some artists were influenced by the Magi, and Botticelli's famous *Primavera*, for instance, can be interpreted as a magical image, after the planetary remedial ideas of Ficino.)

Cornelius Agrippa is a typical magus of the type who followed upon Pico and Ficino. Written In 1510, though not published until 1533, his survey of magic entitled *De occulta philosophia* describes the Creation in three fold terms below God:

The intellectual world — angels — ceremonial magic — theology
The celestial world — stars —celestial magic — mathematics
The elemental world — elements — natural magic —physics
    animals, vegetables, minerals

As each world influences the one below it, so the magician, by manipulation of the elements of a lower world can bring down the influences of a higher world. The three volumes of his book deal with each level of magic in turn which correspond to the threefold division of philosophy into physics, mathematics and theology.

Natural Magic describes the theory of the four elements and goes on to the occult or hidden virtues in things of the sub-lunar world which have their correspondence in stellar or planetary images. He also describes the etheric link between all physical things. (Ficino's *spiritus* or Spirit of the World.)

Much of his work is taken up with describing the planetary correspondences of plants, animals, stones and other substances, and how by various arrangements and usages the influences not only of the celestial or vital world can be drawn down but also the spiritual or angelic forces of the highest world. Here he extends from Ficino's Natural Magic, which dealt only with 'natural' forces.

> For such is the concordance of the world, that celestial things draw super-celestial things, and natural things, supernatural things, through the virtue running through all and the participation in it of all species.

From this he goes as far as to cite alleged ancient Egyptian practice of attracting spirits into idols so that the latter told the future. And here we begin to see a technological spirit creeping in that Ficino and Pico would certainly have denounced as part of the abuses of an evil magic.

Together with his chapters on fascination, poisons, fumigations, philtres, ritual gestures and words of power we begin to find a reversion to the recipe book of the medieval sorcerer. It may well be that the Church had much justification in condemning magic in so far that it seems so easily degraded.

Celestial Magic deals very much with number, and cites the ancient marvels of the world, the earth works, megaliths, pyramids, and so on, as created by mathematical magic. Number, to quote Pythagoras, has a higher reality than natural objects, therefore the magic of mathematics is superior to Natural Magic. Agrippa analyses the lore and virtues of the various numbers from one to twelve and also the numerological significance of the Hebrew alphabet. This is also related to harmony (the musical scale is of course composed of seven steps, using twelve separate semitones, deriving from whole number division of a vibrating string) in its relation to the soul of man and to the stars. There is much on celestial talismans and he describes in detail the magical images for attracting the forces associated with the planets, the zodiacal signs and the decans; together with the principles of constructing images for special intentions.

In a significant passage Agrippa says that the really powerful magic can be performed only by one who has 'mounted higher than the heavens, elevating himself above the angels to the archetype itself, with whom he then becomes cooperator and can do all things'.

According to our diagrammatic analyses, the only thing above the angels is God. Agrippa is therefore either saying that we must attune ourselves completely to God, or else that what we call God is nothing but a sea of archetypes, able to be operated on by any who can contact them. This seems to be, once more, the confusion between the Creator and the 'collective unconscious' or 'basic matter' that we have seen to exist in other contexts. Either Agrippa is become 'at-one-ed' with God, or else he is stepping between God and the Creation. Again we have a knife-edge situation of profound moral and theological implication and see reasons for the church's grave reservations in such matters.

Ceremonial Magic deals with 'religious magic', and is, to some degree, an attempt to reconcile the miracles of Christ, for instance, with the operations of a magician. This is a distinction important to make, for otherwise it may be falsely thought that the magician is nearer to God the more miraculous the works he can perform. This is to be seen in lesser form today in many esoteric students who think that psychism, or astral projection, or mediumship are evidences of 'spiritual development'.

Agrippa posits two types of magic — the pure, divine kind, which operates directly by the power of God the Creator, and the lesser kind which depends upon knowledge of the natural sympathies of things. Both operate by faith, hope and love, but the former by faith, hope and love for the Creator, the latter by faith, hope and concern for the success of the operation and the truth and relevance of the 'occult' linkages of natural and celestial forces.

The Qabalah is introduced in this book, with the theory that the Holy Sephiroth (and their associated numeration and Names) act upon the corresponding nine orders of angels, then upon the nine celestial spheres, and then on men and the sub-lunar world (Figure 22).

This is a development of the synthesis of Christian angelology with Hebrew Qabalah and Orphic Hymns and Pythagorian mathematics, formulated by Pico, and developed and extended by John Reuchlin and Trithemius of Sponheim.

In its highest sense, to put it in the words of Dr Frances Yates in *Giordano Bruno and the Hermetic Tradition:*

... the highest dignity of the Magus is seen to be the Magus as priest, performing

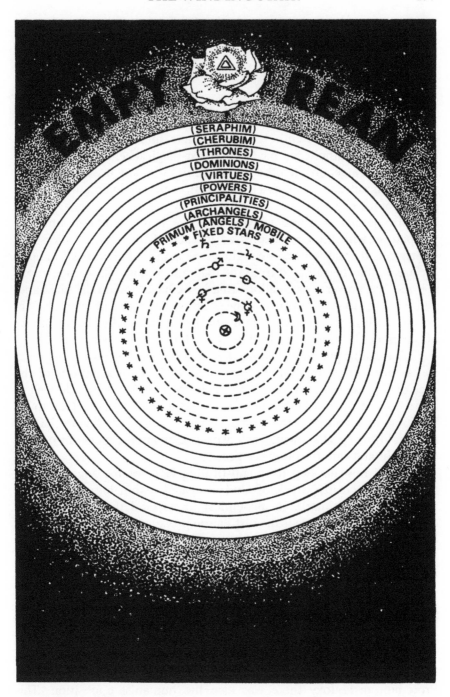

Figure 22

religious rites and doing religious miracles. His "marrying of earth to heaven" with Magia, his summoning of the angels with Cabala, lead on to his apotheosis as religious Magus; his magic powers in the lower worlds are organically connected with the highest religious powers in the intellectual world.'

There is, and was, of course, considerable theological opposition to such a view, and from both Protestant and Catholic sides. The Protestant side expects religion to be entirely free of magic, and indeed suspects and condemns the Catholic for magical or quasi-magical beliefs and practices. The Catholic side, on the other hand, denies that any use of magic is a part of religion, and sees it as a lower form, or perversion of, the spiritual powers of the Church.

With neither of these views would we agree, although one can sympathise with the fears expressed in each of them. And unless one clearly gets the mechanics of it right, there is indeed great risk of abuse. We are, as may be gathered from the diagrams so far, talking in terms of a 'three-tier' universe or creation. That is, we have God on the one hand, with his Creation on the other — the Creation consisting of hierarchies of angelic intelligences and similar spiritual beings; the archetypal dynamics of the Inner Creation; and the Outer Creation or the physical world.

These can be placed one above the other like tiers on a wedding cake, as has been done for example by Dante; or in representations of the Tree of Life that take account of the Four Worlds. We would do well to avoid the trap latent in this type of representation of equating God to his Creation, by recourse to the type of diagram we had in Chapter III, the three-fold pie chart showing each aspect of creation dependant on and directly linked with the others (Figure 23).

We can now develop it by substituting God for the angelic world, which is the creative work of God delegated within his creation, but all *within* God himself. In alchemical terms God then becomes the alembic in which proceeds the distillation process of refining matter and consciousness to a higher state of being. The *ros* or dew of the distillate of the created *crux* or light being a higher interpretation of the Mysteries of the Rose Cross.

Having indicated our own higher view of the function of the magical philosophy we do well, however, to trace through some of the lines that led to the denigration of this highest of arts and sciences, the results of which we see in our own day, for it may serve as a warning of what traps to avoid for the future.

Besides the religious objections to magic from Catholic and Protestant orthodoxy there was also the humanist opposition. This stemmed principally from the earlier part of the Renaissance which

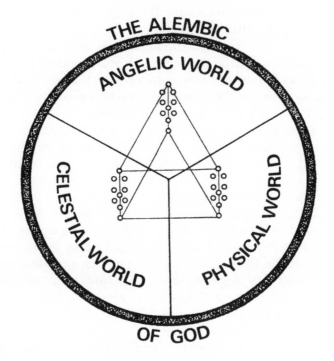

Figure 23

had rediscovered the higher features of Roman (as opposed to Greek) civilisation and cultivated a taste for good Latin (as opposed to medieval scholastic Latin), history, rhetoric and literary style, with little interest for Greek speculation in philosophy, theology and science (including magic).

The humanist, if a Christian, looked to pagan virtues as exemplified by great Romans, and concerned himself, like Erasmus, with a recovery of learning by making Christian literature available to all by the help of the newly discovered printing press with moveable types. The trend was back to the Gospels themselves rather than to the Neo-Platonic speculations dear to the Greek type of mind.

Admirable though this was in its way, the humanist distrust of metaphysical speculation and the mathematical framework associated with it led to a later Reformation fear and hatred of such studies. The University of Oxford, for instance, famed for its mathematical and philosophical studies, met an onslaught of book burning in 1550, when Edward VI's commissioners gutted libraries because '...books wherein appeared Angles or Mathematical Diagrams, were thought sufficient to be destroyed because accounted Popish, or diabolical, or both'. Henceforth, in an officially Reformation country, the whole course of studies of the University changed, to that of Latin humanism.

The destruction of the monastic libraries by the Anglican England that had lost all the liberal humanist breadth of an Erasmus, led John Dee, the great English Elizabethan magus, to travel on the continent in search of learning, for his attempts to rescue such books as survived led him to be suspected as a 'conjurer' and Papist sympathiser.

Dee is a key figure in that he was an eminent mathematician, in modern scientific terms, as well as a student of magic, and he was also a devout Christian. He made contact with the hermetic traditions that continued to survive in the continental church (without the magic), and was philosophical teacher of 'number in the three worlds' to the circle of Sir Philip Sidney who looked back with sympathy to John Colet and Thomas More who had made the first steps in adapting Christian theology to Neo-Platonism. Colet was influenced by Ficino and wrote two treatises on the Dionysian angelic hierarchies, and More translated Pico della Mirandola's biography, and in his *Utopia*, the religion of the Utopians is akin to religious Hermeticism. More saw it as a palliative to the disasters of religious intolerance that were to sweep the West and which indeed cost him his own life.

There was contemporary with John Dee a more radical magician, Giordano Bruno who, though generally hailed as a martyr in the cause of science, was in fact steeped in magic. He had little time for the efforts of Dee, More or Colet for synthesising the Hermetic literature with Christian orthodoxy, but openly came out with a Hermetic Gnosticism that drew inspiration from the new world view of Copernicus, that the Sun, not the Earth, is centre of the Universe. Bruno saw God as a great magician producing innumerable worlds in an infinite universe, and the way to God as being for man an infinite expansion of consciousness to the 'size' of God. For this to be feasible the doctrine of reincarnation had to be reintroduced. This has much in common with the occult monism or pantheism of today deriving from Hindu sources. Bruno paid heavily for this unorthodoxy, however, and was burned at the stake by the Inquisition.

Another ex-Dominican, Tommaso Campanella, was the last of the Italian Renaissance Magi. He also fell foul of orthodoxy, was tortured and spent much time in prison, though he performed magic with the sympathetic Pope Urban VIII and died a Christian, attended with much honour.

Campanella, Dee and Bruno have one thing in common in that they all attempted to use their magic for political ends. This was not a selfish interest of party, but stemmed logically from the magical hypothesis that the bringing of higher forces into lower forms, on its larger basis, must be concerned with the formation of a perfect state, a 'model universe', but on national lines, a great experiment in community and religious synthesis.

One sees this tendency in latter-day occult teachers, not on a national scale, but forming closed groups or communities. The results are generally no more successful than the more grandoise attempts of Dee, Bruno or Campanella, if less spectacular in their failure.

Campanella devoted much time to his ideal of a City of the Sun. This was envisaged as set on a hill in a wide plain, and divided by concentric walls into seven circles called after the seven planets. There would be four main roads leading from the four cardinal points to the centre where there would be a circular temple with a great dome, the ceiling of which would be decorated with the stars whilst below, on the altar, would be two great maps, one a replica of the domed heaven above, and the other of the earth. The stars would also be depicted around the walls of the temple, and within would be seven lamps representing the seven planets.

The walls of the city would have paintings on them, inside and out. On the innermost wall, mathematical figures on the temple side, and a map of the world on the outer, together with details of national rites, custom, laws and alphabets. The second wall out would have precious stones and minerals on the inner side, lakes, seas, rivers, wines and all liquids on the outer. The third wall vegetable life and the stellar correspondences of species on the inner side, on the outer side fish and their correspondences. The following walls would similarly show birds and reptiles, and animals. The outermost wall would have on the inner side an encyclopaedia of the mechanical arts, with portraits of great inventors and law givers on the outer, including Moses, Mahomet, Osiris, Jupiter, but with pride of place given to Christ and the Apostles.

All would be ruled by a Sun Priest, assisted by three others, one of Power in charge of military matters, one of Wisdom in charge of all sciences, and one of Love in charge of social and sexual relations, education and medicine. All property would be held in common and there would be no crime. Such harmonious life would be attainable by conforming life to celestial correspondences, for example, conceiving children at the most appropriate astrological moment.

There is a close correspondence here with the City of Adocentyn we have described earlier, and though the practicalities of such a scheme would prove virtually impossible in real life, it is nevertheless a model universe, or mandala, and could well be used interiorly in a magical sense. One sees the abuses, the disaster, that can come in, however, when the true purpose of such an eidolon is lost sight of, and it is applied to circumstances where it will not fit.

Campanella allied himself, for instance, to the ill-fated Calabrian revolt at the end of the sixteenth century, in the hope that allying himself to a revolutionary cause might give him the subsequent opportunity to build his City of the Sun. He later even hoped to influence the Pope to restructure the Papacy on these lines.

We see a similar kind of ambition in relation to the Rosicrucian Brotherhood at the beginning of the seventeenth century, when, as Frances Yates describes in *The Rosicrucian Enlightenment*, the Rosicrucian manifestos centred about hopes for an ideal state of Bohemia holding the balance between Roman Catholicism and the Reformation as a higher synthesis of religion and morals. Unfortunately it collapsed in short order in a matter of months, ground to pieces by the military power machines of the two great contenders.

The Hermetic influence, which owed so much to belief in the great antiquity of the writings, suffered a mortal blow when the scholarship of Isaac Casaubon in 1614 demonstrated that they had not been written until post-Christian times.

There were those, nonetheless, who saw that this was irrelevant anyway, the most important of whom was the Rosicrucian Robert Fludd (1574-1637).

The great dissensions of religious strife rumbled on with military sanctions, and after the Bohemian debacle the opportunity for a Rosicrucian lead was lost and the great tradition reformulated by Ficino and Pico descended into an underground existence where it has continued to our own times, becoming diluted with various oriental fads and outer space fancies that a divorce from responsible scholarship occasions. The underground line can be traced after Fludd and the Jesuit Athanaius Kircher through Francis Barrett (author of *The Magus*, 1801) and the French Catholic magician Alphonse Louis Constant (Eliphas Levi), with a more open, philosophical but less magical line being preserved by the romantic poets through the influence of Thomas Taylor on Blake, Coleridge, Wordsworth and others, as we have discussed previously.

The underground existence was enforced also by the divorce which came about with science. Ironically, the magical approach had encouraged the scientific method, the *right* of man to be an investigator into the mysteries of the creation that the ecclesiastical mind tried to suppress.

The attitude of Bacon is an important one here, that knowledge is justified by results. This indicates a watershed between the functions of science and religion. However, with the close alliance of magic with religion (and even now the thought of magic, justified by results, would cause some to have moral qualms), and the great religious controversies making matters of belief more sensitive, it was very much in the interests of the infant science to divorce itself from the religious ambit. This meant playing down magic, alchemy, astrology, even mathematics, as dangerous and sensitive areas.

Yet the Royal Society, founded in 1660, although regarded as a great force of scientific enlightenment, had amongst its founders convinced and erudite alchemists and astrologers such as Elias Ashmole — and even Newton and Kepler were convinced astrologers. Like Dee, the two latter combined a modern and Renaissance view of science — with Kepler very much a halfway figure, with his controversy with Robert Fludd on the one hand yet his esoteric interest in other directions.

Another semi-underground stream flowing from the Rosicrucian attempt at synthesis of science, religion and politico-social theory is that of Freemasonry, where, like other symbolic systems put into other forms, such as the Tarot cards, we find the preservation of illuminating symbols by those who have little appreciation of their real value and potential.

It is not our intention to attempt a history of magic, even though one written from the 'inside' would be of great interest.* This must await a qualified historian who is also a practising magus, though the work of scholars such as Frances Yates and D. P. Walker at the Warburg Institute are steps in the right direction, taken in conjunction with the literary scholarship of, for instance, Kathleen Raine, the psychological studies of C. G. Jung and the scholarly researches into mysticism of R. C. Zaehner.

We have merely tried to show in a brief fashion some of the links in the tradition, a tradition that stems originally from a fusion of the Christian and the Classical world — the heights of speculative philosophy of the former being taken up by the humanising influence of Christianity, and with further re-injection of forgotten wisdom via Islam, having a profound formative influence on European history of thought, and holding a mediating position whilst ultimately being rejected by the warring factions of religion on the one hand, and of the new technological science and classical humanism on the other.

We feel much has been lost by default. Valuable matter that has fallen between the entrenched interests of contending parties and it is this that we are attempting to revive as a practical system through the studies of this book.

---

* Gareth Knight subsequently fulfilled exactly this with his 1978 book *A History of White Magic,* also known as *Magic & the Western Mind* (1991), intended for the general reader. Re-issued in 2011 by Skylight Press.

EXERCISE FOR CHAPTER IX

A winding stair is there, for you to climb,
It is a symbol of your own true self.

The basic exercise of this and the following chapter is the formulation of a winding stair through the inner senses, to the Inner Creation, and also to a direct mystical awareness of the Heaven World of God.

Be aware of the Christ at the Round Table holding a lamp, see a door appear behind him in the Upper Room. (In another sense this is represented by Daleth, the Door, in the Cube of Space.) See him beckon you to the door and be aware of the door swinging open.

For the time being simply look through the door at visions that may appear beyond it. This is the beginnings of a higher clairvoyance that is Christ-oriented.

In the next chapter we shall describe some of the things that may occur at such time as you are called to step through that door to tread the spiral ways of the inner mansions of the soul and of your Father's house — a veritable stairway through the stars.

CHAPTER X

The Dark Cloud

The passing through to the Inner side of Creation is an experience that can be gained in a number of ways; we have built a system of symbolic images that will form a safe and balanced preliminary to such work. It is now important that we give some indication of the kind of experiences that may be met with there.

All magic is basically a manipulation of the creative imagination, and can be performed in a group or individual manner. Group work is more conducive to quick and powerful results, but has its risks because the group whole is greater than the individual parts, and any psychic unbalance can cause an overburdening of the weakest link in the circle. Either subjective or ritual methods may be used, the latter making physical actions an 'earthing' of the matters that are the subject of meditation, prayer or contemplation, and again these can be an individual or a group effort.

We give here a number of actual techniques, and their results, with the intention that this may prove a stimulus and fund of suggestion for the discerning student. All the material is original and the fruit of personal experience and where we have gone others may follow or break new trails by their own efforts.

The first account is of an initial working with a small group of students. The series was conducted with a view to seeing how far it might be possible to evolve a technique which could be applied by the average student in the environment of his own home with a group of two or three friends. To few is it possible to work under full ritual conditions, so technique was deliberately kept to the simplest possible form.

The method of working was that of an exercise of the creative imagination using the traditional symbolism of one of the Paths of the Qabalistic Tree of Life as a basis. In the particular working that follows, that of the 32nd Path, the traditional symbols to be used as a structure were the Temple of Malkuth (a simple basic form using the traditional colours and Archangel or the Sephirah); the Tarot Trump XXI, called the Universe; the Hebrew letter Tau; the astrological sign of Saturn; and the basic symbolism of the Sephirah Yesod. All other symbolism that occurred was spontaneous. That this other symbolism was as powerfully evocative as the set symbolism may be suggested by the fact that after this working the leader of the group was laid up under the doctor with a swollen foot caused by a particularly virulent mosquito bite, and thus became unexpectedly a parallel of the lame figure met in the middle of the Path. It is not necessarily the aim of such working to achieve these untoward effects but such 'coincidences' give some indication of the power of the creative imagination.

It would, of course, be possible to start such a 'journey' into the Inner Creation from any symbol or symbolic picture. St. Ignatius used scenes from the Bible in his Spiritual Exercises for the Jesuit Order. One could tread through the adventures of the protagonist of *The Chemical Marriage of Christian Rosenkreutz*, said to be a particularly potent exercise, especially if conducted in the seven days following Easter Sunday as in the original tale. Fairy tales, legend or myth could be used — or simply any painting or drawing, rather in the fashion of Mary Poppins. However, the advantage of the Qabalistic Path is that it does give some kind of structure to follow as a guideline, and one can be more free-ranging and adventurous as experience is gained.

The following is the transcript of five people, who visualised what was described by the leader of the group (the author) as images arose spontaneously into his mind.

PATH WORKING — 32nd Path, Tuesday, 8th June, 1965, 9 p.m.
INTENTION: An initial exploration of the inner planes.

We are seated in a circle, in this room, with the small table in the centre on which is a lighted candle. This table in the centre we now see to be shaped like a double cube. It is a ten-sided altar of the Temple of Malkuth, which is the temple representing the physical universe. Underneath our feet is a floor of black and white paving and all about us there is a grove of black pillars shot with gold. There is, in the flame of the candle, reaching right up to the roof, the guardian of this temple an archangelic figure in the colours of Malkuth — citrine, olive, russet and black — the colours that one may see in an apple for example, the colours of the fruits of the earth.

At the far side of the temple, that is, the Eastern side, there is a doorway, central between two other doorways, and over this door-way there hangs a curtain. This curtain is in the form of the Tarot card allocated to the 32nd Path, Trump XXI, the World, or Universe.

Now the guardian of this temple of Malkuth, the archangelic figure of Sandalphon, has moved over to the East and is indicating the veil picture. It shows a great oval wreath of laurels intertwined with lilies and roses.

The centre of this wreath is completely dark, indigo-black. About this wreath are figures at the four corners: at the top left-hand corner there is the representation of the head and shoulders of a man; at the top right-hand an eagle; at the bottom left-hand a bull; at the bottom right-hand a lion. These are the symbols of the four Elements and they have other interpretations at various levels of understanding.

Now we see in the centre of the dark oval, coming as it were from a great distance, a pale naked hermaphroditic figure, having a bright-blue scarf wrapped symbolically about it and holding two spirals, one in each hand, a gold spiral and a silver spiral — and it is a shimmering figure, as if it were an image seen in a deep indigo pool.

Now this figure is beckoning to us and we are going to step through the laurel wreath into this indigo pool. I will go first, with J *(one of the physical group present)* bringing up the rear.

As we step through, the archangel of the temple of Malkuth stays at the threshold behind us. Now we find ourselves floating, as it were, in a deep, very dark indigo mist, as if we were right under the sea. Almost on the bottom, on the bed of a deep indigo ocean. And under our feet we can feel the rough going, as if it were the bed of an ocean. It is sandy but with rocky and uneven surfaces, dark slippery weed, and there are creatures, fish-like creatures, only we cannot clearly discern their shape, floating, swimming around about us — though they do not interfere with us in any way. We are actually in the etheric sea which is all about our planet and links the whole physical universe together.

As we proceed we find that we are approaching somewhere which looks a little lighter and there is a giant figure approaching us. He appears to be lame, and has a large staff and is using it as a kind of crutch. A huge figure about six or seven feet tall, seemingly Greek. It might be Oedipus — he who answered the riddle of the sphinx — or it might be the healing god, Asculepius. He is waiting for us, by a pathway we are to tread.

He is looking at us searchingly and now he turns, limps off, and we follow him, and the way we are going is more in the nature of a defined path now, and we are in what might be called a glade on the sea bed. Instead of trees around us there are great walls of weed trailing upwards; dark shadows all around us; but above us in gold — forming a golden light for itself — the Hebrew letter of the Path — the letter Tau. One is reminded of the relationship between the shape of this letter and the great limping figure that we have met.

We pass on and as we leave this glade the way gets darker and we are now pushing on in absolute pitch darkness. But as we go we begin to feel that we are losing our weight. We are gradually becoming less dense and we are beginning to float upwards, and as we float upwards the dark indigo begins to become more of a blue — deep blue, almost Mediterranean blue, of the sea and we are about to break the surface of the ocean. And suddenly we have broken through and we are just above the surface of the sea, and as we look up we see in the sky, huge above us, the planet Saturn with its great disc-shaped rings around it and its several moons, which we count and find to be nine in number.

And looking down, just before us, we see a barge — a long low black barge. One imagines like the one the three mourning queens came in to fetch the dying Arthur. A great tall figure is in it, in purple, and we get into this barge, and he has — strange though it may seem in a deep sea — a long pole, and he is punting us along, as it were, and we glide over the surface of the sea, conscious of the starry sky above us dominated by this huge stellar figure of the planet Saturn, and we approach an island. And the great dark purple figure pulls up the boat before we reach the island, and we are going to remain a little way off shore.

The island is a grey kind of volcanic rock and upon it, dominating it, is a nine-sided building, shaped something like an old threepenny piece, only with nine sides. And as we watch it the whole island and the building upon it begins to glow and become translucent so that we can see inside a glowing bluey purple greyish bright lozenge, and there, seated on a throne, is a great female figure — a queen or goddess of the Moon.

She has a heavy ponderous build and white pallor of skin one would associate with the Moon. She may well be one of the classical goddesses dedicated to the Moon. And about her are many moon maidens — there do not seem to be any men in attendance upon her.

Now she is holding up her hand in recognition and salutation to us and we will have a few moments silence while each one of us sees if she has any message or token for us individually. This may not be in any particular words, it may be a symbol, or it might just be a feeling of recognition. We will hold this figure in our minds in silence for a few moments.

* * * * * * *

The island is becoming opaque now, and it has a grey volcanic look, indeed much as the surface of the physical moon has. The boat we are in turns about and the great purple figure ferries us back. Under the cloak one can discern the wings of the archangel of the Sphere of Yesod, Gabriel, archangel of the Annunciation and of visions. He ferries us back beneath the great Saturn display in the sky, to a point in the ocean where we step out onto this water and begin to sink down into the darkening depths, becoming heavier as we go, until we are in complete darkness and our feet touch the ground of the bottom of the ocean.

We proceed back the way that we came, and find ourselves in the grove of weed and submarine life which is the glade where is to be found the great golden key of this path and the huge lame club-footed man with the crutch. He salutes us as we pass. We are conscious of the great golden Tau making a faint light on our path.

Back in the dark deep indigo drifting mist or liquid, feeling under our feet the rough sandy surface and about us the fish or larvae of the etheric plane, and now we come to a curtain through which we started originally. There is this oval which we can just make out in a dark grey or blackish wall, and we step through the oval, myself leading, J bringing up the rear, and find ourselves back in the temple of Malkuth.

We are all in the temple now. We are standing about the altar in the centre with the light upon it, the black and white paving underfoot. And the great guardian of this place seals the opening through which we have come and has now gone back to his place in the flame of the altar lamp.

Gradually the vision fades and we find ourselves sitting in this room about the table.

* * * * * * *

This comprised of the first working of what was to become a long series lasting some five years that became less rigidly structured in formal Qabalistic symbolism as time went by. Of subsequent workings, four turned out to be minor Elemental initiations, though this was not realised until the pattern of the four workings was almost complete.

After about twelve months of weekly meetings (and regularity is important, be it weekly, fortnightly, monthly, or quarterly, for it is a method of gauging earthly time on the Inner Creation) a conscious contact was made with a being who gave his name as an ancient Greek philosopher and appeared to the inner eye in this guise. It was of interest that his identity was first given in codified form, by a nick-name by which he was known to his contemporaries, and which had to be looked up in a classical dictionary.

Whether this being contacted was, or is, this historical figure is not a matter of fundamental importance to the work in hand. The important thing is that the name and historical personality form a basis on which imagination can build, in formulating a link in consciousness. Certainly a very real, warm and living contact was made, which by experience left no doubt that there was a beneficent and wise person working with and through the group and who had others with him some of whom he also introduced to form an 'inner' part of the group.

A particular type of working developed whereby members of the physical side of the group asked questions of those on the inner side. The inner communicators in the account that follows are designated X and Y and the members of the physical group A, B, C, D, E and F. None of the latter were 'mediums' or 'mediators' in the specialised sense. The replies to questions came from whoever felt they discerned them, and this varies from question to question. It is for this reason that the replies are given in the form of 'X via A' or 'Y via D' and so on.

MEETING OF 6th JULY 1969 WITH X & Y

1. **A:** We are wondering if it is possible in any way to carry out work under scientific conditions which might give us some recordable results and assess our capabilities in this direction.

2. **X via A:** X looks reflective for a moment and says that this will in fact be a possible approach to our work, or at best one thread that we can pursue. Doing this on smaller topics will aid any work we might do on larger topics. He suggests that we look around in our own environment or circumstances, or in other words the people involved in the group, to see what inadequacies or imbalances, material or otherwise, we might wish to harmonise. So in fact we should look for some really simple, very small but nevertheless important knot, so to speak, on which we can test our strength and see how it is unravelled. That will lead onto similar knots, possibly at first confined just to our own immediate problems, material and otherwise, and then perhaps progressing outwards until ultimately these principles of observation and recording can be applied to even the biggest problems that we may undertake.

3. **B:** I would like X to suggest a specific problem or undertaking we can work on.

4. **X via A:** This seems to follow on from my question. The idea I get again is of knots or tangles. As far as what I am thinking of is concerned X seems to be throwing the ball back very firmly in our court, saying that we may provide the help and the motive power but they are your problems and you should look at the environment around you in the way that you might lay out a pack of cards and examine the situation. And strictly speaking you should behold a tapestry of many threads and colours that weaves a beautiful pattern. If you look at it carefully and analyse it quite simply with the intellect with which you are endowed and a measure of intuition you will find these knots, these tangles. These represent problems upon which to work.

5. **B:** I would like to suggest a problem and to have some indication on how to solve it. That problem is how can we improve our individual communication with the inner planes and with X in particular.

6. **X via C:** I can see him holding out his hands to B saying, 'Do you *know* I'm here?'

7. **B** *(after some hesitation)*: And the answer is No.

8. **X via C:** And he seems to be answering you, 'That is the answer to your question.'

9. **D:** May I ask whether X has any advice for me.

10. **X via E:** I am getting some reaction to that. It is just two phrases actually. 'Follow (or make) your own contact. Follow your own inner light.'

11. **C:** Yes I got 'Follow your own...' but I didn't get any more.

12. **C:** If we selected a large project, such as Nigeria, or race relations, Vietnam, should we, or could we, on our own responsibility, and with any effect, channel the Christ force directly to such areas?

13. **X via C:** The world is very old, and in universal terms it is still very young, but in such small specific areas, such as particular countries, it would not be right to try to do anything in that way. But he is saying that — I can't get his actual words, that is why I am having to get the idea — the root of the problem of Vietnam or Nigeria or anywhere else is in certain conditions of man. And that if one saw those conditions and decided what they were and then directed the Christ force in a positive and not a destructive way — that is if one came up against greed one would not try to destroy it but to direct force positively on its opposite — in this manner we could have some effect. But he is saying that we must still remember that the world is very young and the universe very large and that while these problems are to us of great enormity they, in a way, have their place. There are always two sides to the balance-scale and the negative or apparently evil side has, in a way in this sense, its balance, but that we could work in the way he suggests and have an effect.

14. **F:** Before I ask my question I have something which I think might help give an answer to B's question about the quality of our contact. It has come to me that perhaps our astral images are not as strong as they ought to be and that we are not building them with enough strength and determination. And that perhaps it would be a good idea to formulate for ourselves a very clearly determined call sign which we can use whenever we try and contact X on the inner planes. And if this is clearly defined and one that we all share then this may act to improve the quality of the contacts we make. My question is if he, X, can give us any advice as to how the group of three of us working in Stroud can develop and still serve the large group.

15. **X via F:** He seems to be saying that there is great scope for any combination of people working apart and outside the larger group, and that while we work as a large group together and also work as individuals serving the group, so we can also work in smaller groups of two, three and four. He seems to be saying that we have established quite a strong link with the work we have been doing and should continue to develop this link bearing always in mind that we are part of a large group and that what we do there must be part of the large group's service.

16. **E:** The question I wish to ask is somewhat of a personal one. It is that I have many interests and projects all going forward, if not at cross purpose then cross current one with another. So am I giving service in as effective a way as I might be? And if not, how may I improve it?

17. **X via E:** The impression I am getting is as follows — that I am one who works under the direction and jurisdiction of the Lords of Synthesis and am primarily concerned with acting as a focus in this life for the pattern of the Aquarian Age man. It has been pointed out before by one of the other masters that I am a human synthesis and this raises difficulties because it means that within myself there is a vortex of very many incoming and contradictory forces which have to be resolved to a pattern and the result of this should be harmony through conflict. Therefore there will be very many skeins or threads to the tapestry I have to weave but if the dedication is right, however muddled all else may seem in the short term, the destiny will be achieved.

18. **Y via A:** I seem to get the impression from X that the origination or originators at work behind our group are far far distant in space or far far inside, much farther than even X or Y, and these two are merely representatives of representatives and so on.

19. **C:** I would like to ask Y why it is that when we receive any information from the inner planes we seem to start on one tack and go quite well along it for ages and then it breaks off and seems to stop altogether as it did, or as it seemed to do anyway, with *The Cosmic Doctrine* things that we were getting through.

20. **Y via C:** He is saying something about that if any of us could sit with him at a table and write down what he said and the quality of reception was clear and fine enough, there is much more that could have come in a short space of time. But as we are not able to receive this clearly we had to be shown by pictures and by ideas rather than words, which take much time. That they had said to us at that time that we would be given certain things which must be purely experimental

as the inner planes have not sufficient knowledge how these things would effect or be effective upon the physical plane and only we could show them. And also that perhaps the reception at that time was not clear enough for the project. Those on the inner planes had experimented and the experience was not successful at that time. This does not mean that it is forgotten or abandoned or lost but that the further progress is achieved the further work will be done. But as for other projects he would suggest that they were all part of one whole which is the bringing of the cosmic force to earth, the Christ force to man. He thanks us for our co-operation in the work we tried to do on *The Cosmic Doctrine*, and he will be seeking our co-operation and communicating again.

21. **E:** I had the impression at first of him showing a model of the 3 rings and indicating that everything was cyclic and had times and seasons and that *The Cosmic Doctrine* was the basis of everything and it would come through in whatever we did in some manner or other. I would like to ask Y if the ritual work that we do has any great effect with regard to bringing through *The Cosmic Doctrine*.

22. **Y via E:** The impression I am getting is that it is of very great value in establishing a kind of astral eidolon of the basic principles of *The Cosmic Doctrine* in so far as the ritual we use is based directly upon it and there is no other ritual being used which is so clearly related to it, although of course any other ritual must be based on it, though indirectly, because it is the true pattern. And that with regard to this pattern generally just having the pattern being built again and again in one's mind is of very great use for it can act as a seed from which much can grow, just as a crystal in a saturated solution can suddenly cause the whole crystallisation of that solution or the building up of a great crystal. If one has this basic concept firmly embedded in one's mind it is, even more than the Tree of Life, a seed idea from which much can grow. And the secret of its use is just as with the Tree of Life, not being too rigidly bound by the symbolism and by its occult fencing off from life. But realising how the whole of life — and he stresses the whole of life no matter what area it may be, however mundane, however commonplace, however large, however small, is based on this pattern. Now he is trying to get something else across but I cannot quite pick up what it is. I think he is just saying it would help all of you very greatly if you would take the trouble to draw with coloured pencils or ink, or even construct with wire or any other material the basic construction as described in *The Cosmic Doctrine* and this will also have the effect of ritual in bringing this concept down nearer to the earth plane.

23. **Y via E:** I get the impression that he is saying that this has been a very successful meeting and that he hopes that it will be repeated possibly at regular intervals, the frequency to be determined by us, and that they very much welcome the initiative coming from our side in seeking them out with our difficulties and problems rather than their having to come to us and try and contact us, often without fully realising properly what our problems are. And that if we are more forthcoming and willing to take our problems and lay them before them then very much more can be done, not only for us personally but to help the work ahead as well. So often the inner planes are held in laudable but rather restricting reverence and many of the things that they say, because they have not come through properly, or because they are not completely aware of all the difficulties of communication (and what may leave them in one form may reach us in another), there is no great virtue in our just trying to act out an incomplete or distorted message. If there is any difficulty at all we should not hesitate to refer back to them for we are all brothers and all servants of the one cause. I give you my greeting and the greeting of all initiates and adepts of the Planetary Hierarchy of which you are a part — and he says with something of an enigmatic smile —for we all form part of a complex which could be illustrated by the diagram of *The Cosmic Doctrine*. Greeting my friends.

*   *   *   *   *   *   *

Some remarks may be appropriate on the above. We stated that none of the Group were especially gifted at communication by psychical or telepathic means and that responses tended to come through different people. There was plainly a difference in the overall ability range of those present and, as may be ascertained from statements 5 to 7 above, one member found particular difficulty in the active use of the imagination. The communicator seemed to imply that this particular individual needed to put more faith into his imaginative work.

It should be said that this person played an important part in the working group even if, by the written record, he did not appear to contribute much. Although he seemed to have a certain blockage on the imaginative level he contributed by stability and also by good advice on occasion. In another context he seemed to be able to act as a catalyst, for in forming an experimental group of his own at a later date those with him were able to make contacts far beyond their usual capability even though he himself again appeared to contribute little. This goes to show that the gifts of the individual are many and various in this line of work.

An examination of this whole script will, we trust, serve to indicate something of the nature of the beings of the Inner Creation that were contacted, and may also throw some practical light on the detailed problems, outer and inner, of such communications generally.

The statements 1 to 4 are certainly sage advice that ought to be taken to heart by most occult students. For the real importance of taking small practical down to earth steps is emphasised as opposed to formulating more ambitious schemes that are never in fact ever properly acted upon and followed through.

The larger project seems to have a different appearance from the inner side of Creation as is indicated by statements 12 and 13. Here it is important to try to discern exactly what is being talked about, and much hangs on the use of the term 'Christ force', which is first used by one of the physical group. And indeed as the reply comes via this same person the communicator from the inner side is probably saddled with the concept whether he wishes or not, and has to make the best of it.

It is a somewhat ambiguous term, though much used in occult circles. It is usually found in use where some realisation or experience of the love of God as an experiential reality is having to be accounted for in terms of an occult/Hindu/monist reference system that can take no account of a personal God. By this convention people tend to be called 'entities', and their feelings 'forces'. But if we regard 'the Christ force' as 'the love of God' we can hardly expect to 'direct' it by magical operation or meditation. In practical terms it turns out to be at best an awkward and misleading way of talking about intercessory prayer; at worst a deluded way of talking about certain psycho-magical techniques.

The communicator seems to be regarding it as a psycho-magical technique though impelled by the highest motives. He seems to have what some would consider an over philosophic, even heartless, point of view about it. Though on reflection it may be seen as but confirmation of some of the 'hard' sayings of Jesus to the effect, for example, that 'the poor are always with us' and it was Judas, the socially conscious one, who turned out to be the betrayer of the Real.

There is certainly a tendency to impersonality of a certain kind in many communications from the Inner side of Creation and the question should be asked, but seldom is, whether this is to the good or no, and whether it is correct or no. We see something of another aspect of it in statement 18 of a kind of endless recession into vast distances. This may possibly be a kind of philosophical or epistemological illusion, and we have the same kind of effect operating on the Outer, or physical, side of Creation. The appearance is that we are tiny creatures on a minor planet of an insignificant star in an unremarkable galaxy in a space of inconceivably vast proportions. Yet the mystics of the world tell us that despite this appearance the Creator of it all is one in whom we live and move and have our being and who is closer than breathing, nearer than hands and feet. It would seem that a similar phenomenal environment appears on the Inner side of Creation also.

So we do well to bear in mind that there may be little difference in opportunities for wisdom on either side of the veil that divides inner from outer Creation, with possibly the better ones on our side because of the more objective nature of physical existence.

Nor are difficulties of communication often considered, which is why statement 20 has more than passing interest. It is not often one hears of occult experiments that are admitted to have failed. And we also see further difficulties in expression, for the term 'Christ force' is used again. One can only speculate at what might really have been meant by the term 'cosmic force to earth' that is apparently an equivalent and parallel to 'the Christ force to man'.

Statements 20 to 22 have much to do with a script received in 1922/3 by Dion Fortune, published under the title of *The Cosmic Doctrine*. There is much that one should suspect as to the claims that it is a point by point description of the inner and outer universe. And this the more so in the coming to light recently of some of the teachings of Dr Moriarty, with whom Dion Fortune worked in her early days in occultism. He formed the basis, in somewhat glamourised fashion, for the protagonist of her stories *The Secrets of Dr. Taverner*.

From Moriarty's teachings, which are not of exceptional interest, but an amalgam of various occult theories current at the turn of the nineteenth century, together with certain concepts of his own, it is evident that much of what appeared to be inner plane communication was more in the nature of conscious or unconscious memory. This is not necessarily a denigration of the material but serves to show that all such matter *must* be judged according to its intrinsic merits and that little reliability can be placed on alleged sources.

However, in its basic outline of three rings in the form of a gyroscopic figure, there is an archetypal pattern that holds good for much of the structure of the Creation, though it is going too far to ascribe to it a structure of the psychology of God. And some of the more detailed teachings on 'life swarms' and so on are in places obscure and indeed self-contradictory, relying heavily on an idiosyncratic Hindu type cosmogony. Much the same could be said of H. P. Blavatsky's rather better known *The Secret Doctrine* which also starts from geometric archetypal principles but then develops into detailed but frequently suspect speculation passing as arcane revelation.

The gyroscopic pattern in fact, if laid flat, gives the circled cross pattern which is of basic importance to practical magical working on the one hand, and the structure of the psyche, at any rate according to Jung, on the other (Figure 24). And from this 3 and 4 are derived the archetypal 7 and 12 that figure largely in most occult philosophical and magical systems.

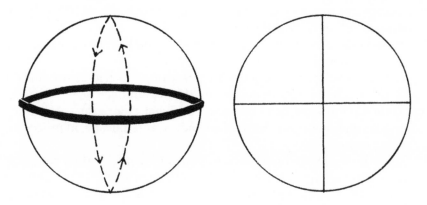

Figure 24

From these fundamentals that are the root of *The Cosmic Doctrine* the injunctions of statements 21 and 22 make sense. They do not imply that that work is by any means infallible. The rituals mentioned, for those interested, were very similar in pattern to those described in the works of W. G. Gray, particularly in *Magical Ritual Methods* and *Seasonal Occult Rituals*. They were not these rituals but derived from similar basic principles.

Further information on these matters was given in a meeting the following month, as well as some other interesting aspects of communication and group work of this type, so we give this further script, which also has something to say about the much vexed and abused subject of reincarnation.

MEETING WITH X – 28.9.69.

1. **F:** How can we best develop ourselves as ritual magicians? We have not had much success so far in the sub-group.
2. **X via F:** All things have their beginning and beginnings may be very small ones. 'Fools rush in where angels fear to tread.'

3. **G:** How should I improve my occult studies?

4. **X via G:** Study the Tree of Life and try to meditate more often.

5. **A:** What should be the future line of the Stroud group in addition to path working and ritual — if there is anything in addition to this?

6. **X via A:** A symbol is given of standing on the edge of a deep chasm, unable to see the other side, darkness in front, throwing a thread out in the darkness to the other side — the group and individuals doing this several times — and then making a way across this strong but slender link. A feeling of pioneering.

7. **X via G:** It seems to be by the methods of path working and rituals rather than by any new form of endeavour.

8. **C:** Is my own particular job with this group finished as my contact seems much less clear than it was in the beginning.

9. **X via C:** You have been contacted on what is for you a well worn groove, and now a new form of contact is, and must be, in process of being made.

10. **X via E:** An image of sun shining on the earth and then clouds of the earth coming in between, though the sun is still shining all the while. The clouds are bearers of rain which fructifies the ground so that when the clouds pass away there will be opportunity for new growth.

11. **X via A:** The impression that it is a question of phase, there is always this cyclic pattern and the pattern may be short or long.

12. **X via E:** In this sun and earth symbolism there is also an allusion to being a priestess of Apollo and having an ancient contact, almost as old as the earth itself. Any interruptions to this contact are very minor, even if the contact were to be cut off or obscured for a whole life time, it would still be relatively temporary and a part of the growth of the spiritual destiny of C.

13. **E:** X stated on an earlier occasion that few people had realised that *The Cosmic Doctrine* was a great practical system as well as a theoretical construction. I would be interested to have him expand on this, as to how we can work out the practical system he referred to.

14. **X via E:** A figure is building up a circle on the floor split into the 12 signs of the zodiac. A vertical circle is travelling round in a clockwise direction cutting through the zodiacal circle at two points. It is going round in time with the year. One stands in this circle looking in the direction of its plane so that at each part of the year one is looking at a different zodiacal sign. This represents one's intention. Another circle is building up vertically, laterally to the other one, which is on one's right and left hand and represents planetary forces, that one works with as tools. The impression is that one works in conjunction with an

astrological ephemeris, working on the general lines of an astrological sign in the appropriate month, when the sun is in that sign, and doing rituals and workings of one kind or another according to particular configurations of the planets. There is also a reminder that the Moon has a certain particular influence in this, in that it does a complete zodiacal revolution itself while the sun goes through one sign. There is an analogue between the moon's movement and the sun's and also an analogue between the sun's annual movement and the great cycles of a lifetime, and ultimately of the Precession of the Equinoxes, which takes one into cosmic cycles and astrology. X says, 'Work for 12 months upon these lines and you will find you have all the practical guidance that you need and probably more!'

15. **X via F:** You should not be too tied up with the terminology given to *The Cosmic Doctrine* by Dion Fortune, but use your powers of visualisation as far as possible, and your own experience and powers of interpretation.

16. **F:** Is there any specific way in which we should interpret our password for the season — *The Fruits of the Earth.*

17. **X via E:** A picture of someone going out and collecting fruit, and the phrase; 'Go out and collect them, the harvest only comes to the harvesters.'

18. **X via C:** When you collect the fruit you also collect the seed for the next cycle of growth. Picture of a plum stone.

19. **X via E:** Picture of a tree which keeps getting bigger and bigger and bigger. Concept that there is fruit in growth itself. Growth is one type of fruit. And all should benefit from this, the one who grows and those around him. Be prepared and willing also to benefit from the growth of others — this is the opposite side of the coil of self-sacrifice. Self-fulfilment should bring benefits for oneself and for all.

20. **A:** Why is it necessary that I should be periodically obsessed about details of my past lives? Are details I have received of these correct — particularly in relation to my last incarnation?

21. **X via E:** There is a difficulty of communication here. It is difficult for X to get straight through to A and also difficult to get through via anyone else because they have lack of relevant data in their minds.

22. **C:** I see X going towards A, and shining. His cloak swells out and C is absorbed almost.

23. **E:** By virtue of this question X seems to have become aware of a personal psychological problem and will very likely do something about it, but it is not something that can really be done by question and answer in the present circumstances. If and when such difficulties occur C should make contact with X for specific guidance at that time.

24. **E:** Why is the doctrine of reincarnation not accepted by the Christian West? If the incarnation of Christ was the incarnation of the Logos, why has not Christianity spread over the entire world instead of being in fact a minority religion on a worldwide basis?

25. **X via E:** There are many questions wrapped up in this question. The West has had the spiritual destiny of the development of the personality to its greatest possible degree and this could only come about to its fullest extent if the general belief is that the one personality is all that we have. The Christian religion has not spread all over the globe because different civilisations have their own destinies to work out and it may be — put pictorially — some sons will work in their father's mansion, some in the fields, some even wandering far away, but all are his sons none the less and will be called home when the day draws to its end. Reincarnation is a fact and this has been held in the East. Although it has had some popular distortions grafted into it, these should not blind one to the main truth. Nor should the fact of the importance of the incarnation of the Logos cause one to take all Christian theology without question.

26. **F:** Is there any way we can improve the effectiveness of our group or is X satisfied that we are proceeding as best we can on a certain line.

27. **X via F:** Make clear your aims and intentions and put your energies into them.

28. **X via E:** We are living in the best of all possible worlds in this regard, though the best may not be terribly good. You are making as much progress as may reasonably be expected in the light of your own circumstances, psychology and so on, but there is always room for improvement, given harder work, dedication, and so on. But we do not live in a perfect world and we are not perfect people so there will always be difficulties of one kind or another. The art of adeptship is learning to live with these things and use them to the optimum advantage.

29. **E:** X goes on to say he is pleased with this type of meeting because it brings a closer liaison between himself and ourselves which will have quite lasting effects in our inner and outer plane relations as well as our own growth. There is one question that E had thought out rather flippantly earlier on which X would like to be asked. That is: where does X go when he is not talking to us?

30. **X via E:** I am a centre of consciousness and am much in contact with all of you all the time although you do not register it, because being members of my ashram you are my physical ears, eyes, hands and bodies, and on the physical plane I learn much through you. It is an analogue of the Christian doctrine of the Church being the Body of

Christ, but on a lower level physical members of a Master's ashram are the physical bodies of the Master, just as inner-plane members of the ashram are part of his consciousness on the inner planes. The Master is in fact an integrating influence, as a kind of group mind over all the members of his ashram, as one may have a group mind over a swarm of bees, and by his uniting principle — which could analogously be put that we are all 'within his aura' — we can link up one with another and with him and with others, and there is much wisdom and strength and comfort available to any of us do we but realise it. It is always there but is all the more powerful if we can consciously realise it also. Something of the nature of this function can be gained by those with sufficient technical curiosity from the Tibetan's book *Telepathy and the Etheric Vehicle*.

Greetings my brethren, and to you and to all of us the fruits of the Earth, for in the light of what I have just said, you must collect them on behalf of all of us.

* * * * * * *

There is little further that need be added to this type of working. The comments on reincarnation must be judged on their merits. This is an issue that seems to contradict the orthodox Christian viewpoint, for if there is the prospect of Heaven for those who believe in the Incarnation, what need is there for reincarnation? To our mind, this is not so devastating a contradiction as it at first might seem. There are apparently souls who do reincarnate, even Christian souls, and if would seem that these do so voluntarily. Other reincarnation may take place involuntarily, particularly by those who believe in it, and thus we see that what we believe may be more important to us than we may realise. What we believe may well in fact be what we get — whether it be heaven, hell, another physical life, here or on another planet, or sheer extinction. This would seem to accord with the general principles of free will.

The occult idea of reincarnation for all that is current in occult circles is based on Hindu ideas deriving from a crude sense of justice, based on 'an eye for an eye; a tooth for a tooth', that finds it difficult to conceive of a personal God or to differentiate between condoning sin or forgiving it. The idea is a comparatively new one in the West, at any rate in this form; to the early Qabalists reincarnation was held to be the lot only of the very wicked.

When all is said and done, the most fruitful and practical form of endeavour is that of working to make the best of current conditions and opportunities, rather than becoming concerned with those of the past or the future. Teaching about such unverifiable matters must always be highly suspect for it relies so much on subjective elements in all the parties concerned.

Experience of types of astral magic tends to fall into definite patterns once experience is gained. At first, in the group mentioned above, all such explorations took place along a fairly well-defined structure of the symbolism of particular Paths on the Tree of Life. This gave way after a time to a freer approach deriving simply from a Tarot Trump. Those present were dealt cards from a pack of Tarot cards and the first one to receive a Trump then had to lead the working, starting off from that Tarot picture, leading where it might.

Again, ability was found to vary, not only between persons, but from time to time. However, as in all things, practice improves performance. At its most basic the working might be little more than a building of the picture on the card in three dimensions and being present 'in' the picture in a contemplative frame of mind. In another case it led off into endless mazes of rocks and caverns getting ever darker and more tortuous until a more experienced member took over and guided things back to light. From a formal Qabalistic point of view it was found possible to start any Path working from virtually any Tarot Trump — which suggests that the sacrosanct and rigid application of Tarot correspondences to the Tree of Life is of little real importance.

On other occasions strange landscapes were found, reminiscent of Lewis Carroll. And whilst some of these never appeared again, others, such as a large library, and various temple structures and environs tended to crop up from time to time.

Eventually, after a regular contact with a specific inner group was made, the pattern of working became more regular — starting off from a particular setting each time, making the personal contact with those behind it, and then going on from there under guidance. This guided work went in phases, and at the end of each phase the whole period of work would be compressed into a particular symbol, often in the form of a jewel. This would be impressed upon each one present to take into themselves as a kind of quintessence of all the experience that had been undergone and achieved by the group.

An important type of work centred around building the form of a temple in the atmosphere high above the earth. This took on, over the months, an amazing solidity, and appeared to act as a staging post, lens, or transformer, for certain spiritual forces or energies.

Once this was built and operating we were taken to a very complex, large and powerful kind of 'cathedral' farther out in 'space', as it were, wherein the central point of radiating force was that of the Christ. This at first came as something of a surprise as all the guides and starting points had been ancient pagan until then, usually Greek, Egyptian or Celtic.

By taking on various geometric formations, together with members of the inner side of the group, beams of light carrying various forces were channelled down via the temple in space to the centre of the Earth itself.

The lower end of this circuit of force was also experienced from time to time. Here, under the crust of the Earth one met a great non-human blacksmith-like being, and a presumably symbolic complex of three caves. The outer one was full of every imaginable kind of traditional elemental creature: elves, fairies, gnomes, in variety too complex to enumerate. Some of these seemed oblivious of our presence, others were much interested and fascinated. The real work took place beyond here though, in a second cavern which was pitch-black save for the light of our torches, and full of the most horrible, deformed and pathetic creatures. They scuttled away from the light into dark corners and crannies. Although creatures of darkness, and of frightening and hideous aspect, they were not, it appeared, evil in themselves, but were various elemental creatures that had been twisted and abused by evil, whether of human origin or otherwise. Taking our courage, faith and spiritual integrity in both hands we had to pass through this cavern (and it appeared that only incarnate humans could perform this task) to a tiny third cavern at the end, which was a spiritual oasis in the centre of this dark and torment, which we reinforced in particular ways that were indicated to us.

This type of working is indicative of a general pattern of bringing spiritual force (and perhaps the term 'Christ Force' which we have disparaged above is as near an approximation to describing it, in spite of its limitations) to bear on areas of pain and fear and darkness. We called it magic, others to whom it has been described recognised it as a particular type of mystical and intercessory prayer.

From time to time individual exercises were also received involving the transmission or manipulation of psychic, occult or spiritual forces. Some examples follow:

1. Breathing Exercise (for country or planet)

Silver disk over head. Activate on in-breath.
Send force down to molten centre of earth, where there is an intelligence, on out-breath.
Bring up from centre of earth through feet, body and head, via disk to high distant point of light on in-breath.
Fountain from the distant point over self and surroundings on out-breath.

2. Healing Exercise

Build figure of Asclepius first with serpent staff, then with the hands held out, fingers up, palms facing forward, force coming from them. Asclepius figure becomes radiant with light and the staff, between hands, changes to an oblong, with the snake inside the oblong, wriggling. The snake becomes made of light too.

Then, palms facing each other, fingers pointing forward, force coming from hands into oblong. Hands could be brought together or drawn apart, the snake becoming more brilliant and active the closer the hands are together.

For self treatment imagine Asclepius figure behind one and with hands coinciding with yours. There is room for experiment with patient. Need not be confined to treatment of physical disease but to all types of disharmony.

3. Jewel Exercise

Visualise ruby centre and metallic rays, small, draw into solar plexus centre, then see jewel concentrated in solar plexus centre, and rays become force raying out to body and aura. For stabilising, and getting onto contact.

Visualise jewel life-size with iron rays. Draw it onto yourself. Gives strength. Visualise jewel as crystal for seeing visions, and as a means of communication. Visualising someone in it establishes two-way contact. Note, the crystal should be a ruby.

Other jewels can be formulated from other temples astrally visited. Centre point or area becoming jewel and pillars or superstructure becoming pattern for setting. This forms a kind of astral talisman for subsequently contacting that force.

4. Sun and Moon Exercise

Before starting, visualise high star-like point of light, forming triangle with the sun over on one's right and the moon over on one's left. Right hand receives force from sun, left hand from moon.

Breath in, gold force passes through you from sun to moon. Breath out, silver force passes through you from moon to sun. This has been found very powerful and could only be performed twice but individuals may differ.

Breath in, silver and gold force comes in together and up to head and into centre overhead. Go into Fountain Exercise (as in F. I. Regardies' *The Art of True Healing*).

5. Integration Exercise

Visualise two golden disks, one coming from heart centre of another and one from heart centre of oneself, as a means of integration. At this point of development in the human race this is of prime importance. Not only can this be done with one person but a whole group, race or nation can be centre of circle. Experiment.

Note (from X): 'All of creation is a particular pattern or set of patterns. But one can create something new by the manipulation of specific patterns into other specific patterns. This is the act of creation. Linking integrates humans into the larger pattern, and man himself as an individual has a set of patterns within him, and is himself a small cosmos. What some men would call their own state of chaos is no more than their perception of opposite pulls — towards centre or towards periphery — in their own cosmos, and in some men this is greater than in others.'

6. Contact with inner Cosmic Doctrine group

An inner group working on *The Cosmic Doctrine* can be contacted by ascending a blue light shaft (13th Path) carrying Cup, first projecting starting point from heart centre. One will come to Tarot Trump II (High Priestess). Place cup before this figure and proceed behind throne and through veil between pillars, into small room with rectangular conference table. You may meet others here.

There is also a Counsellor to this group who should be contacted. He may appear like a business executive in a grey suit. A call sign for him is to see the top of the room open out and to formulate a Greek letter *phi* before a background of stars moving away and outwards (i.e. an exploding or expanding universe as observed by modern science).

Later experiment has tended to show the symbol a truer representation of the real being. (He is Y in the above script.) The anthropomorphic executive figure seems a somewhat two-dimensional projection. He is very ready to answer questions.

Note: If attempting conversation at an astral level, it has been found helpful to visualise oneself too, and to visualise and 'hear' oneself talking to the other party, whose replies come in like manner — though there may also be an admixture of direct mind-to-mind contact. This alternately being positive and negative in astral working is rather like operating a radio-telephone which operates one way at a time only, and it may indeed be a help to say 'Over' as firm indication of end of sentence, and 'Out' at termination of conversation.

7. Close Contact

Visualise six rings interlocking at forehead/throat/heart/solar plexus/ genitals/feet. Heart first then others from top to bottom. Latter has been found almost to induce instant projection. There should be no disk projection from top of head centre; rather one should see and feel a connecting cord going upward to one's own Essential Being, from which one is suspended almost like a pendulum. This close form of contact is probably best only attempted with X or known beings of like stature.

8. Recommended Reading

Read the Gospel of St. John. He knew and realised much, and there is much truth and 'nuggets of gold' to be dug from him.

9. Meditation Symbol

The Three Rings of *The Cosmic Doctrine* can be represented by the circled cross. This simple diagram is as powerful as any complex spheres of lights etc. The lines are *'less lines of force than lines of influence'* and the parts of the circle can represent a number of different things ('grades of influence') like a compass card. In ritual the officers sit at ends of the cross and others sit about the circle. The Elements are not to be identified with any particular part of the circled cross but are simply one set of things which may represent that particular influence.

IMPORTANT NOTES (from Y)
'Some experiments or operations will take time and resources which are not available yet, but utilisation of all your present opportunities will make these further or future opportunities be realised. There is the real end of meditation, and the end meaning of realisation — when things become real in the physical and not just the mental sense.'

IMPORTANT NOTES (from X)

'My purpose is to have you work in conjunction with an inner group to get exercises and practices through, which are to be used and tested by you to see if they are viable, because we cannot on our side properly estimate their best use. *The Cosmic Doctrine* is a great practical system but this has not been realised. It can be used at different levels of development, up to the ultimate goal, which is to achieve the integration of the individual with the Whole—and the Whole with the One. Each one's gifts and talents will be used. We have been working on it for some time on the inner. I will not be concerned on all occasions. It will be difficult at first but as you go on the value will be self-apparent. You may continue with your wish to mediate spiritual forms to Earth, and also develop the ritual side on such exercises as the Pyramid of Mediation, which is best for your purposes but can be used in different ways, incorporating various exercises you have done, such as the Three Caverns.'

*   *   *   *   *   *   *

The Pyramid of Mediation and the Three Caverns are particular formations and visualisations that we mentioned earlier. We do not give precise details, for any who wish to pursue this type of work have been given sufficient for them to make the first approaches themselves and it would not serve any purpose to give highly complex workings designed for a specific context of time, place and personalities.

We have spent much time describing group work, but there is much that can be done by the individual, though indeed it is perhaps true to say that all occult work is group work whether the lone individual realises it or not.

Most of the exercises described can be applied by an individual in almost any circumstances. And the same applies to ritual. This is but a formalised and externalised form of meditation and contemplation and is eminently suitable for individual performance. In fact group ritual, with its greater complexity and occasions for distractions, is likely to be a stumbling and halting performance if those performing it have not had considerable practice on their own individual account.

We have already given sufficient basic principles in Chapter VII for anyone to start their own shrine room or cupboard, together with its 'inner' telesmatic structure. This should spring, preferably, from actual simple working without such equipment — the equipment being introduced to supplement and strengthen existing work. We find it necessary to say this because of a tendency in latter days, now that the technicalities of such matters are more accessible through published books, for some students to furnish themselves with a battery of accoutrements and then not know what to do with them. It is one thing to make or collect them, it is another thing to actually use them, and this is a clear case of getting the cart before the horse.

A simple ritual can be evolved from the structure of the symbolic exercises we have been working on throughout the length of this book. It is based upon burning incense, so it is necessary first to have a functional incense burner. It is not at all necessary to acquire an expensive thurible for this, which is in any case difficult to operate single handed in a confined space. Take an earthenware or fire-proof bowl about four to six inches across, fill it with sand to about an inch of the top and stand it on a tile. Then by placing a piece of charcoal block in the sand, dropping a few drops of methylated spirit upon it, and igniting this, a bed of red hot glowing charcoal will be obtained for putting a few fragments of incense on.

Ordinary charcoal blocks are best, (available from any church or incense supplier), rather than the impregnated self-igniting ones, which tend to give off their own fumes of saltpetre. For the purpose of this small ritual any general incense can be used, though experience and ingenuity will suggest ways of forming a battery of incenses for specific intentions. The only other piece of equipment needed is a small length of glass tubing for picking up methylated spirit, which also acts, for our purposes, as a symbolic spear.

The exercises described in the end sections of the chapters of this book can now be strung together accompanied by a simple physical ritual — though the order is slightly modified.

1. Take a fragment of a charcoal block, place it in the incense bowl, and contemplate it whilst building the Sphere around yourself. Realise it as emblematic of yourself and your own body and being.
2. Take up a few drops of methylated spirit in the glass tube (putting the forefinger over the top retains liquid in the tube by air pressure until the finger is released). Realise the tube to be emblematic of the Spear of Longinus that we visualise transfixing ourselves, with the spirit in the tube the charisma of the Holy Spirit. At the same time, with the inner senses, be aware of the Spear above yourself.
3. Release the spirit into the charcoal, at the same time feeling the Spear come down through you.
4. Contemplate the charcoal block, and yourself as well, as being a Grail, or cup or container for the Holy Spirit, as the block contains the methylated spirit.
5. Strike a match and hold it before you, identifying it with your own spinal column, and the Rod of Power, your own gifts that the

Holy Spirit works upon. Before it burns out, ignite the spirit that impregnates the charcoal block.

6. The flames will lick about the charcoal block. As they do so, visualise this as the Sea of Light about you, and be aware of this about yourself.

7. When the flames die down in a minute or so, a corner of the charcoal will be glowing red hot. Pick up the bowl and hold it before your face and blow slowly and rhythmically upon the charcoal block until it is glowing all over. As you do this rhythmic breathing be aware of the other companions of the Round Table and of your own work or contribution spreading through a whole corpus.

8. When the block is glowing red all over replace the bowl and contemplate it as emblematic of the Upper Room, a source of warmth and light, incandescent with the power of God and human dedication.

9. Take some incense and place it on the glowing charcoal. As the incense smoke rises be aware of your own intention and of the presence of the Christ. See him with your inner eye and be prepared to follow on whatever may transpire, be it mystical contemplation or meditative reflection or magical experience.

10. When finally the work is done it is symbolically ended by dispersing the ash of the block into the sand and clearing away the other utensils that have been used. Remember that the ending of a work of this nature should be as precisely defined as its commencement and performance — though if well done, and properly contacted, the effects may be with you for some considerable time.

The same sequence of symbols could also be subsumed in a prayer, for instance:

In the encompassing love of God	(Sphere)
I dedicate myself to his will	(Spear)
In the development of all my powers	(Rod)
Perceptive to his Love and purpose for me	(Cup)
Conscious of his glorious presence everywhere	(Sea of Light)
I salute my fellow servants of the way	(Round Table)
Looking to the unifying power	(Upper Room)
Of He Who is the True Light	(Light of Christ)
To guide me in the ways of the heights and	(Winding Stair and
of the depths and to bring me close to God	Dark Cloud)
in the working of his ways.	

We are working with psychological devices. This is the element of occult science that is in magic. Powers, forces or contacts made in meditation may be deepened and strengthened in ritual and concentrated into a quintessence in prayers such as the above, which by their mere recitation or recollection, after all the work that has gone into their formation, will make the powers and forces and contacts more readily available to everyday consciousness.

We are forced to talk here in terms of technology. But it would be the surest folly, arrogance and blasphemy to assume that one can 'tap' powers whether of God or of other beings and helpers simply by reciting formulae. The whole thing must be taken in the context of dedication and integrity and with the consciousness of being a branch, amongst very many others, of the True Vine.

This is to work in the true spirit of the dedicated re-discoverers and renovators of Christian magic in the West, Marsilio Ficino and Pico della Mirandola, and those who carried the torch after them such as Robert Fludd. Failure to maintain this pure dedication is to lay oneself open to all the dangers and delusions that critics of magic have always been ready to advertise about what should be the noblest of all arts and sciences.

EXERCISE FOR CHAPTER X

And climbing, though you cannot see,
The mist, the darkness, is my Radiancy.

We spoke, at the end of the last chapter, of a Winding Stair, ascending and descending through a turret off the Upper Room. We did not recommend venturing on to the Winding Stair until a period of simply observing what visions there might be had been gone through. Now is the time, when we have described some of the things that may be met, for the student to venture forth upon the Winding Stair.

It can be trodden in two directions — upwards or downwards.

The descent of the stair, which should be anti-clockwise, is indicative of a descent into one's own inner depths — call it the sub-conscious or unconscious if you will but it has its objective side.

It is important therefore, should we choose to descend, to carry a lamp, which is the Light of Christ. This will preserve us from any perils or illusions of the way, and act as a focus for service in the inner ways rather than the indulgence of an overweening curiosity.

The other alternative is the ascent of the stair, in a clockwise direction. This action is symbolic of a spiritual, as opposed to occult or psychical, quest, and the action of building the symbolism and using it is a commitment to that quest.

At the top of the tower, each one will find what he finds, but in the first instance let him see a cloud of mist. This is a symbol of the blindness of fallen, mortal man. In this, like a neophyte of the Mysteries, hoodwinked and bound, man must enter in faith, to lose himself in it in the sure confidence that he will be found. The entry into the mist as one ascends the winding stair is the beginning of true contemplation and of the colloquy of the soul with its Maker.

The cloud of mist is the same one that received the Risen Christ when he ascended before his disciples, and which will disperse to reveal him at the time of the Second Coming, or more accurately, at his Reappearance.

Whoever perseveres in the call to union within the mist, will bring something back into daily life, and the whole life and activity will spring from an ever deepening divine vitality.

This is a true raising of consciousness, of which there are two kinds, each valid in its own way, but one being higher than the other, because based on a more ultimate reality — on the Creator rather than the Creation. (Though in the end all Creation will be taken up into the Creator, thus bringing about the consummation of a 'higher monism'.) The two types of 'raising consciousness' are indicated by the two ways of proceeding within the Tower of the Winding Stair — upwards or downwards.

Those who read and follow the course of this book will be capable of both forms, in a unique and fruitful synthesis. The two various methods are more often found separately. The first in the contemplative mystics of the Church (and not only the Christian church, for the Christ can work through any form of religion, be it oriental or pagan, even 'irreligion' as long as the heart is open to receive the Divine Beloved). The other in the searchings of the psychoanalyst and in the meditations of the yogi and equivalent Western occult mental systems. Each has its own validity. Regrettably they are often confused one for the other, with regrettable misunderstandings. The process can be placed on the Tree of Life in the manner given in Figure 25.

The symbolic work that we have been doing is a preparation of the soul in the heart centre — in Tiphareth, the central Sephirah. There now is the possibility of descending through the unconscious to the 'inner earth' of Malkuth, or of ascending through the mystical consciousness to the 'inner Heaven' of the 'Earthly Paradise' of Kether (God being in his essence in the Ain Soph, which surrounds all).

The practical pursuit of the occult is very much a process of integration, or reintegration. First and foremost is the process of reintegration of the soul with God. The restoring of the bond of love that was once rejected — as in the parable of the prodigal son.

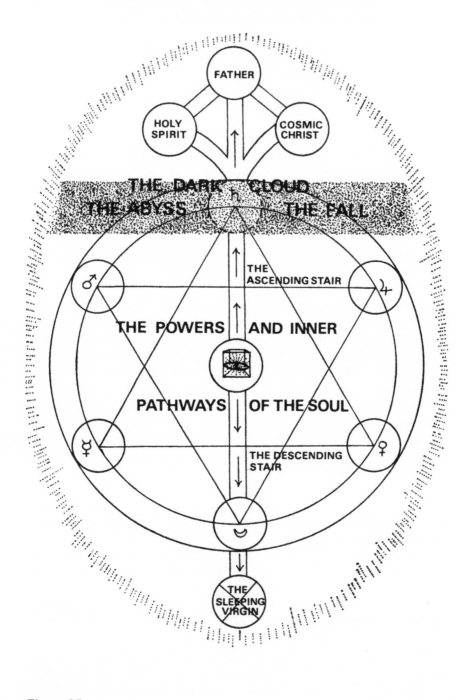

Figure 25

The other process of the restoration of relationships is the internal reintegration of man's own spirit, soul and body — which have become disjointed since the Fall. It is upon this that our relationships with others in the world depends. Had we all inner integration of ourselves and a restored relationship with God there would be no need of legal codes and sexual taboos. All codes of law are based on a falsity — our honour rooted in dishonour stands — that of fallen man's capacity for injuring himself, his environment, and others. St. Augustine saw that the redeemed man could safely follow the injunction: 'Love God, and do what you like.'

The Incarnation of the Logos rendered the possibility to restore things to wholeness — to 'make all things new'. And if so-called Christian man would accept this possibility and live by faith as if that wholeness were fulfilled then there might be some very great surprises. The injunction of Our Lord that 'greater things than this shall ye do' might even come true — which is a far cry from the unfaithful obsession with 'Christian morals' that makes the Church seem like, not an archangel trumpeting the good news of unutterable glory, but a nagging and repressed Victorian governess.

It may be remembered that this is no new phenomenon. When Moses went to Sion to commune with his God on the thundering mountain the original tablets of God's word were broken as a result of the inability of the people to accept them. In their place Moses carved the Ten Commandments — the great 'Thou Shalt Nots.' The Incarnation and the teaching of Jesus should have restored the original true message, for as he said, the old commandments were replaceable by two new ones, to love the Lord God, and thy neighbour as thyself.

The love of 'thyself' is also much neglected in its implications. When the self is reintegrated in true harmony then social harmony will follow. It does not necessarily work the other way about — religion is not a branch of the social services — even if the Christian life may manifest in works of genuine charity.

Much of what passes for dedicated social concern may indeed stem from an internal arrogance or a deep seated sense of guilt. The helping of others, particularly in an occult way, should stem from a loving involvement with the work of God the Holy Spirit in an act of identification with the love of God for another person and acting as a channel for that love. It has nothing to do with manipulating the inner world of others 'for their own good'. This is but a short step from the prying bureaucracy of Hell.

In the last analysis there is little difference between the ways that the soul may tread. They lead all to the same place and the only alternative is extinction. Evil in the end can only be transmuted or destroyed.

There is much spoken in some quarters of the dangers of the occult — and the possibilities of delusion and perdition in labyrinthine psychic ways. It is true some such risk exists. But most students who come to the occult come in dedication and a spirit of truth — and because they have not been led to God by the institutionalised religions of our day.

They may think it is their own spirit that they seek rather than an outside 'personalised' God. But man's spirit is the ultimate truth about himself. And it remains 'unfallen', but dissociated from the rest of the interior man. It is that part of each of us that abides forever in the heart of God.

Man therefore only finds himself when he discovers God. And conversely he discovers God in his fulness only when he finds himself — and is cured of his fallen disintegrated condition. The search for God and the Self are two sides of the same coin.

Some words of Anthony Duncan may serve to summarise the paradox:

A man would search for God?
Let him beware!
He will discover his true self.

A man would seek himself?
Let him beware!
He is in mortal peril of beholding God!'

ACKNOWLEDGEMENTS AND SELECT BIBLIOGRAPHY

In a work as wide ranging as this one, it is plainly not possible to list all the books that have helped to form opinion and give information. The following list is an acknowledgement of those works that are cited or quoted in the text or which have been particularly valuable and informative. The edition noted is that which was consulted.

ALLEN, P. M., *A Christian Rosenkreutz Anthology*, Rudolf Steiner Publications, 1968.

ANDERSON, F., *The Ancient Secret, in Search of the Holy Grail*, Gollancz, 1953

ANDERSON, B. W., *The Living World of the Old Testament*, Longman, 1967.

ANGUS, S., *The Mystery Religions and Christianity, a Study in the Religious Background of Early Christianity*, John Murray, 1925.

ANON., *The Cloud of Unknowing*, Penguin, 1961.

APULEIUS, *The Golden Ass, the Metamorphoses of Lucius Apuleius*, Heinemann, 1915.

ASSAGIOLI, R., *Psychosynthesis, a Manual of Principles and Techniques*, Hobbs Outman, 1965.

BAILEY, A. A., *Telepathy and the Etheric Vehicle*, Lucis, 1950.
— *A Treatise on White Magic — or the Way of the Disciple*, Lucis, 1934.

BARFIELD, O., *Saving the Appearances, a Study in Idolatry*, Harcourt Brace, n.d.

BLAVATSKY, H. P., *The Secret Doctrine* (abridged). Theosophical Publishing House, 1966.

BUBER, M., *I and Thou*, T. &T. Clark, Edinburgh, 1970.

BUCKE, R. M., *Cosmic Consciousness, a Study in the Evolution of the Human Mind*, Dutton, 1969.

BURKHARDT, T., *Alchemy, Science of the Cosmos, Science of the Soul*, Stuart & Watkins, 1969.

BUTLER, W. E., *How to Develop Clairvoyance*, Aquarian, 1968.
— *The Magician, his Training and Work*, Aquarian, 1959.

CHAVASSE, C., *The Bride of Christ, an Enquiry into the Nuptial Element In Early Christianity*, Faber, 1940.

COHN, N., *The Pursuit of the Millennium, Revolutionary Millenarians and Mystical Anarchists of the Middle Ages*, Paladin, 1970.

CRITCHLOW, K., *Order in Space, a Design Source Book*, Thames & Hudson, 1969.

DANIÉLOU, J., *The Lord of History, Reflections on the Inner Meaning of History*, Longmans Green. 1958.

DANTE, *The Divine Comedy* (3 vols), *Hell, Purgatory, Paradise,* Penguin, 1949, 1955, 1962.
— *La Vita Nuova* (Poems of Youth), Penguin, 1969.

DAVIDSON, G., *A Dictionary of Angels, including the Fallen Angels*, Collier Macmillan, 1967.

DAVIES, H., *Christian Deviations, the Challenge of the New Spiritual Movements,* S.C.M 1965.

DODS, M., *Mohammed, Buddha and Christ, Four Lectures on Natural and Revealed Religion*, Hodder & Stoughton. 1878.

DUGGAN. A., *Devil's Brood, the Angevin Family*, Faber, 1957.

DUNCAN, A., *Lord of the Dance, an Essay in Mysticism*, Helios, 1972.
— *The Whole Christ*, S.P.C.K., 1968.
— *The Christ, Psychotherapy and Magic, a Christian Interpretation of Occultism*, Allen & Unwin, 1969.
— *The Priesthood of Man*, Bles, 1973.
— *The Sword in the Sun, dialogue with an Angel*, Sun Chalice, 1997.

FIELD, M. J., *Angels and Ministers of Grace, an Ethno-Psychiatrist's Contribution to Biblical Criticism,* Longman, 1971.

FORTUNE, D., *The Cosmic Doctrine*, Helios, 1966.
— *The Mystical Qabalah*, Williams & Norgate, 1935.
— *The Secrets of Dr. Taverner*, Llewellyn, 1962.

GRAY, W. G., *Magical Ritual Methods*, Helios, 1969.
— *Seasonal Occult Rituals*, Aquarian, 1970.

GRAVES, R. & PATAI, R., *Hebrew Myths, the Book of Genesis*, Cassell, 1965.

GRAVES, R., *The Greek Myths*, Penguin.

HALEVI, Z. b. S., *The Tree of Life, an Introduction to the Cabala*, Rider 1972.

HAPPOLD, F. C., *Mysticism, a Study and an Anthology*, Penguin, 1964.

HERMAN, E., *The Meaning and Value of Mysticism*, James Clarke, 1916.

HOLMYARD, E. J., *Alchemy*, Pelican, 1957.

IGNATIUS, St., *The Spiritual Exercises*, Burns & Oates, 1963.

JAMES, J., *The Way of Mysticism*, Cape, 1950.

JAMES, W., *Varieties of Religious Experience, a Study in Human Nature*, Longman, 1902.

JOINT COMMITTEE ON THE NEW TRANSLATION OF THE BIBLE, *The New English Bible with the Apocrypha*, Oxford and Cambridge University Presses, 1970.

JUNG, C. G., *Memories, Dreams, Reflections*, Fontana, 1967.

— *Psychology and Alchemy*, Routledge & Kegan Paul, 1968.

JUNG, E. & von FRANZ, M. L., *The Grail Legend*, Hodder & Stoughton, 1971.

KEE, H. C. & YOUNG, F. W., *The Living World of the New Testament*, Darton, Longman & Todd, 1960.

LEADBEATER, C. W., *The Masters and the Path*, Theosophical Publishing House, 1927.

LEWIS, C. S., *The Allegory of Love, a Study in Medieval Tradition*, Oxford University Press, 1958.

— *The Great Divorce*, Bles, 1946.

— *Mere Christianity*, Fontana, 1955.

— *Miracles, a Preliminary Study*, Fontana, 1960.

— *The Screwtape Letters*, Fontana, 1955.

MONROE, R. A, *Journeys out of the Body*, Doubleday, 1971.

MORIARTY, Dr., *Aphorisms of Creation and Cosmic Principles*, privately published, c. 1920.

MORISON, F., *Who Moved the Stone?* Faber, 1944,

MULDOON, S. J. & CARRINGTON, H., *The Projection of the Astral Body*, Rider, 1968.

OLDENBOURG, Z., *The Crusades*, Weidenfeld & Nicolson, 1966.

PANNIKAR, R., *The Unknown Christ in Hinduism*, Darton, Longman & Todd, 1964.

PETITPIERRE, R. (Ed.), *Exorcism, Findings of a Commission convened by the Bishop of Exeter*, S.P.C.K., 1972.

PHILLIPS, J. B., *Ring of Truth, a Translator's Testimony*, Hodder & Stoughton, 1967.

— *Your God is Too Small*, Epworth, 1952.

PIXLEY, O., *The Armour of Light, Techniques of Healing the Self and Others*, Helios, 1969.

RAINE, K., *Blake and Tradition* (2 vols), Routledge & Kegan Paul, 1969.

RAINE, K., & HARPER, G. M., *Thomas Taylor the Platonist, Selected Writings*, Princeton University Press, 1969.

REARDON, S. M. G., *From Coleridge to Gore, a Century of Religious Thought in Britain*, Longman, 1971.

REGARDIE. F. I., *The Art of True Healing*, Helios, 1964.

RICE, C., *The Persian Sufis*, Allen & Unwin 1964.

ROLT-WHEELER, F., *Mystical Gleams from the Holy Grail*, Rider, n.d.

de ROUGEMENT, D., *Passion and Society*, Faber, 1956.

RUNCIMAN, S., *A History of the Crusades* (3 vols), Pelican, 1971.

SCHAYA, L., *The Universal Meaning of the Kabbalah*, Allen & Unwin, 1971.

SCHOLEM, G. G., *Major Trends in Jewish Mysticism*, Thames & Hudson, 1955.

SCUDDER V. D., *Le Morte d'Arthur of Sir Thomas Malory, a Study of the Book and its Sources*, Dent Dutton, 1921.

SPENCER, S., *Mysticism in World Religion*, Pelican, 1963.

TEILHARD DE CHARDIN, P., *Le Milieu Divan, an Essay on the Interior Life, Fontana*, 1964.

TUGWELL, S., *Did You Receive the Spirit?* Dorton, Longman &Todd, 1972.

WALKER, D. P., *Spiritual and Demonic Magic from Ficino to Campanella*, Warburg Institute, 1958.

WEAVER, R., *The Old Wise Woman, a Study of Active Imagination*, Vincent Stuart, 1964.

WEIL, S., *Waiting on God*, Fontana, 1959.

WESTCOTT, W. W., *Sepher Yetzirah, the Book of Formation and the 32 Paths of Wisdom*, John Watkins, n.d.

WHICHER, O., *Projective Geometry, Creative Polarities in Space and Time*, Rudolf Steiner Press, 1971.

WHITE, V., *God and the Unconscious*, Harvill, 1952.
— *Soul and Psyche, an Enquiry into the Relationship of Psychotherapy and Religion*, Collins & Harvill, 1960.

WILBY, B. L., *The New Dimensions Red Book*, Helios, 1968.

WILLIAMS, C., *The Descent of the Dove, a Short history of the Holy Spirit in the Church*, Faber, 1939.
— *The Figure of Beatrice, a Study in Dante*, Faber, 1943.
— *The Greater Trumps*, Faber, 1932

WILLIAMSON, H. R., *The Arrow and the Sword, an Enquiry into the Nature of the Deaths of William Rufus and Thomas Beckett, with some Reflections on the Nature of Medieval Heresy*, Faber, 1947.

WITCUTT, W. P., *Blake, a Psychological Study*, Hollis & Carter, 1946.

WRIGHT, J. S., *Christianity and the Occult*, Scripture Union, 1971.

YATES, F. A., *Giordano Bruno and the Hermetic Tradition.* Routledge & Kegan Paul, 1964.
— *The Rosicrucian Enlightenment*, Routledge & Regan Paul, 1972.

ZAEHNER, R. C., *Mysticism, Sacred and Profane*, Oxford University Press, 1961.

INDEX